Deleuze, Kierkegaard and the Ethics of Selfhood

Plateaus – New Directions in Deleuze Studies

'It's not a matter of bringing all sorts of things together under a single concept but rather of relating each concept to variables that explain its mutations.'
Gilles Deleuze, *Negotiations*

Series Editors
Ian Buchanan, University of Wollongong
Claire Colebrook, Penn State University

Editorial Advisory Board
Keith Ansell Pearson, Ronald Bogue, Constantin V. Boundas, Rosi Braidotti, Eugene Holland, Gregg Lambert, Dorothea Olkowski, Paul Patton, Daniel Smith, James Williams

Titles available in the series
Christian Kerslake, *Immanence and the Vertigo of Philosophy: From Kant to Deleuze*
Jean-Clet Martin, *Variations: The Philosophy of Gilles Deleuze*, translated by Constantin V. Boundas and Susan Dyrkton
Simone Bignall, *Postcolonial Agency: Critique and Constructivism*
Miguel de Beistegui, *Immanence – Deleuze and Philosophy*
Jean-Jacques Lecercle, *Badiou and Deleuze Read Literature*
Ronald Bogue, *Deleuzian Fabulation and the Scars of History*
Sean Bowden, *The Priority of Events: Deleuze's Logic of Sense*
Craig Lundy, *History and Becoming: Deleuze's Philosophy of Creativity*
Aidan Tynan, *Deleuze's Literary Clinic: Criticism and the Politics of Symptoms*
Thomas Nail, *Returning to Revolution: Deleuze, Guattari and Zapatismo*
François Zourabichvili, *Deleuze: A Philosophy of the Event* with *The Vocabulary of Deleuze* edited by Gregg Lambert and Daniel W. Smith, translated by Kieran Aarons
Frida Beckman, *Between Desire and Pleasure: A Deleuzian Theory of Sexuality*
Nadine Boljkovac, *Untimely Affects: Gilles Deleuze and an Ethics of Cinema*
Daniela Voss, *Conditions of Thought: Deleuze and Transcendental Ideas*
Daniel Barber, *Deleuze and the Naming of God: Post-Secularism and the Future of Immanence*
F. LeRon Shults, *Iconoclastic Theology: Gilles Deleuze and the Secretion of Atheism*
Janae Sholtz, *The Invention of a People: Heidegger and Deleuze on Art and the Political*
Marco Altamirano, *Time, Technology and Environment: An Essay on the Philosophy of Nature*
Sean McQueen, *Deleuze and Baudrillard: From Cyberpunk to Biopunk*
Ridvan Askin, *Narrative and Becoming*
Marc Rölli, *Gilles Deleuze's Transcendental Empiricism: From Tradition to Difference*, translated by Peter Hertz-Ohmes
Guillaume Collett, *The Psychoanalysis of Sense: Deleuze and the Lacanian School*
Ryan J. Johnson, *The Deleuze-Lucretius Encounter*
Allan James Thomas, *Deleuze, Cinema and the Thought of the World*
Cheri Lynne Carr, *Deleuze's Kantian Ethos: Critique as a Way of Life*
Alex Tissandier, *Affirming Divergence: Deleuze's Reading of Leibniz*
Barbara Glowczewski, *Indigenising Anthropology with Guattari and Deleuze*
Koichiro Kokubun, *The Principles of Deleuzian Philosophy*, translated by Wren Nishina
Felice Cimatti, *Unbecoming Human: Philosophy of Animality After Deleuze*, translated by Fabio Gironi
Ryan J. Johnson, *Deleuze, A Stoic*
Jane Newland, *Deleuze in Children's Literature*
D. J. S. Cross, *Deleuze and the Problem of Affect*
Laurent de Sutter, *Deleuze's Philosophy of Law*, translated by Nils F. Schott
Andrew Jampol-Petzinger, *Deleuze, Kierkegaard and the Ethics of Selfhood*

Forthcoming volumes
Justin Litaker, *Deleuze and Guattari's Political Economy*
Nir Kedem, *A Deleuzian Critique of Queer Thought: Overcoming Sexuality*
Sean Bowden, *Expression, Action and Agency in Deleuze: Willing Events*

Visit the Plateaus website at edinburghuniversitypress.com/series/plat

DELEUZE, KIERKEGAARD AND THE ETHICS OF SELFHOOD

∞

Andrew M. Jampol-Petzinger

EDINBURGH
University Press

Edinburgh University Press is one of the leading university presses in the UK. We publish academic books and journals in our selected subject areas across the humanities and social sciences, combining cutting-edge scholarship with high editorial and production values to produce academic works of lasting importance. For more information visit our website: edinburghuniversitypress.com

© Andrew M. Jampol-Petzinger, 2022, 2024

Edinburgh University Press Ltd
The Tun – Holyrood Road
12(2f) Jackson's Entry
Edinburgh EH8 8PJ

First published in hardback by Edinburgh University Press 2022

Typeset in 11/13 Sabon LT Pro
by Cheshire Typesetting Ltd, Cuddington, Cheshire
Croydon, CR0 4YY

A CIP record for this book is available from the British Library

ISBN 978 1 4744 7608 9 (hardback)
ISBN 978 1 4744 7609 6 (paperback)
ISBN 978 1 4744 7611 9 (webready PDF)
ISBN 978 1 4744 7610 2 (epub)

The right of Andrew M. Jampol-Petzinger to be identified as the author of this work has been asserted in accordance with the Copyright, Designs and Patents Act 1988, and the Copyright and Related Rights Regulations 2003 (SI No. 2498).

Contents

Acknowledgements	vi
Introduction: Why Deleuze and Kierkegaard?	1
1 Kant and the Inheritance of Romanticism	12
2 Faith and Repetition in Kierkegaard and Deleuze	40
3 Kierkegaard as a Thinker of Immanent Ethics	77
4 Kierkegaard, Deleuze and the Self of Immanent Ethics	105
5 Faith, Creation and the Future of Deleuzian Subjects	138
Conclusion: Kierkegaard and Deleuze – Philosophers of Existence	155
Appendices	157
Bibliography	159
Index	168

Acknowledgements

This project absolutely could not have been completed without the care and support of many people.

First on this list is my indefatigable dissertation advisor, Sam Haddad, who put in innumerable hours communicating with me both during the initial composition of a dissertation on this book's topic, and also on just about every other related topic in the years that have followed my defence. He not only reflects the best qualities of a faculty member, mentor and friend, but is among that rare class of people that sets a standard for the kind of philosopher and teacher I would wish myself to become: kind, thoughtful, open-minded, hard-working and self-effacing to a fault. He deserves my deepest thanks.

All of my committee members were immensely helpful and assisted through comments and conversation during the composition and defence of a dissertation on this topic – Michael Baur, Shiloh Whitney, John Davenport and Dan Smith.

Dan Smith deserves credit for being a constant source of inspiration and support and for offering his time and thoughts on a project he most certainly could have said 'no' to. John Davenport, in addition to being an excellent interlocutor on all things Kierkegaard, was the person who has the credit of first introducing me to Kierkegaard as a graduate student, and who allowed me to write a terrible final paper that ultimately contained the seeds of this very project.

Others have been immensely helpful along the way in Fordham's Philosophy Department: Crina and Daryl, who were such friends to me during stressful times, and Brian Johnson who is just a lovely person.

I want to acknowledge the institutional support of Fordham University, which helped me to do research abroad years ago related to the dissertation version of this project, and also the Hong Kierkegaard Library, personified by Eileen Shimota and Gordon Marino, where I spent a lovely summer meeting wonderful people and mostly reading Jean Wahl.

Acknowledgements

I also can't avoid thanking the wonderful, irreplaceable friends and family who assisted at varying intensities of activity and passivity during the course of writing this book: my friends, Mo, Dermot and Scott, who kept me alive during hours of darkness, my wonderful sister and father, who were insistently encouraging and curious, and my incredible partner, Erin, whom I love and who has an inexplicable faith in me even when I do not. I also want to remember my mother, whose love of learning, endless curiosity and passion for the world lives in me in all my philosophical pursuits. She is here in this book as well.

Special thanks to Carol MacDonald and the wonderful team at Edinburgh University Press, who made this process smooth and pleasant and let my project be their project. I also want to thank Eden Seifu, who painted the extraordinary image on the cover of this book, complete with birds and lilies.

Earlier versions of Chapters 2 and 3 appeared in journals as 'Faith and Repetition in Kierkegaard and Deleuze', *Philosophy Today* 63.2 (Spring 2019), pp. 383–401, and 'Kierkegaard as a Thinker of Deleuzian Immanent Ethics', *Symposium: Canadian Journal of Continental Philosophy/Revue canadienne de philosophie continentale* 24.1 (Spring 2020), pp. 118–137, respectively. I would like to thank these journals for allowing me to make use of this material.

Introduction: Why Deleuze and Kierkegaard?

It may seem strange, at first sight, to bring together the philosophers Gilles Deleuze and Søren Kierkegaard in a book. Kierkegaard's theological commitments, when contrasted with Deleuze's avowed 'tranquil' atheism, as much as the former's somewhat marked preference for thinking about suffering, dissatisfaction, anxiety, and the like, make for an apparent strong incompatibility with Deleuze's atheistic philosophy of joy, affirmation and innocence. Perhaps for the length of an interesting paper, but is an entire book really necessary to inspect what these two philosophers might have had to say to one another? In reply, this book stands as an effort to show not only how much these two philosophers did indeed have in common, but also to show how thoroughly Deleuze's thought is linked to Kierkegaard's work and how much of Deleuze there is, in one form or another, in Kierkegaard. To begin this project, my goal here is to assess what Kierkegaard's relationship is to Deleuze at present at the most general level, and also to say something about what has already been said regarding the two, by philosophers of both Deleuzian and Kierkegaardian persuasions.

A Tale of a Missed Connection

Among the more obvious reasons for bringing Deleuze's and Kierkegaard's work together in this way is the fact that the two philosophers so manifestly share a set of conceptual preoccupations and interests. Despite the fact, for example, that Nietzsche is often cited as *the* point of reference for Deleuze's avowed anti-Hegelianism, one could hardly find a better representative of philosophical anti-Hegelianism than Kierkegaard, whose volumes of pseudonymous writing take frequent aim at Hegel or – at least, as some interpreters have argued – Hegel's representatives in the Danish academic system.[1] In fact, if we were to compare the sheer volume of references to Hegel in Nietzsche's work alongside those in Kierkegaard's work, my suspicion is that the latter would dwarf the former, both in number and intensity of acrimony.

Similarly, one can find numerous references to a set of concepts – particularly unusual or distinctive concepts, concepts that strongly characterise both Kierkegaard and Deleuze's work – that would closely associate the two thinkers. The concept of 'becoming' is central to Kierkegaard's existentialism as much as to Deleuze's metaphysics; the category of 'repetition', which we will analyse more closely in the second chapter; the categories of difference and paradox; even emphases on broad theoretical topics like 'aesthetics' and 'theatre' show marked similarities of preoccupation between the two thinkers. Some terms are even close enough to suggest concealed references from Deleuze's work to Kierkegaard's: the pairing of 'humour and irony' that Deleuze investigates in *The Logic of Sense*, *Difference and Repetition* and *Coldness and Cruelty* finds strong resonance with Kierkegaard's use of these categories in the *Concluding Unscientific Postscript to* Philosophical Fragments and *The Concept of Irony*. More substantively, Kierkegaard's scepticisms about the validity of rational morality and his desire to pursue a form of ethics beyond the limits of rational morality resonates with Deleuze's own avowed scepticism about moral judgement. His rejection of traditional metaphysics resonates with the Deleuzian notion that traditional ontological ideas about identity and substantiality need to be reconsidered. An emphasis on the concrete and the inescapability of immanent existence fits here. And we might also cite the profoundly experimental style of philosophising that Deleuze evinces in his work – his commitment to uncovering a style of writing that avoids the pitfalls of conventionally didactic philosophy – and notice the way in which Kierkegaard's pseudonymous authorship, as much as the pragmatic composition of the 'upbuilding' discourses, which fall somewhere beyond both the philosophical and aesthetic paradigms, reflects a novel approach to philosophical thought and writing.[2] From these similarities, we have the impression that rather than posing an opposition based on the theological disparities between Deleuze and Kierkegaard, we might recognise in each of these thinkers a kind of philosophical iconoclasm that ought to (and, as I argue below, does) bring the two philosophers into rigorous and productive intellectual contact. The better question of their relationship might be why it has been so long coming that these philosophers have been overtly brought together, rather than how such contact might be possible.

Introduction: Why Deleuze and Kierkegaard?

Kierkegaard's Presence

One important feature specific to Deleuze's relationship to Kierkegaard – and although this may be primarily of interest to scholars of Deleuze, it ought also to interest interpreters of Kierkegaard who might wonder how this superficially 'un-Kierkegaardian' philosopher would read Kierkegaard – is the strong exegetical value that a richer understanding of Kierkegaard's thought allows for understanding Deleuze. One thing we notice in this regard is the outsized status of Kierkegaard's writings in Deleuze, for a figure who remains so under-acknowledged on the Deleuze side of scholarship. Although Deleuze did not compose any single monograph specifically on Kierkegaard – having instead written on both friends and foes like Kant, Leibniz, Nietzsche, Bergson, Hume and Spinoza – from a cursory survey of Deleuze's works, we find that starting as early as his 1956–1957 lectures on the subject of grounding (recently translated as *What is Grounding?*) Kierkegaard is already an important reference point, figuring as a primary source for the development of some of Deleuze's most basic insights into the important category of repetition, as well as questions about empiricism and the relationship between appearance and truth.[3] And from that point in 1956 onwards, Kierkegaard will serve as a near-constant reference point in Deleuze's work, both in what he published alone and with his co-author Guattari, for purposes of off-handed commentary as well as for closer engagement and analysis. Indeed, as will be evident over the course of this book, in nearly all of Deleuze's most important works – as just a sampling, in *A Thousand Plateaus*, *Difference and Repetition*, the *Cinema* books and *What is Philosophy?* – Kierkegaard's name appears precisely at those points of greatest depth, when we find Deleuze hard at work at his most strenuous efforts of philosophical creation. Arnaud Bouaniche, one of just a handful of readers to directly analyse the debt that Deleuze paid to Kierkegaard in his work, comments in this regard: 'Far from being secondary or marginal, [Kierkegaard's appearances] touch the very nerve of [Deleuze's] thought, and even, more profoundly, touch what it means to "think" for him.'[4] In *Difference and Repetition*, for example, when Deleuze discusses just what it means to produce a philosophy liberated from the constraints of traditional philosophical thought (where the chapter heading is simply the major theme of the book: 'Repetition and Difference'), it is only Kierkegaard whose name gets invoked alongside that of Nietzsche.[5] In the late *Cinema* books, where Deleuze articulates a theory of time, along with an account of aesthetic creation and the 'powers of the false', Kierkegaard's name is cited repeatedly for support. The Danish philosopher is present in Deleuze and Guattari's account of becoming in *A Thousand Plateaus*, appears alongside Marx and Nietzsche in *Bergsonism*, and recurs in Deleuze and Guattari's profound account of 'belief in the world' in *What is Philosophy?*

And if these more or less overt references to Kierkegaard writings were not enough, we in fact find nigh-innumerable oblique or surreptitious invocations of Kierkegaard peppered throughout Deleuze's writings: comments on the 'private thinker' (in *Nietzsche and Philosophy* and elsewhere), on the 'passion' or 'pathos' of thought (*Cinema* books), on the concept of 'qualitative difference' and 'the leap' (*What is Grounding?*), on the 'raising of consciousness to the second power' in *Difference and Repetition*, and more.[6] Phrases and fragments from Kierkegaard's books even appear like leitmotifs throughout Deleuze's writings, sometimes with a seemingly deliberate obscuration of their origin in the Danish philosopher's work: 'only movements concern me', 'the possible, or else I will suffocate', 'give me a body, then' – each of these turns of phrase, inevitably recognisable to the seasoned reader of Deleuze, will be discovered to link us to some obscure passage or other in Kierkegaard, as if charting a secret course deep into the heart of Deleuze's thinking.[7] They return with the persistence of a *ritornello* – offering themselves for recurrent and deeper analysis as to the nature of these elements as among the very building blocks of Deleuze's thought.

Given this persistent reference to Kierkegaard, it should perhaps come as no surprise to discover that, in sum, Deleuze evinces a familiarity with virtually *all* of Kierkegaard's pseudonymous publications, as well as with the latter's unpublished notebooks and doctoral dissertation, across the total body of his writings.[8] From a glance at Deleuze's bibliography, we can even see a more-than-passing familiarity with some significant contemporaneous literature on Kierkegaard, and we know very well of his high esteem for some of the twentieth century's major advocates for Kierkegaard's work.[9] From this we have the impression that Kierkegaard indeed played a strong, if somewhat understated, part throughout Deleuze's intellectual life, one which is substantially overlooked if the reader is guided by superficial assumptions about the compatibility or incompatibility of the two philosophers' theological commitments. Indeed, as this book hopes to demonstrate, a richer understanding of Kierkegaard's work, and of Deleuze's interpretation of Kierkegaard, will be invalu-

Introduction: Why Deleuze and Kierkegaard?

able to a thorough understanding of some of Deleuze's most important philosophical ideas.

Kierkegaard Connections

Before looking a bit more closely at some literature that has already been produced linking these two philosophers, I want to highlight one additional motivation to consider these philosophers in conjunction that comes specifically from some encouraging and exciting developments in Kierkegaard scholarship itself. By this, I mean to refer to the wonderful work of contemporary scholars like Clare Carlisle, Steven Shakespeare, Michael O'Neill Burns and Ada Jaarsma, among others, who have recently done much to bring Kierkegaard more strongly into dialogue with materialist and post-structuralist themes in continental philosophy. While drawing on a longer tradition of so-called 'postmodern' readings of Kierkegaard, these authors have more overtly questioned the assumed division between secular and theological thinking, and have opened Kierkegaard's work to contemporary materialist and 'immanentist' philosophy in ways that I believe will have a long-lasting impact on Kierkegaard scholarship.[10] What these philosophers offer in their interpretations of Kierkegaard are opportunities for broaching a dialogue between studies in the philosophy of religion and theology and Deleuze in a way that has only just begun to be explored.[11] We will have the opportunity to discuss several of these philosophers' works in subsequent chapters of this book, but it stands to mention here the way in which a linking of post-secular theology and contemporary materialist thought has opened new paths for the interpretation of philosophers like Kierkegaard. These interpreters show us how much is left to draw from Kierkegaard's work, especially for those interested to explore the theological or post-theological stakes of Deleuze's thought.

Deleuze/Kierkegaard Research

Of course, the terrain of English-language scholarship on Deleuze's relationship to Kierkegaard is not entirely untrod. In recent years a number of authors have begun to shed light upon the relationship between these two, perhaps most notably in reference to ideas about 'belief' adapted from the *Cinema* books and *What is Philosophy?* Two essays from D. N. Rodowick's *Afterimages of Gilles Deleuze's Film Philosophy* discuss these themes, as does an essay by Joe

Hughes in a collected volume entitled *Deleuze and the Body*.[12] Paola Marrati, in an excellent book on Deleuze's film philosophy, mentions – but does not explore at length – the Kierkegaardian connections in the *Cinema* books.[13] The category of 'possibility' has also been taken as an opportunity for comparison between Deleuze and Kierkegaard's work, notably by Arjen Kleinherenbrink and Ronald Bogue, where special interest is taken in Deleuze's positive adaptation of Kierkegaard's notion of possibility.[14] Perhaps somewhat surprisingly, on the Kierkegaardian side of the equation there has been a slightly more comprehensive consideration of the two philosophers' relationship: Niels Erikson discusses Deleuze in his book on Kierkegaard's category of repetition, and Deleuze is an important point of dialogue for Kierkegaard's notion of becoming in Clare Carlisle's *Kierkegaard's Philosophy of Becoming*, which stands as a key moment for drawing Kierkegaard in a more or less explicitly 'Deleuzian' direction in Kierkegaard scholarship.[15] Christine Battersby – whose work we discuss in Chapter 4 – writes more or less across traditions to bring Deleuze and Kierkegaard together for a profound investigation of their approaches to identity in her book, *The Phenomenal Woman*.[16] Somewhat more didactically, Jon Stewart includes Deleuze in his survey of Kierkegaard's reception in France, and José Mirando Justo – in an exceptionally attentive piece of scholarship – manages to situate nearly all of the major Deleuzian references to Kierkegaard in a collected volume on Kierkegaard's influence on Francophone philosophy.[17] Despite confining myself primarily to English-language scholarship in this connection, it is also worth highlighting the very generative French-language article on Deleuze as a 'reader' of Kierkegaard, quoted above, which similarly notices Kierkegaard's remarkable persistence in Deleuze's oeuvre.[18]

These pieces give a strong indication of the potential for scholarship exploring some of the existential motifs in Deleuze's thought and seeking to understand Kierkegaard's work better in terms of the principles of becoming at work in Deleuze's philosophy. And in this context this book is intended to contribute to the possibility of conceptual exchange between Kierkegaard and Deleuze by pursuing one particular line of interpretation based around to these two philosophers' common interest in ethics and its relationship to the self. Here, my intention is to show that these two philosophers can be read together to develop a coherent account of ethics independent of the conventional categories of moral good and evil, and that in so doing we will discover a corresponding conception of the self

Introduction: Why Deleuze and Kierkegaard?

adequate to the conceptual presuppositions of such an ethics, as well as appropriate to both Deleuze's and Kierkegaard's more general critiques of substantialist metaphysics. In this way, we will have given some sense of what is possible when we attempt to think 'between' these two philosophers, bringing Kierkegaard into dialogue with the rigorous immanentist metaphysics that Deleuze can offer, and bringing Deleuze into dialogue with the more obviously humane elements of Kierkegaard's existentialism. In what follows, I present a general overview of the course and argument of the book, showing how I will first establish some philosophical common ground on the original influences of these two philosophers, before moving on to indicate the importance of the categories of ethics and selfhood for an understanding of these two philosophers more specifically.

Chapter Outline

I begin this book by establishing some background sufficient for associating the Deleuze and Kierkegaard, sketching a historical background that leads us inexorably from the critical revolution that Kant introduced, through the thought of the German Romantic period, to arrive at the work of both Deleuze and Kierkegaard. In beginning with Kant's critical philosophy I show how it is Kant's scepticism of the possibility of noumenal self-knowledge that leads inevitably to the close connection between categories of personal identity and ethics in the subsequent history of philosophy. Specifically, we will see that it is Kant's reliance on practical philosophy to re-establish the possibility of a philosophically knowable sense of self, that leads to the problematisations of identity in Romantic philosophy. Sketching a trajectory of inheritance that leads from Kant, through dialogue between Fichte and Hölderlin to Romantic-era philosophers like Kierkegaard, I set the stage for a comparison that goes by way of Deleuze's own inheritance of Kant's problematic through Nietzsche. Thus – I argue – both Kierkegaard and Deleuze inherit a notion of 'dissolved' subjectivity from the post-Kantian period that sets the stage for their own reckoning with the relationship between ethics and selfhood in their work.

Having established this background on relationship between ethics and selfhood in Kant, in the second chapter I look at one particular topic in Deleuze and Kierkegaard's bodies of work that brings these two themes together as well as bringing together Deleuze and Kierkegaard themselves – namely, the concept of repetition, which figures for both philosophers as an important category for their work on time, subjectivity and ethics. In the category of repetition, we will see an important normative aim for both philosophers that also amounts to a picture of selfhood under conditions of dissolution and immanence. These two accounts, I argue, are remarkably similar, both in terms of their conceptions of the close relation between subjectivity and the category of repetition, as well as for their interest in the notion of self-overcoming at the heart of their normative ideal. It is because to these close similarities that I argue that it will be necessary to correct one popular misreading of Deleuze's thought regarding Kierkegaard's work; specifically, Deleuze has too often been read as a narrow critic of Kierkegaard's account of repetition, especially concerning Deleuze's somewhat obscure use of the phrase 'for all times' to distinguish his own sense of repetition from that of Kierkegaard. Here I argue that this reading of Deleuze both misrepresents Kierkegaard as having a simpler conception of repetition than he does, but also misrepresents Deleuze's own evolution in his relationship to Kierkegaard on this account, from an earlier, 'narrower' reading that places Kierkegaard outside Deleuze's notion of repetition, to a later, more appreciative reading that places Kierkegaard firmly within Deleuze's account of repetition. On this account we will see how Kierkegaard's work can actually be used as a valuable tool for understanding Deleuze's notion of self-overcoming in repetition, where Kierkegaardian faith figures something like the dispossessive move away from one's own identity that Deleuze describes in *Difference and Repetition* and elsewhere.

In the third chapter, I move from this somewhat narrower, metaphysical account of Deleuze and Kierkegaard's ethics to the broader normative philosophies at the basis of the two thinkers' works. Here, I argue that contrary to contemporary readings of Kierkegaard's ethics as a form of divine command theory or virtue ethics, in fact Kierkegaard's normative philosophy will best be understood as a form of immanent ethics of the sort that Deleuze describes in his work on Spinoza and elsewhere. In making this argument, I draw from Deleuze's account of the difference between an immanent ethics and a transcendent morality in *Spinoza: Practical Philosophy* and *The Logic of Sense* in order to show how, given the critique of rational morality at the heart of *Fear and Trembling*, and given the projects of 'becoming' at the basis of his signed discourses, Kierkegaard's ethical philosophy is in fact a reflection of his rejection of transcendence in favour of immanence. I consequently am

Introduction: Why Deleuze and Kierkegaard?

obligated to address one obvious concern that both Deleuzians and Kierkegaardians may have with such an account of Kierkegaard's ethics: namely, the fact that transcendence seems to serve as such an explicit touchstone for Kierkegaard's religious thought. Having once responded to this critique, I introduce an important upshot to my inclusion of Kierkegaard within the canon of immanent ethical philosophers – namely, that for interpreters of Deleuze who have remained suspicious of his apparent penchant for self-destruction, Kierkegaard offers a valuable humanistic counterbalance. Here I specifically read the work of Tamsin Lorraine, who, in her book *Deleuze and Guattari's Immanent Ethics*, makes an appeal for accounts of Deleuzian ethics that make space for the conditions of emergence of 'fledgling subjects', rather than simply valorising the destruction of identity so often associated with Deleuze's thought. Kierkegaard's ethics, I argue, may well serve as a case of immanent ethics that better accommodates the real needs of subjects in the process of emergence under conditions of marginalisation and exclusion.

The fourth chapter of the book aims more directly to fulfil the promise of the book's title to provide to a concept of selfhood adequate to both Deleuze's and Kierkegaard's understandings of immanent ethics. Here I draw upon a number of Deleuze's writings where he specifically invokes Kierkegaard's thought in order to provide a set of conceptual tools for the thinking of selfhood outside of the boundaries of substantialist notions of identity. I subsequently link these concepts to related notions in Kierkegaard's work – especially the concepts of transparency and immediacy – in order to provide a distinctly Kierkegaardian contribution to the question of selfhood under conditions of change and becoming.

The fifth and final chapter of the book serves to open some of the preceding themes of selfhood and ethics to future lines of research regarding more political topics. Here the category of belief in Deleuze serves as a tool for thinking through the ways in which a Deleuzian-Kierkegaardian notion of selfhood might involve a stronger sense of the presence of collective identity within individual experience. I use this close connection between selfhood and political collectivity in Deleuze to introduce some recent writings on Kierkegaard as an implicitly political philosopher, especially the work of Michael O'Neill Burns and Ada Jaarsma, both of whom find an important place for the opening of political possibility in the open-endedness of Kierkegaard's existentialism. This account points towards the possibility of future work on political themes in both Kierkegaard and

Deleuze that take up from their common appreciation of belief as a central normative category.

Notes

1. This is, for example, the basic argument of Jon Stewart's *Kierkegaard's Relations to Hegel Reconsidered*.
2. See Kierkegaard, *The Sickness Unto Death*, p. 5, where Christian upbuilding authorship is described as resembling 'the way a physician speaks at the sickbed'.
3. The translator of Deleuze's *Grounding* lectures has also followed Deleuze into what might be considered broadly 'Kierkegaardian' territory, with his own book on the importance of 'singular' entity in Deleuze.
4. Bouaniche, 'Deleuze lecteur de Kierkegaard', p. 127, translation my own.
5. Deleuze, *Difference and Repetition*, pp. 5–11.
6. Kierkegaard's pseudonym 'Johannes Climacus' describes himself as a 'private thinker [privatiserende Tænker]' in *Concluding Unscientific Postscript*, p. 63; 'pathos' is omnipresent in Kierkegaard's work, but also specifically comprises a full section of *Concluding Unscientific Postscript*, pp. 387–555; the principle of a 'passion' or 'paradox' of thought appears in *Philosophical Fragments*, p. 37; the principle of repetition as a 'raising of consciousness to the second power' is in *Repetition*, p. 229; 'the leap' and 'qualitative difference' are discussed in *Concept of Anxiety*, p. 40.
7. 'Only movements concern me' or 'I pay attention only to the movements' is taken from *Fear and Trembling*, p. 38; 'give me a body, then' is likely adapted from Camus, 'The Myth of Sisyphus', p. 39, but is itself a quote from Kierkegaard's *Journals and Papers, Vol. 6*, p. 320; 'the possible, or else I will suffocate', has long been recognised as an adaptation of *The Sickness Unto Death*, p. 38, where Kierkegaard's pseudonym writes: 'without possibility a person seems unable to breathe'. A recent reading of the translator's introduction to the work of Benjamin Fondane – himself an important French interpreter of Kierkegaard – at last revealed the proper origin of Deleuze's unique paraphrase of this passage: Fondane uses it as an adaptation of Kierkegaard's scenario in a 1933 review of Sickness Unto Death for the *Cahiers du Sud*, p. 42 (quoted in Baugh, 'Introduction', pp. xxi–xxii).
8. For illustration of Deleuze's references to each of Kierkegaard's texts, see Appendix A. This, contra Kleinherenbrink, 'Art as Authentic Life', p. 99, where he claims that 'Deleuze only refers to *Fear and Trembling*, *Repetition*, and some passages from the *Papirer*'.
9. Deleuze's very first publications included reviews of Knud Løgstrup's

Introduction: Why Deleuze and Kierkegaard?

'Kierkegaard und Heideggers Existenzanalyse und ihr Verhältnis zur Verkündigung', Régis Jolivet, 'Le problème de la mort chez M. Heidegger et J.-P. Sartre', and Helmut Kuhn, *Encounter with Nothingness: An Essay on Existentialism*. Among the several advocates of Kierkegaardian thought that Deleuze references, Jean Wahl (*Études kierkegaardiennes*) and Pierre Klossowski (discussed in the next chapter) stand out.

10 See Carlisle, *Kierkegaard's Philosophy of Becoming*; Burns, *Kierkegaard and the Matter of Philosophy*; Shakespeare, *Kierkegaard and the Refusal of Transcendence*; and Jaarsma, *Kierkegaard After the Genome*.
11 One excellent exception to this relative silence is Daniel Barber's *Deleuze and the Naming of God*, which however avoids any mention of Kierkegaard.
12 Rodowick, 'The World, Time', pp. 97–114; Bogue, 'To Choose to Choose', pp. 115–132; Hughes, 'Believing in the World', pp. 73–95.
13 Marrati, *Gilles Deleuze: Cinema and Philosophy*.
14 Bogue, 'The Art of the Possible'; Kleinherenbrink, 'Art as Authentic Life'.
15 Eriksen, *Kierkegaard's Category of Repetition*; Carlisle, *Kierkegaard's Philosophy of Becoming*.
16 Battersby, 'Scoring the Subject of Feminist Theory'.
17 Stewart, 'Kierkegaard as a Forerunner of Existentialism and Poststructuralism', pp. 421–474; Justo, 'Gilles Deleuze: Kierkegaard's Presence in his Writings', pp. 83–110. Part of the reason for the somewhat greater comprehensiveness of scholarship from the Kierkegaardian side has to do with the absolutely massive, multi-volume *Kierkegaard Research: Sources, Reception and Resources* project, which aims to provide systematic scholarship on just about every dimension of Kierkegaard's thought.
18 Bouaniche, 'Deleuze lecteur de Kierkegaard', p. 127.

1
Kant and the Inheritance of Romanticism

To better understand the relationship between Deleuze and Kierkegaard, it will be helpful to first situate these two philosophers with respect to a particular history of post-Kantian philosophy from which they both derive several of their basic concerns and preoccupations.[1] In looking at this tradition of post-Kantian philosophy, we will come to better understand two important vectors of both Deleuze's and Kierkegaard's thought. On the one hand, we will gain some understanding of the broader philosophical orientations of these two philosophers, especially around some common scepticisms regarding the adequacy of rational thought to grasp the specificity and materiality of existence. On the other hand, we will learn something about a specific philosophical narrative that serves to link ethical and psychological (in the sense of 'rational psychology' or 'the study of the soul') problematics in Kantian and post-Kantian philosophy and see how this association carries over into the close connection between ethical and psychological-existential issues in Kierkegaard's and Deleuze's work. By looking at the post-Kantian tradition, we will see that questions about ethical obligation and the possibility of moral judgement carry an important weight for questions about the nature of the self and indeed about the possibility of stable personal identity more generally. Here I simply want to situate these two philosophers at the end of a philosophical trajectory that leads from the Kantian critique of the possibility of self-knowledge, through a post-Kantian attempt to resuscitate the validity of the noumenal self, and finally towards a Romantic rejection of the possibility of apodictic self-knowledge. This sequence will show how questions about personal identity as they are inherited by both Kierkegaard and Deleuze are grounded in problematics associated with moral judgement and rationality, and also justify my premise that for both Kierkegaard and Deleuze the question of self-knowledge and the nature of the self remain central inheritances from the Kantian and post-Kantian tradition. I will subsequently investigate some more specific points of contact, around the concept of repetition in Chapter 2, and the concept of non-prescriptive ethics in Chapter 3. In the fourth chapter I will return to these reflections on the nature of the self in order to sketch how each of these thinkers elaborates their own reformulation of the nature of personal identity, especially in line with some of the more Romantic 'aesthetic' elements inherited from the immediate post-Kantian period. For the time being, I simply want to present two related itineraries through the post-Kantian tradition – one leading from Kant, through Fichte and Hölderlin, to Romantic-era figures like Kierkegaard, as well as a closely related itinerary leading through Nietzsche to Deleuze. Showing how these two trajectories arrive at the kinds of concerns that shape Kierkegaard's and Deleuze's thinking should more than adequately position these thinkers in terms of a common foundation in their sceptical approaches to selfhood, categorical ethics and the kinds of philosophy adequate to these themes.

Kant and the Cognition of the Self

Any account of the post-Kantian tradition and its scepticisms about self-knowledge of course must begin with the work of Kant himself, who, in the *Critique of Pure Reason*, begins the trajectory that I intend to describe with his critical bracketing of the possibility of noumenal self-knowledge. In that work, Kant observes that although human beings must presuppose the existence of a transcendental unity of apperception (what we might typically recognise as the 'I' or the 'self') as a condition for the possibility of the cognition of objects, nonetheless for Kant this 'I' is not itself an object of experience. In the 'B' deduction of the *Critique*, Kant writes:

> The **transcendental unity** of apperception is that unity thought which all of the manifold given in an intuition is united in a concept of an object. It is called **objective** on that account, and must be distinguished from the **subjective unity** of consciousness, which is a **determination of inner sense**, through which that manifold of intuition is empirically given for such a combination.[2]

In this passage, Kant intimates a distinction that he will go on to elaborate, separating the nature of transcendental apperception – by which we are given the 'I' whose activity is recognised as present in every act of cognition – from the empirical experience of the 'self' as an object of intuition governed by the very same unity of apperception that makes the cognition of empirical objects possible. In distinguishing between these two dimensions of self-knowledge or self-reflection, Kant is clear to indicate the basically active, 'thinking' nature of the transcendental unity of apperception (what we, again, might most naturally refer to as the 'I' which attends all my experiences) and the effectively receptive nature of the self experienced or known only through several acts of empirical cognition. A few pages later, in the same deduction, Kant goes on to clarify the importance of this distinction as far as the nature of the philosophical knowledge of self is concerned:

> In the transcendental synthesis of the manifold of representations in general, [...] hence in the synthetic original unity of apperception, I am conscious of myself not as I appear to myself, nor **as I am in myself**, but only **that** I am. This **representation** is a **thinking**, not an **intuiting**. Now since for the **cognition** of ourselves, in addition to the action of thinking that brings the manifold of every possible intuition to the unity of apperception, a determinate sort of intuition, through which this manifold is given, is also required, my own existence is not indeed appearance (let alone mere illusion), but the determination of my existence can only occur in correspondence with the form of inner sense according to the particular way in which the manifold that I combine is given in inner intuition, and I therefore have **no cognition** of myself **as I am**, but only as I **appear** to myself.[3]

Here we see the consequence of the distinction Kant draws between the consciousness of self in the form of our self-representation as thinking things, and our capacity for knowledge under the conditions of the critical philosophy: it is because the self as an object of cognition is only known through the faculty of inner sense as an object of experience, subject to the conditioning of the activity of the transcendental unity of apperception, that the self is capable of being known and at the same time can only be known as an object of appearance. In other words, with respect to the self as it really is, a human being is capable of knowing abstractly that it exists and perhaps in principle something about the nature of its activity, but strictly speaking nothing about what it is, nor about what sort of philosophical properties might be attributed to it as it exists in itself.[4]

Kant elaborates this distinction several times over the course of the *Critique*, always in order to draw this distinction between the 'I' as an act of thinking and the self as an object of possible knowledge:

> [Since] I do not have another self-intuition, which would give the **determining** in me, of the spontaneity of which alone I am conscious, even before the act of **determination**, in the same way as time gives that which

is to be determined, thus I cannot determine my existence as that of a self-active being, rather I merely represent the spontaneity of my thought, i.e., of the determining, and my existence always remains only sensibly determinable, i.e., determinable as the existence of an appearance. Yet this spontaneity is the reason I call myself an **intelligence**.[5]

In other words, as Deleuze comments upon in the second chapter of *Difference and Repetition*, in the first *Critique* Kant adds to the problem of the determination of the subject the concept of a 'form in which the undetermined is determinable (by the determination)' – so that the activity that is represented to the individual as its own (i.e., the activity of thought that gives the individual a self of identity 'on account of which I call myself an **intelligence**') is separated from the passivity in which the individual has a cognition of itself in experience.[6] He writes:

> The activity of thought applies to a receptive being, to a passive subject which represents that activity to itself rather than enacts it, which experiences its effect rather than initiates it, and which lives it like an Other within itself. To 'I think' and 'I am' must be added the self – that is, the passive position (what Kant calls the receptivity of intuition); to the determination and the undetermined must be added the form of the determinable, namely time.[7]

Here it is on account of the introduction of the form of time (the form of sensibility belonging to inner sense and to which all objects of experience, whether appearing in space or not, must belong) that the individual is forced to experience their own activity as that of an 'Other' – represented to oneself as 'one's own' but neither inhabited as one's own nor concretely known. In this very basic distinction between knowledge as applicable to oneself as an object of possible experience, and reflection as applying to the 'I' as an activity that happens, perennially, 'behind one's back' (so to speak), an effective philosophical alienation of self from self is achieved.

This account of the self as a mere possible object of phenomenal experience becomes a specific philosophical problem for Kant in the famous 'Paralogisms' section of the *Critique of Pure Reason*, where Kant indicates the limitations that critical philosophy must set to the possibility of rational psychology.[8] In that section (revised substantially between the first and second publication), Kant identifies four properties which, outside the realm of critical philosophy, might have been attributed to the self by virtue of rational reflection alone. These are the concepts of: substantiality – the self-subsistence without dependence of the subject; simplicity – the unity of the self rather than its division into multiple selves; personality – the identity of the self across time; and distinction or non-materiality – the 'detachment' of the self from all matter.[9] These central propositions from the tradition of rational psychology themselves establish no less than the very knowledge of myself who I am, my integrity as an individual and my distinction as a thinking thing, as Kant recognises. And in bracketing the possibility of attributing such properties to the self a priori Kant effectively concludes the philosophical project of a possible rational psychology, writing:

> It would be a great, or indeed the only stumbling block to our entire critique, if it were possible to prove a priori that all thinking beings are in themselves simple substances, thus (as a consequence of the same ground of proof) that personality is inseparable from them, and that they are conscious of their existence as detached from all matter. For in this way we would have taken a step beyond the sensible world, entering into the field of **noumena** [. . .]. Yet that danger is not so great here is one approaches nearer the matter.[10]

And he concludes this section of the *Critique* by writing:

> The dialectical illusion in rational psychology rests on the confusion of an idea of reason (of a pure intelligence) with the concept, in every way indeterminate, of a thinking being in general. I think of myself, in behalf of a possible experience, by abstracting from all actual experience, and from this conclude that I could become conscious of my existence even outside experience and of its empirical conditions. Consequently I confuse the possible **abstraction** from my empirically determined existence with the supposed consciousness of a **separate** possible existence of my thinking Self, and I believe that I cognize what is substantial in me as a transcendental subject, since I have in thought merely the unity of consciousness that grounds everything determinate as the mere form of cognition.[11]

Julian Wuerth, giving an account of Kant's basic argument in the 'Paralogisms' summarises thus: 'Our pure apperception [. . .] avoids the fate of empirical apperception, of providing knowledge of ourselves merely as phenomena, [. . .] but it does so at the cost of complete indeterminacy, so that "the consciousness of oneself is therefore far from being a cognition of oneself".'[12] Deleuze writes: 'What Kant saw so profoundly in the *Critique of Pure Reason* [was] the manner in which the speculative death of God entails the fracture of the I, the simultaneous disappearance of rational theology and rational psychology.'[13] Although we will see later how a concept of the 'death of God' is involved in the 'fracture' of the subject, for the time being it is sufficient to know that it is in rejecting the claim of rational psychology to be able to derive conclusions about the self from the mere 'I think' that the essential features of any rigorous knowledge of the self – for example, knowledge of the self as a substantial, simple, self-identical and non-material being – fall to nothing.[14] In the distinction between the phenomenal and noumenal realms a certain alienation from the self (as much as from knowledge of the world as it exists in itself) follows. And consequently, it will be necessary either to resolve this issue by either a definite surrender of the possibility of apodictic self-knowledge, or by adopting some set of conceptual tools adequate to resuscitating or reconstructing this knowledge, the latter of which is precisely what Kant sets out to do.

KANT'S PRACTICAL RESURRECTION OF THE SELF

Having established the impossibility of self-knowledge through the framework of theoretical philosophy, Kant will go on to inextricably link the projects of speculative self-knowledge and moral philosophy to one another through his practical approach to the resuscitation of the self, using practical reason in order to attribute, among other things, the properties of freedom, indestructibility and personality (identity over time) to the self as necessary conditions for the possibility of moral responsibility.[15] Kant, in other words, appeals to a moral point of view to provide grounds for an account of personal identity that he cannot adequately present in terms of theoretical philosophy. And as we will see later, it is not just Deleuze's and Kierkegaard's common uptake of the theoretical opacity of the self that is ultimately traceable to Kant's bracketing of noumenal self-knowledge, but also their common reconsideration of relationship between selfhood and ethics that inevitably ties their thought to the tradition of post-Kantian philosophy. If anything, it is because of this close connection between ethics and the possibility of self-knowledge in post-Kantian philosophy that Deleuze and Kierkegaard's moral scepticism – that is to say, their rejection of rational, 'categorical' morality in the name of an immanent or non-prescriptive ethics – necessarily shapes their understanding of what it means to be a self.

Because Kant's account as developing a 'practical' resuscitation of the self is going to bear particular importance for Deleuze's and Kierkegaard's eventual rejection of a Kantian framework of morality, it is worth discussing just how Kant aims to resuscitate the self in his practical writings – specifically in the *Groundwork of the Metaphysics of Morals*, and the *Critique of Practical Reason* – where he argues for two points particularly relevant to our interest in questions of personal identity. First, we will see that Kant argues that the moral domain gives us access to something closer to a noumenal self in the form of a 'personality' (*Persönlichkeit*) (what Kant refers to as the 'actual self' over and against the merely phenomenal self of cognition); and, second, we will see that the requirements of moral responsibility – including the requirements of one's belief in the ultimate justice of the universe through the securing power of God – make it necessary to make various categorical assertions about the nature of the self in terms of both its identity and persistence. Kant will call these latter propositions 'pure rational beliefs [*reine Vernuftglauben*]' as they are secured through an exercise of practical, rather than theoretical, reason. And yet these will bear epistemological priority over the agnosticism of our speculative thought, simply to the extent that our purely speculative vocation appears as secondary to our primary moral vocation.[16]

Groundwork to the Metaphysics of Morals: 'freedom'

In Kant's *Groundwork of the Metaphysics of Morals* he argues that just as, in the theoretical domain, concepts of our understanding can be given a positivity through their application to objects of experience, in the practical domain we have a consciousness of an activity that is not merely empty in terms of the predicates applicable to it, but one which contains in addition to this something of the positivity absent in the account of mere transcendental apperception. Here Kant speaks of the self as it exists 'in itself' as belonging to a 'world of understanding', in which the subject

> puts himself in a different order to things and in a relation to determining grounds of an entirely different kind, when he thinks of himself as an intelligence endowed with a will, and consequently with a causality, than when he perceives himself as a phenomenon in the world of sense (which he actually is as well) and subjects his causality, according to external determination to laws of nature.[17]

These 'determining grounds' that Kant distinguishes from the grounds of causality in the world of sense he initially defines merely negatively, pointing to the absence – in the world of the understanding – of the conditions of necessity that determine a subject to act by outside causes. But as he elaborates the nature of this freedom from the causality of outside sources he also adds to this account a positive determination – namely, the concept of autonomy has 'the property of the will of being a law to itself'.[18] And this, while not granting the individual any speculative insight into the way that the self exists in itself, nonetheless will allow the individual application of these concepts in their practical use in a manner 'analogical' to their theoretical use, in thinking of the self as endowed with the property of freedom. In revising the second edition of the *Critique of Pure Reason*, Kant therefore returns to the section on the paralogisms of pure reason in order to add a caveat to the suspension of all speculative knowledge of the self as an object of rational psychology. He writes:

> But suppose there subsequently turned up – not in experience but in certain (not merely logical rules but) laws holding firm a priori and concerning our existence – the occasion for presupposing ourselves to be **legislative** fully a priori in regard to our own **existence**, and as self-determining in this existence; then this would disclose a spontaneity through which our actuality is determinable without the need of conditions of empirical intuition; and here we would become aware that in the consciousness of our existence something is contained a priori that can serve to determine our existence, which is thoroughly determinable only sensibly, in regard to a certain inner faculty in relation to an intelligible world (obviously one only thought of).
>
> But this would nonetheless bring all attempts of rational psychology not the least bit further. For through this admirable faculty, which for the first time reveals to me the consciousness of the moral law, I would indeed have a principle for the determination of my existence that is purely intellectual; but through which predicates? Through none other than those that would have to be given to me in sensible intuition, and thus I would have landed right back where I was in rational psychology, namely, in need of sensible intuitions in order to obtain significance for my concepts of the understanding, substance, cause, etc. [...]. Meanwhile, I would still be warranted in applying these concepts in regard to their practical use, which is always directed to objects of experience, according to their analogical significance to their theoretical use, to freedom and the free subject, since by them I understand merely the logical function of subject and predicate, ground and consequence, [and so on].[19]

In other words, Kant here argues that under the guidance of our practical use of reason, we discover an exercise of our intelligence that is independent of the conditions of sensibility and which – while not providing us with any real insight into the nature of the predicates we use – nonetheless can provide us with the occasion to apply concepts of our understanding to the self in a manner 'analogical' to their speculative usage. Hence Kant here already begins to open the door to a broader application of speculative capacity to our noumenal selves by appeal to practical reason, as disclosing to us a world in which the self is at is 'in itself', as a moral agent.

The *Critique of Practical Reason*: the postulates of practical reason
In the *Critique of Practical Reason*, Kant goes even further in this direction of drawing upon the rational subject's practical capacities in order to argue for the existence of various properties of the self that can be validly attributed to it by virtue of its moral 'vocation'. Here it is the important priority of the practical function of reason, over its mere speculative theoretical use, that entitles Kant to make claims regarding certain properties belonging to the individual that would otherwise trespass beyond what can be known using speculative reason alone. Here Kant argues that it is because the practical interests of reason have priority over reason's interests as a speculative faculty that those propositions which are inseparably bound up with the self's moral aims must be accepted even where – as purely theoretical claims – they pretend to go beyond the limitations of what can be known through mere speculation. Kant writes:

> If pure reason of itself can be and really is practical, as the consciousness of the moral law proves it to be, it is still only one and the same reason which, whether from a theoretical or a practical perspective, judges according to a priori principles; and then it is clear that, even if from the first perspective its capacity does not extend to establishing certain propositions affirmatively, although they do not contradict it, *as soon as these same propositions belong inseparably to the practical interest* of pure reason it must accept them – indeed as something offered to it from another source, which has not grown on its own land but yet is sufficiently authenticated.[20]

In other words, human beings are authorised and even obligated to take those postulates for true which necessarily follow from their moral obligations as members of a world of understanding, even without having any possibility of achieving insight into their validity from a speculative perspective.

Chief among the propositions determinable through the practical use of reason, Kant goes on to argue, are those related to the possibility of practical reason's 'highest good' – that is, to the demand that happiness should be distributed 'in exact proportion to morality (as the worth of a person and his worthiness to be happy)'.[21] In other words, practical reason may make demands about theoretical reason to the extent that these are necessary for the supposition of the possibility of a kind of distributive justice regarding happiness. And two important postulates follow from the practical assumption of a highest good: first, that the self must be immortal in order to therefore be susceptible to a kind of repayment in this way, and second, that a 'holy', 'blessed' and 'wise' being (that is, a God) must exist capable of providing for this good.[22]

Elaborating upon this first postulate – namely, the necessary immortality of the human soul – Kant specifies that such a belief involves (1) the capacity of the self for an 'endless progress' towards conformity with the moral law, and (2) the existence of a 'personality' (*Persönlichkeit*) or identity over time sufficient for the imputation of moral responsibility in the course of this improvement or degeneration.[23] Indeed just such a claim had been made earlier as the very basis for the possibility of attributing a sense of identity to the self, given the suspension of rational psychology under the critique of pure reason. In a handwritten note from the time of the *Groundwork*, Kant writes: 'We cannot [. . .] – at the same time as we better ourselves – believe that we had another personality [*Persönlichkeit*] at that time and on that account fail to be punished – as nearly all men believe.'[24] In other words, in order for its just reward or punishment to be possible, the self must be sufficiently recognised as 'the same' self over time (and even over infinite time). And given the priority of the practical use of reason over the speculative use that allows for the application of such categories where these do not necessarily contradict the principles of speculative reason, here we are permitted to attribute the very same 'personality' to the self that had been denied to it as a paralogism in the *Critique of Pure Reason*.[25]

Thus we have, in Kant, both an attempt to delimit the possibility of knowledge of the self, as well as an effort to base a kind of revised or provisional conception of the self (a mere rejection of identity being undesirable) upon the very possibility of morality. Other philosophers, we will see, will approach the problem of noumenal self-knowledge very differently (for example by questioning the basis of Kant's rejection of noumenal knowledge in the first place). But before moving in this direction, I want to simply highlight the provisional connection between the themes of moral responsibility and personal identity here in order to anticipate some of the basic ideas of Kierkegaard and Deleuze. Both of these philosophers, we will see, will be situated not only in terms of their common concern with the relationship between selfhood and morality in their only philosophy, but moreover in terms of the way that their rejection of Kant's approach to rational morality – the emphasis on transcendental moral rules and the form of moral responsibility related to those rules – will lead them to reject the doctrine of persistent identity in favour of an account of selfhood that privileges becoming and change. For both of these philosophers, the project of overcoming the 'reactionary' nature of rational morality will link their ideas about ethics to a non-Kantian view of personal identity: one in which the normative project of becoming oneself, or even more broadly of simply becoming, will form itself part and parcel of their ethical projects. For both Kierkegaard and Deleuze, the nature of the self will play a pivotal role in the kinds of normative motivations one recognises and takes up. But – crucially for these accounts – these normative motivations will not be based around concepts of morality that involve ideas of transcendental laws, moral obligation or transcendental freedom.

Post-Kantian Philosophies

Having now presented some of Kant's basic insights into the problem of self-knowledge, it will be useful to see how these problems were adopted and reconfigured in the work of those philosophers who followed Kant and whose influence was transmitted to Deleuze and to Kierkegaard by diverse pathways. In presenting this history, we will follow two closely related itineraries. First, we will look at the inheritance of Kant's moral and anthropological problematic by J. G. Fichte and Friedrich Hölderlin as a key pairing for the history of Romantic philosophy that followed. Then we will see how Nietzsche radicalised some of the basic scepticisms of post-Kantian thought, leading to Deleuze's anti-substantialist uptake of these problems. In doing so we will see how both Kierkegaard and Deleuze can be understood in terms of the broad sweep of philosophical thinking centring around the relationship between ethics and self-knowledge beginning at the end of the eighteenth century.

As we mentioned above, one of the key points of reference for the post-Kantian inheritance of the self-knowledge problematic will be the relationship between the post-Kantian philosopher J. G. Fichte (1762–1814), and the poet and philosopher Friedrich Hölderlin (1770–1843). But before elaborating on the specifics of this relationship, it will be worth mentioning some of the hermeneutic reasons for highlighting these particular philosophers for the reading of European philosophy after Kant that we intend to link to the thought of Deleuze and Kierkegaard. And the first reason for this pairing is quite simply textual: although there is not very much known with absolute certainty about what Kierkegaard read of Fichte, we do know for a fact how important both of these philosophers were for Deleuze.[26] Thus when we show, below, why it is that the reply Hölderlin gives to Fichte is so important for an understanding of Kierkegaard's thought, we will be able to draw upon the common ground shared between Deleuze and Hölderlin in order to make an even stronger connection to Kierkegaard. The second reason for using this pair as a reference point for our thinking is related to this: although Kierkegaard's reply to Fichte, which we will see below, is not completely isomorphic with that of Hölderlin, it nonetheless bears enough in common with the kind of sensibility that Hölderlin represented to reflect the general community of thought between Kierkegaard and the Romantic tradition of his time period. In making this claim, it is worth mentioning one recent work which – from a different angle – unintentionally confirms the continuity I am intending to sketch out between Hölderlin and Kierkegaard's thought. In Michael O'Neill Burns's *Kierkegaard and the Matter of Philosophy*, the author presents an account of Kierkegaard's relationship to Fichte that is specifically intended to show the greater continuity between Fichte's thought – specifically Fichte's later thought – and Kierkegaard, for both of whom the self is essentially 'fractured' at its core, in such a way that allows for the open-endedness of human experience and forecloses the possibility of a radically self-positing and self-knowing subject.[27] And yet in making this claim Burns is obligated to draw a sharp distinction between Fichte as he is represented in his earlier work (the work which we will discuss below), and Fichte as he is represented in his later work – especially in his *Vocation of Man* – where he 'finally accounts for something "other" than the absolute "I" which both precedes its emergence and continues to exist as a negative remainder within the activity of the "I."'[28] It is only in drawing this distinction between the earlier and the later Fichte that Burns can clarify why Kierkegaard's initial criticisms of Fichte, in *The Concept of Irony*, for example (where Kierkegaard explicitly discusses the 'early' Fichte) ought to in fact be replaced by a greater sense of continuity between Kierkegaard's thought and Fichte's thought.

Although Burns's line of argumentation, in drawing the distinctions that he does, does appear extremely compelling as far as situating

Kierkegaard's thought within a tradition of post-Kantian idealism, my interest in this place is less to parse the details of any particular philosopher's intellectual evolution than to present a general trajectory of thinking that can be used to jointly situate both Kierkegaard and Deleuze in terms of the problems of selfhood and knowledge introduced above. Consequently, although there is almost certainly something to be gained through a more nuanced and dialectical understanding of Fichte's thought here, in this context I hope that it does not do that thinker too great an injustice to look instead at a critique appearing from outside of Fichte's work – namely Hölderlin's critique – for the way in which this critique will seem to reflect sensibilities belonging to both Kierkegaard and Deleuze. Hence in what follows I will present a general account of the philosophical dialectic of post-Kantian idealism represented in Fichte's and Hölderlin's thought in order to show how, for those who took up Hölderlin's critique, the problem of self-knowledge remained among the central concerns of their philosophy.

FICHTE, HÖLDERLIN, AND THE TRIALS OF SELFHOOD

Fichte's body of work betrays a complicated and sometimes infuriating attempt to place some of Kant's basic insights upon firmer ground with respect to the nature of the human subject. One way in which Fichte does this, across his numerous attempts to establish a foundational science of knowledge, is by attempting to present an account of the subject such that its primary activity – rather than merely applying categories of experience to itself through the activity of reflection – is in fact the activity of a certain kind of self-positing that will allow it to evade the Kantian critique of self-knowledge.[29] In his 1794 *Foundations of the Entire Science of Knowledge*, Fichte argues for this apparently 'self-positing' form of subjectivity by arguing from the 'absolutely certain' proposition 'A=A' to the deduction of the existence of a supposedly self-identical subject ('I = I'), from which it is possible to argue for an absolute, self-positing subject *'whose being or essence consists simply in the fact that it posits itself as existing'*.[30] On Fichte's account, because the absolutely certain proposition 'A = A' requires a subject that is capable 'without any other ground' of asserting a necessary connection between the subject 'A' and the predicate 'A', it follows that 'there is something permanently uniform, forever one and the same' that lies at the basis of theoretical positing.[31] From this, Fichte can claim that we must arrive at the 'unconditionally and absolutely valid' proposition regarding the self (namely that 'I' exist), and hence at the intuition that there must exist a veritable self-positing 'I' at the basis of all our judgements.[32] And this 'self-positing' consciousness, 'in which the subjective and objective is immediately united' can be both known and experienced in an immediate intuition, according to Fichte.[33]

Because Fichte's self-intuition is a priori – that is, because it is a direct intuiting of the activity of the intellect by itself prior to being cognized under any of the forms of its appearance – the consciousness that precedes the distinction between subjective and objective self-consciousness in Fichte serves not only as a ground for objective experience (insofar as it sets the rules for the possibility of judgement about objects), but also is itself an absolute, or unconditioned form of self-consciousness. In other words, this consciousness is immediately conscious of itself and hence has no need for the mediation of the conditions for the possibility of experience that Kant uses to distinguish between the noumenal and phenomenal worlds. Consequently, the kind of bracketing or fracture that Kant describes – in which the subject is intrinsically alienated from its itself by virtue of a cognitive activity that can only present us with objects of empirical intuition – does not apply to Fichte's self. The self here is freed from its alienation by virtue of its absoluteness. For a brief moment, the existential dread of our self-alienation is staved off by our non-reflective self-awareness.[34] Fichte returns us to the state of absolute self-knowledge, even as he dramatically expands the scope of our nature in this act of self-knowledge in a manner that some will consider a form of deification.

The poet Friedrich Hölderlin, writing around the same time as the publication of Fichte's *Wissenschaftslehre*, famously replies to Fichte by effectively re-establishing the Kantian distinction between knowledge and the 'I' that Fichte had sought to overcome. Hölderlin's reply to Fichte's account – expressed most concisely in a short, fragmentary paper entitled 'Judgement and Being' dated from around the time of the *Wissenschaftslehre* and reiterated in a letter to Hegel – is comprised of three interrelated points. First, Hölderlin argues that nothing posed as prior to the distinction between subject and object in the manner of Fichte's self-intuiting 'I' can be properly understood as 'consciousness' on account of the absence of the subject-object distinction that is a necessary element of what we understand by consciousness. Hölderlin writes:

> [Fichte's] absolute 'I' (=Spinoza's substance) contains all reality; it is everything, and outside of it there is nothing; [...] however a consciousness without object cannot be thought [...]; therefore, within the absolute 'I,' no consciousness is conceivable; as absolute 'I,' I have no consciousness, and insofar as I have no consciousness I am (for myself) nothing, hence is the absolute 'I' (for me) nothing.[35]

In 'Judgement and Being', he elaborates upon this notion, pointing out that, since Fichte's absolute 'I' would lack self-consciousness, its 'I'-hood must reduce to nothing that could be considered subjectivity at all. He writes:

> How can I say: I! without self-consciousness? But how is self-consciousness possible? By setting myself in opposition to myself, by separating myself from myself but, the separation notwithstanding, by being able to recognize myself in what opposes me.[36]

Here Hölderlin is arguing that the supposed distinction between subject and object understood to alienate the subject from itself through its cognition also precludes the possibility that anything like an absolute 'I' could even exist. If, as Fichte argues, the 'I' can have a consciousness of itself prior to any objectifying distinction between itself as subject and itself as object, then this consciousness – just by virtue of having no object – also cannot be a subject. As Dieter Henrich writes,

> Hölderlin maintains [against Fichte] that there can be no [...] theoretical distinction between the consciousness 'I' and self-consciousness. And from this he draws the methodological conclusion that that consciousness 'I,' or 'I am I,' is inappropriate as a conceptual starting point for a philosophical system.[37]

This impossibility of conceiving of a 'self' prior to self-consciousness leads to Hölderlin's second conclusion: namely, that the underlying unity behind objective self-consciousness ought not properly be understood as a subject or consciousness, but rather instead as something indeterminate. Henrich paraphrases Hölderlin when he writes that, in thinking of the supposed unity that precedes consciousness, 'one must not think of the supposedly pure consciousness "I" but of something radically prior to all consciousness, something that makes intelligible, even conceivable, the thought "I" and with it the fact of self-consciousness'.[38] Hence, Hölderlin will prefer to use the term '*Seyn*' (Being) 'to refer to that which underlies both the fact of, and our understanding of, the I and self-consciousness'.[39] This subjective ground will be deeply obscure and even mysterious to us, despite constituting – ultimately – something akin to most basic unity of our very identity prior to the distinction between subject and object in which our own selves appear to us as objectified and hence phenomenal objects.

From this point follows perhaps the most paradoxical element of Hölderlin's thought, namely his claim it will be impossible to render any judgement regarding this supposed prior unity of subject and object, owing to the way in which judgement is itself a form of separation that must obscure the very nature of this 'unity's' essence. In 'Judgement and Being', he writes:

> *Judgement* – is in the highest and most strict sense the original separation of the most tight unity of object and subject in intellectual intuition, that separation which makes object and subject first possible, the judgement [*Ur-theilung*, original-separation].[40]

Here, we see the unique paradox that Hölderlin aims to articulate regarding the problem of noumenal self-knowledge. On Hölderlin's account, if we are to gain some knowledge of our selves through an objectifying cognition, then we will necessarily be left with a mere appearance that obscures what it is to be a self. If, on the other hand, we aim to think of the unity preceding consciousness as something other than this objectified self, then we are left with a mode of existence utterly unlike any kind of 'self' that we are familiar with, one for which, the more we aim to capture its nature in terms of some kind of comprehensible judgement, the more we will be misled in the direction of something fundamentally unlike this prior unity.

Consequently, as Hölderlin reiterates, in place of a relationship to what grounds my very identity, I am restricted to a kind of reflection upon myself as a mere appearance, but at the same time one which allows me to retain a kind of indirect awareness of the very paradoxicality of this awareness. On Hölderlin's account, it is because my self is both known to me as obscure, and unknown to me as what it really is, that I am condemned to a kind of cyclical movement of understanding and alienation. In subsequent writings, Hölderlin will theorise the nature of this alienation, in which what is most natural and proper to my identity is nonetheless held at an alienating remove, so that I am condemned to a kind of perpetual exile, until I am left with only one alternative: to learn to appropriate the very fact of my basic alienation.[41] In Jean Beaufret's masterful reading of Hölderlin's late essays on Sophocles, he argues that – for Hölderlin

– it is the Kantian '*Umkehr*' (turning-away) of God's face – that is, our alienation from any access to the noumenal realm in which we might make sense of our own basic identity – that constitutes a basic break in my subjective experience of time. Like Oedipus, condemned to an endless wandering in exile after the events at Thebes, the Hölderlinian subject is 'split' by a *caesura*, so that he can no longer recapture his original sense of identity.[42] 'The god "who is nothing but time" – time being itself reduced to a pure "condition" [...] – is this not the very retreat or *détournement* ["turning-away"] of God, such that He leaves man faced with the empty immensity of an endless sky?'[43] Here it is the separation of noumenal and phenomenal reality that casts the individual into an insuperable isolation from reality. And yet, within this context, it will be possible to recover something like an appropriation of this very alienation, in which the hero learns to accept and even affirm their own state of affairs as their very destiny as a human being.[44] Here it is not through the Kantian commitment to the moral law, but rather through an ambiguous and 'existential' acceptance of one's status as a wanderer under the conditions of mere appearance that the individual comes to reappropriate their identity. As we will see, this kind of reconciliation with the very phenomenality of existence will become a common theme for both Deleuze and Kierkegaard. The difficulty of living with a basic alienation from oneself, coupled with an understanding of this alienation as itself deeply a part of one's identity, serves as the complicated context for one's ethical striving. Hence it is in adopting a position of suspension, never fully confident in one's way of taking up identity, but also perpetually reconciling oneself to this lack of certainty, that one can come to proper normative relationship to oneself.

Kierkegaard

If the indications immediately preceding have not made it clear, I think there is good reason to contextualise Kierkegaard's approach to philosophy in terms of this tradition which leads from Kant, through Fichte, to Hölderlin.[45] Although it is by no means my intention to claim that Kierkegaard's work or approach to philosophy is merely an extension of this philosophical context, nonetheless within this set of background assumptions we can clearly recognise a set of philosophical preoccupations that will serve to guide the general study of Kierkegaard's work. Like Hölderlin, Kierkegaard will provide us with a picture of human subjectivity that is predicated on a basic opacity of ourselves to ourselves. Like Hölderlin, something in our relationship to his 'alienation' will require that we learn how to live with or appropriate our own basic opacity, as well as our own limitations as dependent, finite creatures who – unlike Fichte's self-positing subject – are unable to get behind the contingency of their own existence. And because of this, we will see that the basic normative questions of our existence are not about how we obey categorical moral obligations but rather about how we ought to relate ourselves to a self whose very existence will always be a problem. Later, we will have a chance to better sketch how it is that Kierkegaard comes to rethink the nature of selfhood beyond the substantialist metaphysics that Kant brackets in his *Critique*. For now, we can see how Kierkegaard reacts to the particular post-Kantian tradition that forms the immediate context of his thought. Throughout Kierkegaard's writings, we will see that several themes will remain central: both a sense of the basic alienation or displacement that distances the individual from any absolute insight into their own nature, as well as a kind of normative restlessness that seeks to appropriate this awareness in a way that can remain adequate to one's human needs. What we find markedly in Hölderlin and Kierkegaard alike (and what sets these all apart from Kant's 'moral' resuscitation of self-understanding) is the sense that human experience is fundamentally an experience of distance from the absolute certainty, coupled with a suspicion that rationality will remain insufficient to resolve this sense of displacement.

Nietzsche and Klossowski

If the preceding account of post-Kantian philosophy showed how Hölderlin, through a critique of Fichte's concept of the self-positing subject, could give us an account of selfhood suspended from the grounds of its own existence, in what follows I want to go one degree further in this account in order to show how – while still drawing explicitly upon Hölderlin's thought in *Difference and Repetition* and elsewhere – for Deleuze, Nietzsche will become a key representative of the Kantian destruction of rational psychology.[46] Although we will look more directly at how Deleuze himself reads Nietzsche in the next chapter, in this chapter I want to interpose an intermediary between Deleuze and Nietzsche, specifically because this intermediary will serve to provide us with an explicit link between Kant's suspension of rational psychology and the 'dissolution' of the self that Deleuze will take up from Nietzsche. Thus, much of what follows will draw explicitly from the French philosopher (critic and author) Pierre Klossowski's work on Nietzsche, specifically because of the unique role that this author's reading of Nietzsche plays in Deleuze's work.[47] Klossowski, as readers of Deleuze will know, comprises one half of an important exchange of ideas that Deleuze undertakes about Nietzsche during the second half of the twentieth century. An early translator and interpreter of Nietzsche, several of the basic coordinates of Klossowski's reading of Nietzsche specifically – and of his own approach to questions of personal identity more generally – were already fairly well established as early as the 1930s.[48] After the publication of *Nietzsche and Philosophy* in 1962, Deleuze and Klossowski exchanged ideas on Nietzsche at the 1964 Royaumont conference on Nietzsche, after which Klossowski's paper, entitled 'Forgetting and Anamnesis in the Lived Experience of the Eternal Return', would come to be published as one of the central chapters in his landmark *Nietzsche and the Vicious Circle*, published in 1967.[49] In the interim, Deleuze published on Klossowski in 1965 ('Klossowski or Bodies-Language', later reprinted as an appendix to *The Logic of Sense*), while also mentioning Klossowski's reading of Nietzsche in *Difference and Repetition*, where he refers to Klossowski as 'renew[ing] the interpretation of Nietzsche' with his essays from the preceding decade.[50] Thus any interpretation of Nietzsche that intends to serve as an introduction to Deleuze's thought about personal identity ought to begin with a consideration of Klossowski.

NIETZSCHE

Klossowski's reading of Nietzsche on subjectivity is mainly comprised of two parts. The first of these consists in Klossowski's account of the relationship between selfhood and God, to the extent that this relationship is undermined by Nietzsche's famous proclamation of the 'death of God', while the second of these consists in Klossowski's interpretation of Nietzsche's so-called 'lived experience' of the Eternal Return, in which the theme of subjective dissolution explored in the earlier work is placed in conversation with a concept of subjective multiplicity. Placing this reading of Nietzsche in particular at the end of a sequence that includes the dialogue between Fichte and Hölderlin finds its justification in Klossowski's own indebtedness to the Hölderlin: Klossowski began his career as a translator with translations of Hölderlin's poetry in 1930, and the idea of subjective alienation at the heart of Hölderlin's work retains a persistent theme throughout Klossowski's writings. We will see that this experience of epistemological and existential alienation – together with the specific project of overcoming this condition through a kind of *amor fati* – confirms a continuity between Kant, Hölderlin and Klossowski's unique interpretation of Nietzsche.

The first of Klossowski's premises regarding the relationship between God and the self – one which is laid out as early as his first works on the Marquis de Sade from the 1930s – is that it is indeed God's very existence (or at least, His existence in the form of the moral rules providing normative protection to one's 'neighbour') that secures the coherence and identity of the individuated self.[51] On Klossowski's account, one function of God's existence is to secure for human beings – and especially for human beings of different social statuses – a certain moral value that prohibits individuals from abusing, harming or even simply ignoring the Other. In Klossowski's *Sade My Neighbor*, which underwent substantial revisions away from its more Catholic orientation between its initial publication in 1947 and its republication in 1967, he writes that '[even] at the lowest run of [social] hierarchy, [the individual] finds his individual significance because he participates in an edifice whose cornerstone is God'.[52] It is consequently with the death of God – already contained in the Marquis de Sade's work but made famous by Nietzsche – that the ontological basis upon which was secured the rights of one's neighbour vanishes, allowing for the very possibility of the practical excesses made famous in Sadean literature.[53] Klossowski, drawing upon a Nietzschean argument famously presented in the second essay of the *On the Genealogy of Morality*, argues that it is with the loss of this sense of moral value for others that the individual subject themselves is no longer able to secure a coherent form of identity. This is because, as Nietzsche had claimed, the self – comprised of a certain subjective depth experienced by the individual as what they will come to call their 'soul' – is in fact nothing other than the effect of an otherwise outwardly directed aggression, turned back against the agent themselves under conditions of moral prohibition. As Nietzsche argues in *Genealogy*: 'All instincts which are not discharged outwardly *turn inwards* – this is what I call the *internalization* of man: with it there now evolves in man what will later be called his "soul."'[54] As Klossowski argues, in his interpretation of Nietzsche, the speculative death of God – whether this derives from a broader cultural rejection of the theology or from a philosophical bracketing of theology in the manner that we find in Kant – results in a death of the self specifically due to the absence of a restricting moral code sufficient to secure the protection of the Other. Hence, the self has no condition for the reflux of externally directed aggression which itself comprises the soul. 'If God dies', Klossowski writes, 'the individual self loses not only its Judge, but loses also its Redeemer and Witness: but if it loses its eternal Witness, it loses also its eternal identity. The self (*moi*) dies with God.'[55]

This absence of a coherent self which arises through the death of God must result, according to Klossowski, in a felt dissolution of subjectivity that brings us to the second element of his account. Given the link between coherent selfhood and the moral constraint exercised upon the individual by its belief in God, it makes sense that Nietzsche's reckoning with the death of God and the absence of a theologically grounded moral framework should result not only in the dissolution of Nietzsche's experience of coherent subjectivity, but also in an 'opening up' of that subjectivity to a plurality of possible identities, 'all its possible identities, already apprehended in the various *Stimmungen* of the [. . .] soul' in the absence of any stabilising sense of self.[56] Like Hölderlin's account of the long wandering that leads the individual to a kind of acceptance of his phenomenal existence, Klossowski's reading of the Eternal Return centres upon a loss of identity that compels the individual not merely to despair of their own selfhood, but also leads them to appropriate and reconcile themselves to a generalised experience of the fortuitousness of identity. On Klossowski's account, the Nietzschean individual is left not in absolute disarray after the elimination of their identity, but rather given the opportunity to inhabit a world where selfhood is at once an uncertain and fortuitous quality – arising only under arbitrary historical conditions and subject to arbitrary material circumstances.[57] The Nietzschean subject consequently learns to reappropriate their own identity, not as something deeply grounded in their nature, but rather just as a fortuitous identity, unconstrainted by the necessity of any teleological necessity. For this reason, Nietzsche's experience of identity is no longer one of ownership – a kind of proprietary relationship to one's self – but rather is a matter of what Klossowski calls a 'resonance' between Nietzsche's own self and the fortuitous selfhood to which, like he, all other names in history are subject. In this sense, Nietzsche is himself subject to the fortuitousness of his identity in the same way in which Napoleon was subject to the fortuitousness of his identity, and the same for all other names in history. Consequently, at the same moment that Nietzsche experiences a certain individuation of his identity through a reflection on the uniqueness and fortuity of arriving at the particular form of selfhood that he has, he also experiences a kind of sympathy or harmony with each of these other cases of identity as equally fortuitous across time. Hence Klossowski's reading of the famous letter that Nietzsche writes to Jacob Burckhardt: 'At bottom I am every name in history.'[58] As Klossowski understands it, through the release of substantial identity the now-contingent soul discovers an aptitude

> for an always-inexhaustible metamorphosis, its need for an unappeasable and universal investment, in which various diverse extrahuman forms of existence are offered to the soul as so many possibilities of being – stone, plant, animal, star – but precisely insofar as they would always be possibilities for the life of the soul itself.[59]

In other words, the Nietzschean self here adopts an experience of 'impersonality', in which their fortuitous identity is both affirmed as fortuitous and also recognised as arbitrary. In place of the deep kind of existential appropriation hoped for at the bottom of a substantial account of selfhood, the self is here experienced as essentially alien, and yet also appropriated and affirmed in that condition of alienation.

Consequently, one finds in Klossowski's Nietzsche two qualities that substantially reiterate some of the developments we saw in Hölderlin's account of subjectivity: first, the alienation from the self that follows from the loss of noumenal knowledge in what Deleuze will later call 'the simultaneous disappearance of rational theology and rational psychology'; and, second, the emergence of a kind of resonance of the individual with a plurality of possible identities – an affirmation of one's very phenomenality that gives one a kind of impersonal or pluralised identity. Hence we can see the development of the trajectory left open as early as Kant's work on the possibility of noumenal self-knowledge: in the absence of this self, and moreover in the absence of the sense of moral responsibility that Kant can alone marshal for the purposes of securing a sense of coherent identity, a certain explosion or proliferation of identities takes place. Nietzsche picks up the alienation from the self's 'ground' that Hölderlin so powerfully describes, in order to turn this alienation into an ecstasy of subjective dis-placement and non-identity.

Deleuze

As will become more evident in what follows, this theme of rejecting the metaphysical conception of the self in favour of a form of selfhood closer to a kind of 'fortuitous' or 'phenomenal' identity finds its place in Deleuze's work under the framework of the 'dissolved' subject. Deleuze's account of selfhood, we will see, links together notions of impersonality and contingency, and places the overcoming of settled notions of identity at the centre of his moral philosophy. Like Nietzsche, Deleuze is interested in the ways in which individual selves can relate to an 'impersonal transcendental field, not having the form of a synthetic personal consciousness or subjective identity' prior to individuation.[60] And it will possible, on Deleuze's account, to remount to this impersonal field, through a process of dis-individuation or de-personalisation, so that one can once again experience the ambiguity of identity and even select from among its various directions of becoming.[61] It is through such a process – and in particular through the dis-identification with one's narrow 'personal' interests – that individuals can break with calcified forms of identity, and release a form of individuation 'without a name, without family, without qualities, without self or I'.[62] In this aspect of his thought, Deleuze restages some of the main ideas that we have described above, from Kant to Nietzsche: the self is no longer understood as a substantial subject in the manner of a noumenal ground, but rather as a kind of phenomenal appearance that we are invited to affirm or even to overcome. Moreover, in Deleuze the notion of selfhood as in some sense 'secured' through a kind of moral obligation as we see in Kant is implicitly endorsed – although in a negative sense – in Deleuze's own account of selfhood as a function of the kind of immanent ethics that we will discuss in Chapter 3. As we will see, Deleuzian selfhood cannot be adequately secured by an appeal to notions moral obligation or responsibility, but, rather, in overcoming these notions of moral obligation the self will be relieved of calcified forms of its own identity. In this way, a close theoretical relationship between ethics and personal identity will be maintained, but here under a different heading: a novel understanding of the self will be linked to a radical critique of conventional morality. And, indeed, this will serve a primary point of contact between Deleuze and Kierkegaard: the idea that a critique of rational morality entails a critique of the conventional conception of the self. And, reciprocally, a new conception of what it means to be a self will help shape our understanding of philosophical normativity.

Conclusion

What we have seen in this chapter is an extended history of the relationship between the categories of ethics and the notion of the philosophical subject or self. Moving from the Kantian conception of the self as subject to a radical critique (it's placement outside the limits of philosophical knowability) we saw how subsequent philosophers elaborated notions of selfhood that attempted to consolidate and also reckon with this apparent inaccessibility of the self. From Kant to Nietzsche, we sketched the maintenance of a concern with the wide-reaching effects of the bracketing of noumenal self-knowledge. Moreover, by looking at how Kant himself anticipated the possible consequences of his account through his attempted moral resuscitation of the self, we laid out in advance one of the main premises of this book: namely, that any significant revision to our conception of ethics must have significant ramifications for our understanding of the nature of selfhood. Philosophical criticism of the conventional notions of moral responsibility, obligation, freedom, and so on, will also have strong implications for philosophical ideas about selfhood and personal identity.

Beyond this, we have introduced some important hermeneutic tools for thinking about the relationship between Deleuze and Kierkegaard – namely, evidence to suggest that despite their apparent divergence as far as theological commitments are concerned, nonetheless they share a number of common inheritances from the Kantian and post-Kantian traditions that form the background of much of their thinking. It is not without good reason that both Deleuze and Kierkegaard express a kind of scepticism of substantialist metaphysics, nor is it surprising that both philosophers test the limits of philosophical speech and writing in a way that has been partially anticipated in post-Kantian philosophy. Both these philosophers, grappling with questions of morality, identity, and the very possibility of philosophical knowledge, find themselves inevitably linked through an inherited history of Romantic philosophy. And we will see that their own appropriations of these questions have more in common than one might have predicted.

Notes

1. One excellent resource for the tracing of Kierkegaard's relationship to this tradition – in particular with an eye towards drawing out a materialist and idealist reading of Kierkegaard – is Burns's *Kierkegaard and the Matter of Philosophy*, where the author situates Kierkegaard primarily in terms of a Fichtean undermining of the self-positing subject, which we discuss below. Carlisle, in her recent *Philosopher of the Heart*, also dedicates a chapter to the Romantic context of Kierkegaard's education, although her focus there is more on the uptake of certain aesthetic ideas; Carlisle, *Philosopher of the Heart*, pp. 91–111. On Deleuze's inheritance of post-Kantian philosophy, see Graham Jones and Jon Roffe (eds), *Deleuze's Philosophical Lineage* and *Deleuze's Philosophical Lineage II*.
2. Kant, *Critique of Pure Reason*, p. 250 [B139].
3. Ibid., pp. 259–260 [B157–158], emphasis in original.
4. Ibid., pp. 414–415 [A345/B403].
5. Ibid., p. 260 [B 157].
6. Ibid., p. 259 [B157]; Deleuze, *Difference and Repetition*, p. 86.
7. Deleuze, *Difference and Repetition*, p. 86.
8. Kant, *Critique of Pure Reason*, pp. 411–458 [A341–505/B399–432].
9. Ibid., pp. 445–447 [B407–410].
10. Ibid., p. 447 [B410].
11. Ibid., p. 445 [B427].
12. Wuerth, 'Paralogisms', p. 213, quoting Kant, *Critique of Pure Reason*, p. 260 [B158].
13. Deleuze, *Difference and Repetition*, p. 87.
14. Kant, *Critique of Pure Reason*, p. 454 [B423]: 'In this way, then, a cognition going beyond the bounds of possible experience yet belonging to the highest interests of humanity disappears, as far as speculative philosophy is concerned, in disappointed expectations.'
15. On the centrality of moral responsibility, see Kant, *Nachlaß*, p. 295 [R5646].
16. Kant, *Critique of Practical Reason*, p. 241 [5:126]. On the 'prerogative' of practical reason over speculative, see ibid., p. 237 [5:121].
17. Kant, *Groundwork*, p. 66 [4:457].
18. Ibid., p. 56 [4:446].
19. Kant, *Critique of Pure Reason*, p. 457 [B431].
20. Kant, *Critique of Practical Reason*, p. 237 [5:121].
21. Ibid., p. 229 [5:111].
22. See, for example, ibid., pp. 239–240 [5:124].
23. Ibid., p. 238 [5:123]: 'This endless progress [taken as the object of a will in conformity with the moral law, is] possible only on the presupposition of the *existence* and personality of the same rational

being continuity *endlessly* (which is called the immortality of the soul).'
24 Kant, *Nachlaß*, p. 295 [R5646], translation my own.
25 Kant, *Critique of Pure Reason*, p. 414 [A345/B403]; Kant, *Critique of Practical Reason*, p. 246 [5:133].
26 Kangas, for example, mentions that 'one of the few certainties' about Kierkegaard's engagement with Fichte is that he read *The Vocation of Man* sometime before 1835, although specifics beyond that are speculative, Kangas, 'Fichte', p. 65. To my knowledge there is no evidence that Kierkegaard read Hölderlin (there is no entry for Hölderlin in the Princeton *Cumulative Index to* Kierkegaard's Writings, for example). With reference to Deleuze, see, for example, comments on Fichte in 'Immanence: A Life' and on Hölderlin (amongst many) in *Difference and Repetition*, p. 58.
27 Burns, *Matter of Philosophy*, p. 7.
28 Ibid.
29 Heath and Lachs, 'Preface', p. xiv.
30 Fichte, *Science of Knowledge*, p. 98, emphasis in original.
31 Ibid., p. 96.
32 Ibid., p. 97.
33 Fichte, *Wissenschaftslehre*, p. 528, translation my own.
34 For a helpful summary of Fichte's position with respect to the concept of 'immediate intuition', see Larmore, 'Hölderlin and Novalis', p. 147.
35 Hölderlin, 'Letter to Hegel', p. 189.
36 Hölderlin, 'Being Judgment Possibility', p. 191.
37 Henrich, 'Hölderlin at Jena', p. 104.
38 Ibid.
39 Hölderlin, 'Being Judgment Possibility', p. 191.
40 Ibid., pp. 191–192. Hölderlin here spaces out the portions 'Ur' and 'Theilung' in order to derive a (spurious) etymology of the concept of judgement (*Urteil*).
41 Here I follow Jean Beaufret's interpretation of Hölderlin's late poetological writings on 'Oedipus' and 'Antigone', in Beaufret, 'Hölderlin et Sophocle', which also serves as a resource for Deleuze's later concept of the 'fractured' self. See Deleuze, *Difference and Repetition*, p. 316; Deleuze and Guattari, *A Thousand Plateaus*, p. 529; and Deleuze, *Essays Critical and Clinical*, pp. 28 and 56. For additional discussion of Beaufret's essay see Ronald Bogue, 'The Betrayal of God', pp. 9–29.
42 Hölderlin, 'Remarks on Oedipus', p. 201.
43 Beaufret, 'Hölderlin et Sophocle', p. 21, translation my own.
44 Ibid., p. 25; quoting Kant, *Religion Within the Boundaries*, p. 92 [6:47–48].
45 Studies on Kierkegaard's relationship to Fichte, Kant and figures in

German Romanticism are readily available in Stewart's *Kierkegaard and his German Contemporaries*. Ronald M. Green has published much work on the relationship between Kierkegaard and Kant and the 'debt' relationship between the two; see, for example, Green, *The Hidden Debt* and Green, *Kant and Kierkegaard on Time and Eternity*. On Kierkegaard's relationship to Romantics like Schlegel, and a comparison of their respective conceptions of irony, see Söderquist, 'Friedrich Schegel', pp. 185–233. Söderquist claims, interestingly, that Kierkegaard was apparently unfamiliar with Schlegel's own use of the term 'indirect communication' in his work, although he was aware of the Schlegelian premise of the imperfect nature of philosophical speech to capture absolute truth, 'Friedrich Schlegel', p. 190.

46 Deleuze describes Hölderlin as the 'descendent' of Kant in *Difference and Repetition*, p. 87.
47 Deleuze, *Difference and Repetition*, p. 87.
48 Klossowski published the important 'Nietzsche, Polytheism, and Parody' in 1958, as well as 'On Some Fundamental Themes of Nietzsche's *Gaya Scienza*' as an introduction to his translation of *The Gay Science* in 1956, both of which expressed some of the basic principles of the link between the death of God and the death of the subject. But Klossowski was already exploring related ideas about the nature of personal identity in his first publications on the Marquis de Sade in the 1930s.
49 See Klossowski, *Cahiers de Royaumont*, pp. 236–244. Klossowski dedicated *Nietzsche and the Vicious Circle* to Deleuze.
50 Deleuze, *Difference and Repetition*, p. 312, fn. 19. On the intellectual relationship between Deleuze and Klossowski see in particular Douglas Smith, *Transvaluations*, pp. 140–184.
51 Klossowski, *Sade My Neighbor*, p. 19.
52 Ibid., p. 53.
53 Ibid., p. 70: 'Does not the denial of God involve the denial of the neighbor?'
54 Nietzsche, *On the Genealogy of Morality*, p. 57 [Essay II, §16].
55 Klossowski, 'Don Juan selon Kierkegaard', p. 140, translation my own. See also Klossowski, *Sade My Neighbor*, p. 51, and Klossowski, 'Temps et Agressivité', p. 103. For an extremely helpful discussion of Klossowski's view of the self, as well as the complicated itinerary that his intellectual development takes, see James, *Persistence of a Name*, especially pp. 8–65 on the Marquis de Sade.
56 Klossowski, *Nietzsche and the Vicious Circle*, p. 57; see also Klossowski, 'Nietzsche, Polytheism, and Parody', p. 117, and 'On Some Fundamental Themes', p. 8.
57 Klossowski, *Nietzsche and the Vicious Circle*, p. 71.
58 Nietzsche, 'To Jacob Burckhardt', p. 686.

59 Klossowski, 'Nietzsche, Polytheism, and Parody', pp. 118–119.
60 Deleuze, *Logic of Sense*, pp. 98–99.
61 Ibid.
62 Deleuze, *Difference and Repetition*, p. 90.

2

Faith and Repetition in Kierkegaard and Deleuze

In this chapter, I want to develop some of the associations of the preceding chapters in order to compare Deleuze and Kierkegaard on the concept of 'repetition', which serves both philosophers as a critical metaphysical and practical concept. By focusing on this concept, I will show not only that Deleuze's and Kierkegaard's ethical or practical philosophies share much in common, but will also defend Kierkegaard against certain limitations that Deleuze ascribes to his conception in his earlier work. To this end, I will also respond to an important criticism frequently levelled against Kierkegaard from the perspective of Deleuzian scholarship, to the effect that Kierkegaard's conception of selfhood is too much grounded in a resuscitation of substantial identity to adequately reflect the sort of values and premises of Deleuze's philosophy. In replying to this claim, I hope to show both that a rigorous understanding of Kierkegaard's work already accounts for this critique, and also that Deleuze in fact corrects this criticism in his later work, evolving in his understanding of Kierkegaard to more properly appreciate Kierkegaard's thought. What we will see, in what follows, is that for both Kierkegaard and Deleuze, the critical question of their normative thought is how one might best adapt oneself to the fact of becoming, so that the Kierkegaardian notion of 'faith' will have much in common with the Deleuzian ideal of 'becoming-active' or 'self-overcoming', as articulated in works like *Nietzsche and Philosophy* and *Difference and Repetition*. In the next chapter, I will broaden this account, in order to show that in fact this common ground on the topic of repetition reflects a more general shared 'immanent-ethical' conception of morality in Deleuze and Kierkegaard, before we go on to sketch the features of a synthetic account of selfhood across Deleuze and Kierkegaard's writings in subsequent chapters.

In this chapter, then, I will begin by situating the category of repetition in the work of both Deleuze and Kierkegaard before elaborating the two philosophers' normative understanding of this concept. This will be followed by an account of Deleuze's criticisms

Faith and Repetition in Kierkegaard and Deleuze

of Kierkegaard's concept, before showing how Kierkegaard might reply to these criticisms, and defending a Kierkegaardian conception of faith as repetition. This will serve to situate the Deleuzian and Kierkegaardian accounts in their relationship to a conception of selfhood that will be developed in subsequent chapters.

Repetition in Difference and Repetition

In the second chapter of *Difference and Repetition*, Deleuze provides an account of three forms of repetition that he claims correlate to distinct 'syntheses of time' related to the transcendental exercise of various faculties of subjectivity.[1] Deleuze's intention here is to sketch an account of subjectivity in which various faculties are linked to diverse forms under which repetition can be conceived, so that his account of time is intimately linked to an account of the nature of subjective experience for human beings.[2]

The first of these modes of repetition constitutes what Deleuze calls the synthesis of the 'lived present, the living present' (*le présent vécu, le présent vivant*), and emerges through a passive 'contraction' of a series of repeated elements in time. Deleuze describes the pre-reflective subjectivity associated with this mode of repetition as appropriating diverse material elements from which a certain difference is extracted in such a manner as to generate a 'habit' or 'expectation' of what is going to happen next. For Deleuze, a succession of even identical phenomena across time would be insufficient to establish repetition, on account of the fact that the world in which such repetition take place would amount to a mere *mens momentanea* ('momentary mind') that would be unable to retain these phenomena sufficiently to establish their repetitive relationship to one another. Each 'repeated' element would remain, in its temporal vanishing, unrelated to any element of which it was supposed to be the repetition and, consequently, the fact of repetition would have no basis on which to appear. Thus, the phenomenon of repetition only appears in relation to a mind constituted by and at the same time as what it understands as a contemplative 'contraction' of those elements whose repetition it establishes. In other words, subjectivity here is inextricably linked to repetition as a material phenomenon: they arise as two sides of the same coin.

On Deleuze's account, this first form of repetition arises when the contemplating mind, by uniting into a single experience the distinct elements of a repetition, synthesizes these in the form of an impression that serves as the basis for a distribution of the three dimensions of time in its immediate experience: the sensible mind of the present distributes a 'past' and a 'future' on the basis of this synthesized experience of repetition.³ Here, it is the repeated impressions of an empirical experience that generate an anticipation of the future as a dimension of the habituated present experience, just as much as it comprises a past 'depth' corresponding to the quantity of repeated experiences. It is through the repeated encounter with several similar types of events that I experience an intensity of expectation correlating to the depth of my past experience, just as much as I am led to anticipate a certain consequence (the 'B' that regularly follows 'A') with a given degree of certainty as my felt experience of the future. The subject's immediate, repeated experience is consequently united as a single phenomenon containing a depth of impression as well as a felt generality of experience that is itself the dimension of futurity.⁴ Deleuze calls the mode of subjectivity that corresponds to this experience of habit 'the dissolved self' (*le moi dessous*) or 'larval subject' (*sujet larvaire*) and argues that it corresponds to a conception of repetition in its primary mode as a material repetition of discrete events across time. In this first account, therefore, we are presented with the unification of an experience of the sensible present, a concrete repetition of identical events across time, and the felt dimensions of the past and future as aspects of the immediately felt present. This comprises Deleuze's account of the 'first' type of repetition.

From this first account, Deleuze goes on to argue for the necessity of a second form of repetition grounded in the necessity of accounting for the apparent sequencing of repeated elements involved in this first form of time. For Deleuze, the immediate experience of repetition that constitutes the synthesis of habit requires another dimension for its existence, in which this assumed first repetition takes place: on Deleuze's conception, there could not be a felt repetition of the present were it not the case that there existed some form of time 'in which' this supposed repetition took place. Hence, if the living present is an experience of time based on the repetition of a series of presents that pass, producing a phenomenon of depth that is then reflected in an anticipation of the future, then a second form of temporality must exist in order to establish the context in which these presents can be embedded, and in terms of which there can be said to exist a present that passes. Hence a second form of time will be implied in this first mode of repetition, which leads us from the immediate present of the first form of repetition to a second form of repetition that unites a second faculty of subjectivity (memory), a second primary dimension of time (the past) and a second conception of repetition, understood as a trans-temporal instantiation of the 'self' within each event. Explaining the basis for this conception of the past, Deleuze writes:

> The claim of the present is precisely that it passes. However, it is what *causes* the present to pass, that to which the present and habit belong, which must be considered the ground of time. [. . .] At the moment when [active memory] grounds itself upon habit, memory must be grounded by another passive synthesis distinct from that of habit. The passive synthesis of habit in turn refers to this more profound passive synthesis of memory.[5]

In this passage, we see Deleuze giving an argument for the necessity of the second synthesis of time which will serve as the basis on which passing presents are capable of passing or, as he puts it, the condition under which alone they have a 'right' to pass. Indeed, Deleuze will talk regularly about the past, with its strong Platonic valences, in terms of the a priori Idea that can serve to adjudicate between 'claimants' to a certain kind of character. In other words, the present has a 'right' to pass only in the sense of basing this right on an appeal to some ideal past capable of adjudicating between diverse pretenders to this right.[6] Following Bergson, Deleuze enumerates three main properties belonging to this ideal form of the past, the first being its 'contemporaneity' with the present even at the very moment that it passes, the second being its 'coexistence' with itself as a totality at each moment of the passing present, and the third being its 'pre-existence' as a presupposition of the passing present, therefore not requiring a past present in order for it to exist as past.[7] These qualities of contemporaneity, coexistence and pre-existence constitute the properties of what Deleuze will call the 'pure' or a priori past: rather than a material passing of the present, we are invited to consider something like the 'insistence' of the past in the form of a pure, a priori ground of temporality, along with a distinctive mode of subjectivity and form of repetition associated with it.

Because this a priori past is in fact a priori and not a case of the present which has subsequently come to be past, Deleuze understands the faculty of subjectivity adequate to this form of temporality as nothing other than memory, here understood otherwise than in terms of the empirical exercise of recollection of a present-become-past, but rather as an involuntary 'reminiscence' of the pure past as such.[8]

Recollection here serves as a transcendental capacity for evoking or invoking the 'sense' of the past that accompanies each concrete recollection: it serves not to bring into the present a past that is no longer, but rather to grant access to the past as a dimension of time, allowing the human subject to find the present that it seeks even as it still remains empirically present.[9] The transcendental exercise of memory invokes the 'pastness' of the present in its occurrence, and allows us to enter into a consideration of past presents through our access to a transcendental past as such.

In speaking of this transcendental exercise of the faculty of memory, Deleuze presents repetition not as a material repetition of something that happened and therefore might happen again, but rather as the recurrence of the contemplating self in the present of each moment, serving as the condition allowing us to recognise ourselves across all sorts of past experiences and serving to unite these as elements in a sequence of our experienced life.[10] Invoking the Proustian experience of recollection, in which the individual finds herself, all of a sudden, plucked out of her present in order to identify with an overarching subjectivity that coexists beside each of her diverse particular memories, Deleuze writes: 'This is what we call metempsychosis. Each chooses his pitch or tone, perhaps even his lyrics, but the tune remains the same, and underneath all the lyrics the same tra-la-la, in all possible tones and pitches.'[11] Here Deleuze is describing a kind of general repetition that accompanies the diverse moments of experiences and allows us to place ourselves at various points in our lived past, where it is we who repeat at the level of generality within each particular case of recollection. On this account, a second mode of repetition brings together the transcendental exercise of the faculty of memory upon a pure past with a notion of repetition as a form of generality, as opposed to the material and particular repetition of the first case.[12] To the initial triad 'the present-habit-particularity' Deleuze appends a second triad, 'the past-memory-generality': the past as the element in which both present and future take place, memory as the transcendental faculty of this element, and generality as the form under which repetition appears in this faculty.

To this second mode of repetition Deleuze ultimately appends a third mode of repetition that he argues will be necessary as a precondition for even the pure past on which the passing present depends, just as the pure past served as a condition and presupposition of the present in the second mode of repetition. And despite the obscurity of Deleuze's comments on this account, we can glean a certain argument for the necessity of this third mode of repetition and the forms of temporality and subjectivity associated with it, in the 'grounding' relationship that Deleuze describes between the first and second dimensions of temporality. Here, Deleuze suggests that the described relationship between the first and second modes of temporality – the past's 'grounding' character in allowing the present to pass or giving it a 'right' to pass – in fact introduces too much into our conception of time to the extent that it serves primarily to account for the present as an empirical phenomenon. As Deleuze puts it, 'the shortcoming of the ground is to remain relative to what it grounds, to borrow the characteristics of what it grounds, and to be proved by these' – in other words, the conception of the past that we retain, in viewing it in terms of the present that it serves to condition, presents us primarily with what is necessary and sufficient for a representation of our empirical experience.[13] In basing our understanding of the past on the presupposition of the present that appears for us in experience, the past shows up for us as nothing other than this present's reflection, adjusted sufficiently to make that present possible, but without adequate attention paid to what belongs to the past just insofar as it is a dimension of time as such. Thus the question of what time is independently of its relationship to the immediate, empirical present remains unanswered. This is what Deleuze means when he said that the ground always 'points beyond itself' and is 'in a sense "bent" and must lead us towards a beyond': the pure past leads us in the direction of a third synthesis that will reflect more accurately what time is like for itself rather than in terms of its conditioning our experience in the first and second modes of repetition.[14] Deleuze calls this third synthesis or mode of temporality 'the pure and empty form of time' (*la forme pure et vide du temps*) or the 'unground' of time.[15] When time is understood independently of the qualities that it gains from empirical experience, we can begin to consider it in its pure or a priori form. Here we will find a triad of the form 'the future-thought-Eternal Return' to complete the set of triads, 'the present-habit-particularity' and 'the past-memory-generality', of the first and second modes of repetition.

In order to articulate the nature of this most primordial form of time, Deleuze begins by presenting four different aspects or dimensions in terms of which time can be understood entirely a priori. For each of these, he draws upon one of four 'time-determinations' (*Zeitbestimmungen*) that Kant mentions in the 'schematism' section of the first *Critique*, where these schemata are given as mechanisms for the attribution of the categories of the understanding to objects of intuition.[16] For Deleuze, each of these determinations is essentially a constructive element of temporal experience as it is understood independently of movement: rather than thinking about an object or individual as moving 'through' time, here we think about the ways in which time makes itself manifest, qualitatively, in terms of its various elements. This way of thinking about time accounts, for example, for the very distinction between the present, past and future as dimensions rather than the empirical phenomenon of movement through time, and in this sense it reflects time as what does not appear in any object of experience but rather as a pure form.

The first a priori time-determination that Deleuze discusses consists of what he simply calls the 'form' of time: it is the mere fact of time existing independently of movement, which makes possible – without resembling – the movements that happen within it. This is comparable to Kant's notion of time as a pure form of intuition and presents time as a condition under which empirical events take place, to the extent that it is separable from those empirical events. The second determination of time Deleuze calls time's a priori 'order', which comprises time's threefold division into a past, present and future, which is then determined in the image of a 'totality' (*ensemble*), in which time's multiple dimensions are embodied in a symbolic representation.[17] In the English translation of *Difference and Repetition*, Deleuze's term '*ensemble*' is translated as 'totality' so that the '*ensemble du temps*' is understood as a 'totality' or 'collection' of time as such.[18] But it is important to notice that in referring indirectly to the Kantian determination of time as a '*Zeitinbegriff*' there is an obscure intimation of another important dimension of this 'totality' of time – namely in the fact that the German suffix '*-inbegriff*' can refer both to time as a 'totality' or 'collection', but also to the notion of an 'exemplar' or 'embodiment' of time.[19] In this sense the 'totality of time' that Deleuze refers to is equally a kind of incarnation of time as such, sufficient to being encountered 'as' a representation of time by a concrete individual. Thus what Deleuze here calls the 'totality' or 'whole' of time, as one of the four a priori determinations of temporality, can be understood as a figuration or symbolisation of time itself. Deleuze wants to use this notion of time as incarnated in a symbol in order to present the dramatic image of a task or event – some symbolic act presented as a kind of challenge for the individual – that stands for time for that individual. This 'totality' of time therefore serves to link the abstract dimensions of time in the 'time-order' to a dramatic or literary notion of temporality: one in which an individual is in principle engaged in an encounter with temporality that requires their utmost. As we will see, Deleuze will link this aspect of the pure and empty form of time to various aesthetic representations – indeed it will figure as the archetypical model of narrative art wherein an individual must struggle to overcome their own identity in a conflict with time as such.

This notion of time as a possible object of encounter is elaborated by Deleuze in terms of the last of the four time-determinations – what Deleuze calls the 'series' of time, which refers to the a priori set of relationships possible for the individual in their very confrontation with temporality: here the 'order' of time as comprising a past, present and future is restaged in terms of the set of possible forms under which an individual is capable of relating themselves to the 'totality' of time as such. Thus, although Deleuze maintains the language of empirical time in speaking of the series of time as including a 'before', 'during' and after', in fact what we understand in terms of this series is not a flowing temporal sequence, but rather a set of modes under which an individual relates themself to the challenge presented by time as a task 'too large' to accomplish. Thus in speaking of the 'before' of time Deleuze means not the empirical period of time that takes place prior to some event taking place, but rather to the way of being in which an individual experiences that event as 'too big' for them.[20] Here Deleuze refers, for illustration, to the story of Oedipus, for whom the major event of the narrative – Oedipus's predicted murder of his own father and marriage of his mother – has already empirically taken place in the time 'before' the narrative occurs, and yet Oedipus, who as yet cannot and will not accept his own accomplishment of this act as his very destiny, nonetheless lives the event in the 'before' of the series, refusing to see himself as capable of performing the task that amounts to a destruction of his own sense of self.

It is only subsequent to an intensive process of change and becoming that Oedipus 'becomes capable' of the indicated event, so that he moves from the 'before' of the time series to the 'during' of the time series – what Deleuze also names the '*caesura*' of the event – in which he is capable of recognising himself as equal to act in question. Oedipus '[projects] an ideal self in the image of the act', and thus 'becomes capable' of accomplishing the task otherwise recognised as impossible.[21] It is only after this process of becoming, in which the individual immerses themself in the temporality represented by the symbolic event, that the individual arrives at the 'after' of the series, consisting in what the event effectively 'brings about' for the individual: the very limits of the individual's identity have been overcome, destroying the self which stood before it, thereby bringing about a new self or identity unbounded her previous constraints. As Deleuze puts it in *Difference and Repetition*,

> [when the symbolic] future appears, this signifies that the event and the act possess a secret coherence which excludes that of the self; that they turn back against the self which has become their equal and smash it to pieces, as though the bearer of the new world were carried away and dispersed by the shock of the multiplicity to which it gives birth.[22]

Here it is by passing through the encounter with the symbolic totality of time that the self loses the coordinates of its previous identity in order to make room for a new, unsettled or unstable identity – in any case an identity that had been inconceivable from the perspective of the prior self that it no longer is.

It is because of this sequencing of the before, during and after of the series of time that we can recognise in the event described something like the ability of an individual to come to an affirmation or reconciliation with the very nature of temporality as such. What each figure does, in identifying a symbolic event which they recognise as impossible for themselves, is to define a limit beyond which they are incapable of affirming the becoming associated with temporality as such. Indeed, the very problem established in the image of the symbolic act is just how one can come to change in such a fundamental way such that one will no longer recognise oneself across the boundary of the indicated event. For Oedipus, it is the inability to become the individual that he knows he must become, at such gross odds with his own sense of identity, that determines the sequence of his tragedy. Deleuze also cites Hamlet as another example of this temporal gap between the before and after of the series: 'time is out of joint' for Hamlet who struggles to accomplish the destiny that he is so famously conscious of from the very start of the play.[23] Here the self that arises from the accomplishment of the task is not nothing simpliciter, but rather is 'nothing' in relation to the self that went before: it is excluded by the kind of identity available to the individual prior to the accomplishment of the event, and therefore represents the pure becoming that is proper to time itself.[24]

From these four determinations of time, we therefore have a sense of the structure of Deleuze's forms of repetition as they are related to the present, past and future: each of these in fact reflects a different way of thinking about the nature of repetition, coupled to a different dimension of time emphasised and a different faculty of subjectivity. To the dimension of the living present is linked the faculty of sensibility or habit, and a concept of repetition as a material recurrence of identical events across the flow of time. To the dimension of the a priori past is linked the faculty of memory, and a concept of repetition as a general recurrence of the 'self' across diverse events. And to the dimension of the future is linked a faculty of thought in which an event is represented as 'too great' for that individual, but which can be brought about through a process of self-overcoming. But why – having sketched out the faculty of subjectivity and the dimension of time associated with this third mode of repetition – does Deleuze account for this form of self-overcoming as a kind of 'repetition'? What is 'repetitive' in the overcoming of one's sense of selfhood and allowing oneself to undergo the change that so dramatically divorces the individual from the person that they knew themself to be? In order to better understand just what is meant by repetition in this context, and why it is related – as Deleuze repeatedly claims – to the Nietzschean concept of the Eternal Return, it will be necessary to take a brief detour through Deleuze's important consideration of time in *Nietzsche and Philosophy*. There we will see why it is that Deleuze understands an encounter with the totality of time as a form of repetition, as well as why this experience is critically related to a notion of overcoming the reactivity of 'being-human', specifically, so that to bring about the Eternal Return will mean something like overcoming the egoistic and identity-preserving characteristics proper to humanity as such. This will, of course, prepare the ground for the consideration of Kierkegaard's notion of faith as its own form of self-overcoming in his account of repetition, below.

Nietzsche and the Eternal Return

The concept of the Eternal Return occupies a paradoxical place in Nietzsche's writings. Although the idea clearly constitutes an important element of his thought, it remains one of the most obscure elements of his philosophy and ultimately is a rare topic of discussion in his published work. Despite this, Nietzsche clearly valued the concept highly, and writes besides his first mention of the concept in August 1881, '6000 feet above the sea, and far higher above all things human!'[25] In section 341 of *The Gay Science*, published the following year, Nietzsche presents the basic premise of the Eternal Return in the form of an imagined encounter between an interpolated reader and a 'demon,' who invites you to imagine

> [that] this life as you now live it and have lived it, you will have to live once more and innumerable times more; and there will be nothing new in it, but every pain and every joy and every thought and sigh and everything unutterably small or great in your life will have to return to you, all in the same succession and sequence. [. . .]
> Would you not throw yourself down and curse the demon who spoke thus? Or have you once experienced the tremendous moment when you would have answered him: 'You are a god and never have I heard anything more divine.'[26]

In *Thus Spoke Zarathustra*, a version of the account is represented in the central 'On the Vision and the Riddle' chapter, where Zarathustra encounters a passage marked 'Moment' (*Augenblick*) and pronounces:

> See this moment! [. . .] From this gateway Moment a long eternal lane stretches *backward*: behind us lies an eternity. / Must not whatever *can* already have passed this way before? Must not whatever can happen, already have happened, been done, passed by before? / And if everything has already been here before, what do you think of this moment, dwarf? Must this gateway too not already – have been here?'[27]

The category of the Eternal Return, as we saw in the last chapter, also plays a significant part in Pierre Klossowski's interpretation of Nietzsche, where much of Nietzsche's thoughts about identity are supposed to follow from his supposed 'lived experience' of the Eternal Return. But as we will see, it is Deleuze's synthesis of the ontological account of the Eternal Return with a normative consideration of that account that gives us a fuller picture of this concept.

In *Nietzsche and Philosophy*, Deleuze distinguishes the concept of the Eternal Return into an 'ethical' doctrine related to the nature of individuals' willing and an 'selective ontological' doctrine related to the abstract properties of 'forces' that we will discuss below. When Deleuze speaks of the Eternal Return as an 'ethical' doctrine he means by this the notion of using the hypothesis of an infinitely returning and recurring universe as a test, serving to distinguish between those kinds of souls capable of accepting and willing the reiteration of their own form of life, and those – as Deleuze puts it – 'like those old women who permit themselves an excess only once', making their decisions 'only on the condition that it be said the day before: tomorrow I will give it up'.²⁸ In other words, in the ethical doctrine of the Eternal Return we separate out, normatively, those who are capable of fully affirming their own way of life, and those whose life remains provisional in some way – something that individuals are willing to accept for the time being, but ultimately resentful of or dissatisfied with. On Deleuze's account, to take as one's principle Nietzsche's motto, 'whatever you will, will it in such a way that you also will its eternal return', will separate out all those who can only do what they do half-heartedly, and so serves as a selective ethical thought distinguishing subjects of willing on that basis.

And yet, on Deleuze's account there is something unsatisfactory in this notion of the Eternal Return as a merely ethical and selective standard for willing. This is because separating out those capable of willing in the way he describes does not adequately prevent the inclusion, in this grouping, of even the most degraded, uninspired and nihilistic ways of being alongside the more creative and life-affirming ways of thinking. This is because, rather than stating that one must will a particular thing or possess a certain kind of personality, the ethical doctrine says simply that 'if' you have uninspiring and base ways of being, so long as you will this manner of life eternally you will satisfy the ethical standard of the test. The Eternal Return as a selective thought 'is content to eliminate certain reactive states, certain states of reactive forces which are among the least developed. But reactive forces which go to the limit of what they can do in their own way [...] resist [such a] selection.'²⁹ In other words, if the doctrine of the Eternal Return remained a merely normative doctrine, it would remain consistent and compatible with even the most reactive and un-creative modes of being having a share in the Eternal Return. What Deleuze's Nietzsche seeks is instead an understanding of the Eternal Return in its ontological significance, such that it is capable of enforcing or bringing it about that the universe it comprised of only those forces that truly affirm their own existence: of active, affirmative forces not only capable of willing their own return but of actually themselves returning so that reactive forces are perpetually vanishing.

This latter, more robust conception of the Eternal Return, goes closer to the account of repetition as a force of change and transformation described in *Difference and Repetition*, and it will show how Deleuze makes the Eternal Return into a fully ontological principle. But to understand how the Eternal Return is understood as a distinctive mode repetition requires a slightly richer understanding of the some of the basic elements of Deleuze's notion of force and his basic account of the category of becoming.

In the second chapter of *Nietzsche and Philosophy*, Deleuze distinguishes between what he calls 'active' and 'reactive' forces, whose basic relationship to one another constitutes a kind of tension or conflict. According to Deleuze, 'active' forces are those that 'go to the limit of what they can do', expressing the full extent of their capacities at each moment and in that sense realising a perfect coincidence between their way of being and their ways of behaving. There is, for these active forces, no 'doer' behind their 'deeds', simply because there is nothing belonging to the force in question beside the effects that it brings about at every moment of its existence.[30] Reactive forces, on the contrary, fundamentally act only by separating other forces from their own actions: they respond to the behaviour of active forces, they take up from the effects of active forces in order to determine how it is that they ought to behave and, critically, they impute to active forces a distinction between those forces and what they do. If we were to imagine active and reactive forces in terms of more familiar, empirical relationships between individuals, 'active' forces would be those which act, create and behave innocently, unreflective of the motives or consequences of their actions, and are fundamentally spontaneous in their estimation of their own actions and behaviours. 'Reactive' forces, on the other hand, would depend upon the behaviour of active forces in order to determine what it is that they value: their fundamental perspective 'says "No" on principle to everything that is "outside," "other," "non-self,"' and so they develop a set of values about how to be and act as 'reactions' to what has been presented to them by active forces.[31] Perhaps more critically for the perspective from which Deleuze is coming, it is reactive forces that attribute to active forces a kind of substance or identity behind what it is that they bring about: it is only by first imputing an ability to choose or refrain from doing the kinds of things that follow from their nature that reactive forces are able to attribute genuine moral responsibility to active forces.[32]

The crucial connection between this conception of reality as a composite of active and reactive forces and the concept of the Eternal Return as an ontological principle has to do with the way in which the forces described change from one kind of force into another. On Deleuze's reading, reactive forces are capable of causing active forces to 'become reactive' through a kind of attribution of moral responsibility to these forces: 'an active force *becomes reactive* [. . .]

when reactive forces [...] separate it from what it can do'.[33] But despite this clear account of what it is for an active force to 'become reactive' in this way, it is not clear what it means for a reactive force to 'become active' in a comparable way. As explained above, it is evidently not enough for a reactive force to 'go to the limit' of what it does, since such an account does not sufficiently distinguish between the most degraded and nihilistic forces and more joyful and affirmative forces. For a reactive force to 'become active' cannot mean for it to simply express its reactivity 'to the limit', but will rather mean for it to participate in a more complicated process according to which it 'transmutes' itself through its own self-destruction in the name of a future or unknown affirmation.[34]

This means that reactive forces participate in a process of 'becoming active' not by directing themselves negatively against active forces (that is, 'going to the limit' of their own nature), but rather through a directing of their endemic negativity towards themselves in such a way as to being about their own destruction or annihilation.[35] This liberation of negativity from the self-preservative interests of reactive forces 'makes negation a negation of reactive forces themselves'.[36] And in this turning of their negativity back upon themselves, reactive forces remount to a form of negativity that takes on an unexpected appearance: here negativity does not serve as a means to the ends of reactive impulses, but rather represents a kind of joy of destruction in which the negativity proper to reactive forces is affirmed for itself. Negativity, in being released from the condition of serving the self-preservative instincts of reactive forces, shows itself in this case as an expression, or mode, of affirmation.[37] Consequently, reactive forces do not 'become active' by going to the limit of their reactive way of behaving (the lazy, spiteful or life-depreciating way in which they act under the 'ethical' test of the Eternal Return), but rather they become-active when they turn towards an active destruction of themselves, 'willing their own downfall', and finding in this activity an expression of affirmation and joy.[38]

In discussing the nature of this process of 'becoming-active', Deleuze refers us to an important concept that he had previously only hinted at: on Deleuze's account, the process of becoming-active is specifically bound up with an overcoming of what means to be 'human' because, as Deleuze says, what is essential to the human being is its own unique manner of being affected. Human beings have a distinctive mode of 'sensibility' or capacity for 'being affected' which coincides with their very tendency to become reactive: what it is to be human, for Deleuze, is to become-reactive, so that becoming-reactive is the distinctive form of affection to which human beings are susceptible. Deleuze writes: 'Is it not [that] man is essentially reactive? [That] becoming-reactive is constitutive of man? *Ressentiment*, bad conscience and nihilism are not psychological traits but the foundation of the humanity in man.'[39] In other words, because the sensibility or manner of being affected proper to human beings is their becoming-reactive, the movement of becoming-active – that is, of having a different way of being affected or mode of sensibility – necessarily entails a kind of overcoming of the very humanity of the individual. 'Becoming-active' means overcoming what it is to be a human being (what Nietzsche famously described in terms of the *Übermensch*) in this sense.

This phenomenon of becoming-active is therefore tied to the category of repetition (we have not forgotten this question!) because, for Nietzsche, to bring about a repetition is nothing other than the affirmation of the existence of a distinctive form of becoming. According to Nietzsche, in a world whose very essence is becoming and change one can only approximate a world of stable identities by affirming and thereby subjectively eternalising the phenomenon of change that one inevitably finds in the world. Hence to affirm the becoming of the world means to attribute a kind of stability or provisional identity to a world which fundamentally refuses to accept such an identity. And Deleuze clarifies that in a world for which neither simple change nor simple identity is possible, 'repetition' – that is, the appearance of possessing an identity but specifically in the form of an absent identity or as something which is not an identity – is the only possible approximation to a (non-existent) world of stability. 'Returning is the being of that which becomes', writes Deleuze, echoing Nietzsche: 'That everything recurs is the closest approximation of a world of becoming to a world of being.'[40] In other words, because becoming-active is the only form of fundamental becoming that can be the object of an affirmation this form of becoming appears for Nietzsche as a of repetition or Return, such that we can say that repetition (Return) is the proper consequence or product of becoming-active.

Bringing together what has been said here with the syntheses of time described above we can at last say something about the normative and ontological values of Deleuze's conception of time: for Deleuze, repetition in his 'third' sense refers to the practice of giving oneself over to becoming in such a way that through this practice of giving-over we overcome our natural tendencies towards self-preservation; we overcome our 'all-too-human' resistance towards change; and we consequently manifest an affirmation of change that allows us to become new people. It is by appeal to our 'singularity' – a term that Deleuze uses to refer to our identity over and against our all-too-human forms of individuation – that individuals can come to relinquish control over their lives, and allow themselves to become one of the infinite number of 'selves' which might be assigned to them by fate. To repeat in this context will mean to permit oneself a change of identity by coming to affirm, against one's reactive instincts, their own 'becoming' in concert with the becoming of the rest of the universe.

Having thus traced this long trajectory that links *Difference and Repetition* to Deleuze's reflections on the Eternal Return in *Nietzsche and Philosophy*, we can now gather together what we have determined, in anticipation of a comparison with Kierkegaard's ideas about repetition. Deleuze is intentional about linking his own conception of repetition to Kierkegaard's own thought, although, as we will see, he also wants to indicate various limitations to Kierkegaard's conception as well. What is relevant for the time being is the idea that repetition, for Deleuze, has to do with a certain kind of dramatic and challenging encounter for the human being wherein, by overcoming one's identity-privileging instincts and opening oneself up to the possibility of radical transformation, the individual learns to affirm becoming as such. In what follows, we will examine Kierkegaard's own threefold account of repetition in order to show how both an affirmation of change and a hostility towards the reactive and 'all-too-human' concerns of the individual are replayed in Kierkegaard's notion of faith. From this we will have the grounds to show the limitations of Deleuze's eventual criticisms of Kierkegaard.

Kierkegaard's Repetitions

The concept of repetition (*Gjentagelse*) in Kierkegaard, like the concept of the Eternal Return in Nietzsche, has a paradoxical status. It is, on the one hand, the eponymous subject of an entire obscure, novelesque work from 1843, written under the pseudonym 'Constantin Constantius', entitled *Repetition*, as well as the subject of some sixty-odd pages of unpublished journal entries written shortly after *Repetition*'s publication composed as an expected reply to a critic.[41] The concept is also afforded an exceptionally high status in a handful of references to both the book and the concept repetition in the also-pseudonymous *The Concept of Anxiety* and elsewhere.[42] And yet – as translators Howard and Edna Hong note in their historical introduction to *Repetition* – the category itself is ultimately 'sparsely represented' in Kierkegaard's writing, and – as interpreter Niels Eriksen observes – the notion is 'overshadowed by other key notions, such as the moment of vision (*Øieblikket*) and the paradox' beginning immediately after 1844.[43] Reflecting on the apparent absence of the concept in Kierkegaard's work, the Hongs are compelled to go so far as to assume that today we simply lack the totality of Kierkegaard's journals and papers (that is, suggesting that repetition simply must be discussed more fully in some missing writing) and, in rectification of this fact, they suggest that an adequate solution would be simply to take references to 'spontaneity after reflection' and even 'faith' as stand-ins for this category.[44] In other words, from this perspective, one could just as well take virtually the entirety of Kierkegaard's pseudonymous work – hundreds upon hundreds of pages of passionate reflection on the Christian notion of faith – as a long and passionate consideration of the category of repetition itself. Repetition would here serve, effectively, as the central preoccupation of almost all his work.[45]

Where it is discussed, the category of repetition appears under a variety of forms, not all of which are affirmed as the 'highest' or most important framing of this concept. According to André Clair, who discusses the category in his book *Pseudonymie et Paradoxe*, the concept of repetition covers at least four different levels, of which the highest level – the 'spiritual repetition' which is the ultimate intended topic of Kierkegaard's book – is divisible into no fewer than three different stages.[46] Here the category of repetition refers not simply to a repetition in the material world as it exists outside of subjectivity, but rather to repetition as a kind of subjective task for the individual who has diverse experiences of this phenomenon. And although Clair disagrees with this notion, I will here defend the claim that it is indeed possible to sketch a conception of Kierkegaardian repetition that in its division surveys roughly the three spheres of existence – the 'aesthetic', 'ethical' and 'religious' spheres – for which Kierkegaard is so well-known.[47] Deleuze himself implies much the same thing in his sketch of Kierkegaardian repetition in *What is Grounding?* – his fullest consideration of Kierkegaardian thought prior to *Difference and Repetition*.[48] For this reason, and for the sake of highlighting the symmetry that I claim will hold between Deleuze's and Kierkegaard's conceptions of this category, I will present the concept of repetition

Faith and Repetition in Kierkegaard and Deleuze

here in terms of Kierkegaard's so-called three stages of existence. As we will see, each of these stages unites – as it does for Deleuze – both a primary faculty of subjectivity, a primary form or mode of repetition, and a primary dimension of time. And in doing so I will also show how Kierkegaard's highest stage, corresponding to faith and the repetition of the future, fulfils the necessary features of a kind of Nietzschean self-overcoming, again emphasising the important element of an individual's 'singularity' and their capacity for transformation.[49]

Three Repetitions

The first mode of repetition that Kierkegaard discusses in his pseudonymous writings corresponds broadly to what he describes as an 'aesthetic' point of view. In his unpublished reply to the critic J. L. Heiberg, Kierkegaard's pseudonym Contantin Constantius describes this conception of repetition in terms of the practical capacity for 'sagacity' (*Klogskab*) by which he means to refer to a kind of prudence or skilfulness in dealing with an otherwise undesirable experience of repetition. 'As yet, freedom has only a finite relation to its object and is qualified only aesthetically ambiguously. Repetition is assumed to exist, but freedom's task in sagacity is continually to gain a new aspect of repetition.'[50] Here Constantius already introduces several of the important elements of the 'aesthetic' conception of repetition that he will elaborate elsewhere: repetition consists in an ultimately material mode of recurrence (that is, a sequence of 'finite' events that one seeks to 'gain a new aspect' of), and the individual's relationship to this form of repetition is to aspire towards 'gaining' or extracting a certain difference from it. In the first volume of *Either/Or*, the character known only as 'A' – taken in Kierkegaard's work as the archetypical representative of an 'aesthetic' mode of existence – elaborates the category of sagacity in terms of the boredom that will inevitably confront us if we lack the ability to find such new aspects of repetition. He calls his method of resolving the difficulties of boredom a 'rotation of crops'. It is through a constant variation of how one approaches or thinks about a repeated material object that one is capable of extracting from repetition a kind of enjoyment. 'Think of our school days', he writes.

> We were at an age when there was no aesthetic consideration in the choosing of our teachers, and therefore they were often very boring – how

57

resourceful we were then! What fun we had catching a fly, keeping it prisoner under a nutshell and watching it run around with it! What a delight in cutting a hole in the desk, confining a fly in it, and peeking at it through a piece of paper! How entertaining it can be to listen to the monotonous dripping from the roof![51]

In this passage the Aesthete describes his process of accommodating himself to repetition by adopting unique ways of appropriating or approaching this repetition, so as to stave off boredom. In this way, the Aesthete brings together a very material form of repetition (the repetition of a single event or daily routine) with a kind of subjectivity – the immediate, 'sensible' worldview of the Aesthete – and a distinctive mode of temporality (repetition in the present).

Thus we find, in this first approach to the concept of repetition, several of the main elements of Deleuze's own original conception of repetition. For Deleuze, recall that the first form of repetition comprised a repetition of material elements sharing an actual identity across time. These elements were then brought together in an immediate sensibility whose function it was to 'draw a difference' from this material repetition in the form of a habit or expectation of the future.[52] And although in this context Deleuze's notion of repetition is not considered from the perspective of boredom, nonetheless there is an everyday prudence involved in Deleuze's notion of this kind of repetition that resembles the 'sagacity' of Kierkegaard's account. Repetition here remains a function of sensibility or *'aiesthesis'*, the repeated event is undeniably empirical and a function of the temporal present, and the manner of repetition is that of a simple identity across time. Here we are already intimated of some strong similarities between Kierkegaard's and Deleuze's conceptions of repetition.

Kierkegaard's second stage of repetition is related to a particular form of ethical subjectivity that, across his body of work, is frequently associated with Stoicism. In the unpublished reply to Heiberg, Constantius writes that – by contrast to the tolerant or dissatisfied attitude towards repetition represented by the aesthetic mode of subjectivity – under an ethical framing, 'freedom's supreme interest is precisely to bring about repetition, and its own fear is that variation would have the power to disturb its eternal nature'.[53] Here Constantin argues, in other words, that the interest of the individual from an ethical point of view is no longer to tolerate an otherwise undesirable phenomenon of repetition – repetition taking place inevitably in the material world – but rather to realise a potentially unattainable form of repetition within one's subjectivity. In this context the problem of the subjective experience of the individual is not the inevitable repetition of the outside world, but rather the perpetually changing, vanishing nature of life. It is thus by adopting a certain ethical stance that an individual is capable of overcoming the change of everyday life, thereby bringing about a certain repetition within themselves or in terms of their persistent identity.

André Clair, in describing this Stoic approximation of repetition, refers to the 'immobile fixation in impassivity [*fixation immobile dans l'impassibilité*]' that allows the individual to obtain a kind of exemption from the change of the temporal world.[54] In drawing the connection between the ethical worldview and a kind of Stoic or Greek worldview, Constantius invokes an association with Platonic ethics that will otherwise appear consistently across Kierkegaard's works. In *Fear and Trembling*, the pseudonym Johannes de Silentio describes ethical subjectivity in terms of a 'resignation' from finitude that allows the individual to obtain a kind of eternal consciousness.[55] And because this mode of resignation is essentially related to the kind of exemption from temporal change that is so often associated with a Socratic worldview, Kierkegaard's pseudonym deliberately associates this category with the faculty of 'recollection' or *anamnesis*: 'Deeper natures never forget themselves and never become anything other than what they were. The knight [of resignation], then, will recollect everything, but this recollection is precisely the pain, and yet in infinite resignation he is reconciled with existence.'[56] Here we have an account of resignation that in its essentials matches a 'Socratic' approach to the temporally fleeting nature of finite existence: the individual withdraws themselves through a faculty of recollection to the Forms of the Good, Justice, and so on, and in so doing earns the kind of continuity or stability that is otherwise unobtainable for them in the empirical world.

This ethical level of repetition thus unavoidably corresponds, point for point, to Deleuze's second mode of repetition, wherein a Platonic transcendental exercise of memory – what Deleuze calls the 'Platonic reminiscence [that] claims to grasp the immemorial being *of* the past' – points us towards a notion of repetition involving the stability of one's trans-temporal personal identity over and against the variations of the finite world.[57] To Kierkegaard's initial mode of repetition as a reflection of an aesthetic worldview, here we have a repetition that is linked to a faculty of memory or recollection, that understands repetition as the maintenance of a persistent subjectivity distinct from empirical experiences, and that is based primarily in the temporal past as opposed to the present of the first repetition. And this sets the stage for the final and most important formulation of the category of repetition in Kierkegaard, corresponding to a Christian notion of faith or belief, inviting us to link this category to a notion of self-overcoming or transformation.

The third conception repetition that Kierkegaard's pseudonyms describe arises, normatively, as the result of a kind of failure of ethical subjectivity to accommodate the entirety of its own ideal. Looking once again at Constantius's reply to Heiberg, we read that for Constantius, the Stoic conception of repetition falls short precisely on account of a factual sort of circumstance: although ethical subjectivity in principle expects to be able to sustain its own repetition through freedom (it is 'self-sufficient' [*Selbtgenugsam*] and therefore need not rely on external circumstances in order to remain the way that it is), for Constantius ethical subjectivity's self-sufficiency is compromised by an appearance of 'sin' as a kind of 'stumbling block' to its exercise of freedom.[58] Constantius writes:

> If freedom here now discovers an obstacle, then it must lie in freedom itself. Freedom now shows itself not to be in its perfection in man but to be disturbed. This disturbance, however, must be attributed to freedom itself, for otherwise there would be no freedom at all, or the disturbance would be a matter of chance that freedom could remove. The disturbance that is attributed to freedom itself is sin.[59]

In *The Concept of Anxiety*, written under the pseudonym Vigilius Haufniensis ('The Watchman of Copenhagen'), the author explains this phenomenon of sin in terms of its radically factical and yet perplexing nature. He calls the discipline that properly deals with such a paradoxical form of actuality 'dogmatics': 'With dogmatics begins the science that, in contrast to that science called ideal *stricte*, namely, ethics, proceeds from actuality. [. . .] It does not deny the presence of sin; on the contrary, it presupposes it and explains it by presupposing hereditary sin.'[60] What Haufniensis, like Constantius, argues for here, is a notion of sin that must be assumed on account of the paradoxical structure that it possesses. Sin is presented as paradoxical for that fact that although it inhibits moral freedom – that is, as Constantius puts it, it 'belongs' to freedom in some sense – yet at the same time it constitutes a form of inhibition that is neither resolvable by means of freedom alone nor is it extrinsic to freedom in such a way that it exempts one from moral responsibility for this sin. The function of sin in this case is precisely to pose a certain kind of problem to ethics – namely, how we can be both morally guilty, aim to be innocent, and yet remain incapable of bringing about our own innocence – in a way that requires us to step outside of the framework of secular ethics entirely.

What Kierkegaard therefore presents, with the category of sin, is a phenomenon that cannot be accounted for in merely rational terms, since it defies the basic parameters of a rational conception of morality. Sin is a limitation to my freedom, that is attributable to my freedom, and yet it cannot be resolved through my freedom alone.[61] The individual finds herself 'caught' by sin, in some sense, in such a way that she cannot work herself free from it. And yet to be caught in sin in this way in no way diminishes the individual's normative need and desire to free herself. This constraint upon the individual's ability to realise a moral repetition therefore leads to another 'higher' mode of repetition that the ethical mode relates to 'as the totality of living creatures in the ocean relates itself to those in the air and to those upon the earth'.[62] This form of repetition coincides not with the moral repetition of the second stage, but rather with an overcoming of sin through faith.

Kierkegaard's Third Repetition

This third, or 'highest' conception of repetition is initially indicated in *The Concept of Anxiety*, although we will have to look to *Philosophical Fragments* in order to understand how this category is linked to the concept of sin that forces Kierkegaard beyond the ethical framework described above. In *The Concept of Anxiety*, Haufniensis describes repetition as coinciding with a kind of religious normativity that he calls 'second ethics' which deals specifically with the form of 'transcendence' endemic to Christianity.

> [In] *Fear and Trembling* [. . .] the author several times allows the desired ideality of aesthetics to be shipwrecked on the required ideality of ethics, in order through these collisions to bring to light the religious ideality as the ideality that precisely is the ideality of actuality, and therefore just as desirable as that of aesthetics and not as impossible as the ideality of ethics. This is accomplished in such a way that the religious ideality breaks forth in the dialectical leap and in the positive mood – 'Behold all things have become new' – as well as in the negative mood that is the passion of the absurd to which the concept 'repetition' corresponds. Either all of existence comes to an end in the demand of ethics, or the condition is

provided [see below] and the whole of life and of existence begins anew, not through an immanent continuity with the former existence, which is a contradiction, but through a transcendence.[63]

Here we already have a sketch of several of the key elements that we will discover upon an inspection of the category of religious repetition below: first, the association of repetition with a religious ideality that will be elaborated alongside the 'condition' for the possibility of overcoming ethics below; second, we have the notion that the form of repetition picks up where 'the ideality of ethics' leaves off, through its very 'shipwrecking'; and, third, we have the notion of a kind of transcendence or break with the continuity of personal identity that moves us from a prior mode of existence to a new one. But in order to properly understand how these elements relate to one another in faith, it will be necessary to look at that concept as it is presented in Kierkegaard's *Philosophical Fragments*, so as to get a better structural understanding of the relationship between faith, temporality, and the overcoming of one's limitations in sin.

In *Philosophical Fragments*, pseudonym Johannes Climacus discusses the relationship between faith and sin in terms of the uniqueness of their temporal character. In that work, Kierkegaard's author is primarily interested in the question of whether it is in fact possible for a 'moment in time' to possess what he calls 'decisive' significance.[64] In order to distinguish this critical category ('decisive significance') from its opposite (what he calls mere 'occasional' significance) Climacus appeals to the familiar Socratic understanding of temporal existence as a mere opportunity for the recollection of eternal knowledge in the occasion of an encounter. For Plato (here Climacus makes no distinction between Socrates and Plato) in encountering an object of empirical experience – for example, two equal-length sticks as described in the *Phaedo* – we are stimulated to recall, through an act of *anamnesis*, the eternal Form of equality supposedly accessible to us through a kind of innate knowledge. In this account, the empirical event of encounter serves as a mere 'occasion' for the recollection of the truth, insofar as it serves simply to point us towards some truth which ultimately bears the greater significance. The 'moment' of encounter in this case bear an only relative, 'occasional' value, on account of primary or decisive significance resting in the recalled object (the Forms) existing outside of time. On this picture of knowledge, temporal events cannot bear the sort of decisive significance that eternity, embodied in the Forms recalled, bears. In asking whether it is possible for historical moments in time to bear 'decisive significance', therefore, Climacus is asking after the possibility of finding some kind of circumstance under which the historical moment at which some truth is learned itself comes to have the kind of significance that eternity bears on the Socratic picture of knowledge. In other words, we ask what could possibly afford temporality the kind of importance owed to eternity.

Climacus's account of sin then is to argue that temporality is capable of bearing the significance of Socratic eternity if what occurs at the moment of knowledge, rather than being a mere exercise of some condition or capacity that already belongs to the individual, is in fact a *reception of the condition* for the possibility of acquiring knowledge. As Climacus puts it, 'if the learner is to obtain the truth, the teacher must bring it to him, but not only that. Along with it, he must provide him with the condition for understanding it, for if the learner were himself the condition for understanding the truth, then he merely needs to recollect, [in which case] the moment is to be understood only Socratically.'[65] In this passage we are given the tools to understand the significance of Climacus's conception of 'faith' as an 'organ' for understanding the truth: on Climacus's account, what occurs in faith is not simply that the individual comes to recognise the truth (here embodied as Christ, who is Himself 'the Truth'), but rather that she receives the condition for the possibility of recognising this truth, and therefore overcomes the limitation ('sin') to which she had been subject up to this point. Hence faith is represented here as a kind of transcendence of the limitations represented by sin in a way that affords time its own distinctive significance comparable to the secular significance of eternity. The overcoming of sin is – as Haufniensis has put it – a 'religious ideality [that] breaks forth [. . .] not through an immanent continuity with the former existence, which is a contradiction, but through a transcendence'.[66] In other words, there is a break that occurs for the individual who overcomes sin, not through an exercise of her known capacities, but through the fortuity of an event that provides her with the condition for overcoming her own limitations.[67]

So why, ultimately, do Kierkegaard's pseudonyms understand this movement of faith as a kind of 'repetition' to add to the preceding two conceptions of repetition? In this context, there are two senses in which the movement of faith can be understood, from within Kierkegaard's texts, as specifically a kind of repetition. The first of these has to do with the way in which – as Climacus describes it – the acquisition of faith constitutes both a kind of break with a preceding identity and, at the same time, a 'rebirth' or 'retaking' (the Danish word for repetition, '*Gjentagelse*', literally means 'to take again') of identity. As Climacus writes, the individual who 're-takes' their freedom after having lost it 'sink[s] down into himself again, just as the person did who once possessed the condition and then, by forgetting that God is, sank into unfreedom'.[68] On the next page he goes on:

> Inasmuch as he was in untruth and now along with the condition receives the truth, a change takes place in him like the change from 'not to be' to 'to be.' But this transition from 'not to be' to 'to be' is indeed the transition of birth. But the person who already *is* cannot be born, and yet he is born. Let us call this transition *rebirth*, by which he enters the world a second time just as at birth.[69]

In this sense, through faith, the individual's identity is 'repeated' in the sense that she recovers or re-stages her own prior existence in an act of rebirth.

But there is another form of repetition here that coincides, I believe, with something close to the metaphysical account of repetition that we saw earlier in the Nietzschean concept of the Eternal Return. Whereas Constantius's second conception of repetition was constituted through the repetition of subjectivity beyond the movement of passing time, the third mode of repetition figures a re-taking of subjectivity that constitutes a synthesis of the eternal and the temporal in an affirmation of temporality as such. For Climacus, the 'moment in time' at which the individual acquires faith amounts to an attribution of, as he puts it, 'eternal significance' to a moment of temporal passage, especially through the acknowledgement of a god who Himself reflects a paradoxical synthesis of eternity and time.[70] In other words, faith here coincides with a profound receptivity to change – just as we saw, in Deleuze's account of the Eternal Return, that notion of repetition as an 'approximation' of the world of becoming to eternity through an affirmation of change.[71] Here again, therefore, we find the same kind of similarity between the Deleuzian notion of the Eternal Return and the Kierkegaardian concept of faith: faith constitutes a paradoxical exercise of the faculty of thought; it reflects a kind of movement oriented towards the future over and against the past and present of the second and first modes of repetition; and finally it involves a framing of repetition an as affirmation of change or becoming, over and against the forms of repetition we

Faith and Repetition in Kierkegaard and Deleuze

saw earlier.[72] And similar to the Deleuzian notion of repetition as a mode of self-overcoming, for Kierkegaard we can see that it is by moving beyond the limits of what is possible for the individual (in this case, stepping beyond one's limited capacities to realise one's ethical ideals) that one comes to affirm this form of repetition by becoming, in effect, a 'new person'.

Deleuze's Criticisms of Kierkegaard

Before drawing this comparison of Deleuze's and Kierkegaard's accounts of repetition to a triumphant close, it is first incumbent upon me as a responsible explicator of Deleuze to consider some of the ways in which he himself discusses Kierkegaard's account of repetition in *Difference and Repetition*. What we will see in these criticisms is that Deleuze in fact over-hastily rejects Kierkegaard's account of repetition – most particularly on account of the supposed 'Kantianism' of Kierkegaard's conception of faith – whereby Kierkegaard is supposed to emphasise a notion of unity at the base of his notion of self-overcoming. Although at this point it will be necessary to correct that reading of Kierkegaard and to show that – in fact – Kierkegaard's account of repetition bears all of marks of an indefinite and open-ended process of becoming, it will also be worthwhile to show how, ultimately, Deleuze himself even corrects this initial criticism of Kierkegaard in his earlier work, so that Kierkegaard's notion of repetition will move from somewhere outside the Deleuzian account of repetition to firmly within the limits of Deleuze's repetition.

For the time being, we will take account of several interconnected criticisms of Kierkegaard that Deleuze makes in his earlier works. These criticisms circulate around (1) the aforementioned claim that Kierkegaard's concept of repetition takes place only 'once'; (2) Kierkegaard's involvement of God as a condition for 'wagering' the self in faith; and (3) a supposed depressive affective orientation that limits Kierkegaard's critique of rationality. Let us take a look at each of these three criticisms in turn.

The first, and perhaps most significant, element of Deleuze's critique of Kierkegaard has to do with his claim that the movement of faith has a kind of subjective identity supposedly waiting at its end, even as it involves a temporary suspension of selfhood in the movement of faith described above.[73] This theme is articulated in terms of a distinction that Deleuze draws between Kierkegaardian repetition, which supposedly takes place 'once and for all', and Deleuzian repetition, in which repetition takes place 'for all times'.[74] And indeed this is a criticism that Deleuze repeats in several places in his writings from this period of time. In *The Logic of Sense*, for example, he writes:

> The Nietzschean repetition has nothing to do with the Kierkegaardian repetition; or, more generally, repetition in the eternal return has nothing to do with the Christian repetition. For what the Christian repetition brings back, it brings back once, and only once: the wealth of Job and the child of Abraham, the resurrected body and the recovered self. There is a difference in nature between what returns 'once and for all' and what returns for each and every time [*pour toutes les fois*], or for an infinite number of times.[75]

In this phrasing we might recognise something of Klossowski's wording in *Nietzsche and the Vicious Circle*, where Nietzsche's experience of the Eternal Return is one in which 'all identities are exchangeable, and [...] none of them is stable once and for all [*une fois pour toutes*]'.[76] On Deleuze's account, the experience of the Eternal Return distributes an individual's identity across an infinite number of repetitions, so that at this moment one feels oneself as not having a single identity but rather adopting (even if only in the dimension of possibly) an infinite number of diverse identities. For Kierkegaard, however – so Deleuze claims – repetition is supposed to take place once: it is expected to bring back a concrete object that has been lost and can be returned as a unique object, and the process by which this object is returned ideally only happens once. It is the exclusivity of this conception of identity – that the individual regains a concrete object with its particular identity, rather than dissipating or dissolving that identity in an indefinite number of possible personalities – that Deleuze opposes in these early reflections on Kierkegaardian repetition.[77]

A second, related critique is articulated in Deleuze's observation that God's existence is not only concretely involved in Kierkegaardian repetition (Kierkegaard's account being, ultimately, a Christian one), but moreover is transcendentally presupposed in the 'either-or' character of the wager presented to Kierkegaard's 'knight of faith' who selects from among a set of exclusive possible outcomes. In *Nietzsche and Philosophy*, Deleuze writes that God is 'the perspective presupposed by [the knight's wager], according to which chance is fragmented into chances of winning and losing'.[78] In other words, the exclusive disjunction between one outcome and another (either

Faith and Repetition in Kierkegaard and Deleuze

Abraham kills Isaac, or Isaac survives the test) prohibits their both being realised at once – a distinction that is maintained for the sake of the religious wager, in which one and not the other of the several outcomes (in this case, Isaac's survival) is in fact desired. In *The Logic of Sense*, Deleuze clarifies the Kantian presupposition involved in such a distinction among 'exclusive' possible outcomes: 'The sum total of the possible is an originary material from which the exclusive and complete determination of the concept of each thing is derived through disjunction. God has no other sense than that of founding this treatment of the disjunctive syllogism.'[79]

In other words, in setting the task of faith as that of bringing about a certain desirable, if unlikely, outcome, Kierkegaard invokes a transcendental, even more than a metaphysical, God as the condition for the possibility of this faith. And this transcendentality is, on a Deleuzian account, perhaps the worse aspect of such a conception of God, to the extent that what is named 'God' under certain philosophical accounts may remain more or less amenable to a Deleuzian ontology of difference (consider, for example, Spinoza's immanent God), but God specifically as the ground for the possibility of exclusive disjunctions is just what Deleuze is obligated to reject.

The third element of Deleuze's critique of Kierkegaard has simply to do with Kierkegaard's affective orientation towards the topics of his own reflection. In *Nietzsche and Philosophy*, Deleuze writes:

> Pascal, Kierkegaard and Chestov, knew, with genius, how to take criticism further than ever before. They suspended morality, they reversed reason but, ensnared in *ressentiment*, they still drew their strength from the ascetic ideal. There were the poets of this ideal. What they oppose to morality, to reason, is still this ideal in which reason is immersed, this mystical body in which it takes root, *interiority* – the spider. In order to philosophize they need all the resources and the guiding thread of interiority, anguish, wailing, guilt, all the forms of dissatisfaction.[80]

In other words, at the origin of Kierkegaard's assessment of the world – and more specifically at the basis of his conception of chance, and the function of faith in bringing about some impossible yet desirable outcome – there is supposed to lie a certain disapprobation of existence as it stands: a judgement that the world is fundamentally unjust in its treatment of human beings and consequently that it is need of redemption either in a world beyond or by a movement, that is alone supposed to make the world inhabitable once more.

Having laid out these criticisms, let us consider them one by one.

On Deleuze's first point, regarding the supposed unity awaiting us at the conclusion of Kierkegaard's account, we can see already how the affirmation of becoming that Kierkegaard endorses in his concept of faith by itself will make this notion of unity unavailable to him. For Kierkegaard, the project that the individual pursues in making the movement of faith is 'gratuitous' – it is a movement that an individual makes not out of a sense of moral obligation or on the condition that it be concluded 'once and for all', but rather for the sake of a unique dimension of selfhood that Kierkegaard refers to as one's 'singularity' – the dimension of the self that compels the individual to overcome the limits of her settled identity and seek a form of becoming that can only be achieved through one's unique relationship to God.[81] And consequently this movement of faith, far from involving a conclusory settling of identity after the movement had been made, takes place precisely through a recognition of the indeterminacy with which the same movement will need to be made again innumerable times in the future. It is just this manner in which faith intrinsically involves its reiterability that Kierkegaard dramatises in *Concluding Unscientific Postscript*, when he writes: 'the terror that this [that is, the challenge of losing one's identity in faith] could happen for one-tenth of a second, remains forever'.[82] André Clair, in his comments on Deleuze's reading of Kierkegaard, indicates quite correctly that the claim that the movement of faith is supposed to take place only 'once and for all' for Kierkegaard is flatly contradicted by the letter of Kierkegaard's writing.[83] On my own count, there are no fewer than six specific statements to the effect that the movement of faith is absolutely not 'once and for all', for example when Johannes Climacus mentions, in *Concluding Unscientific Postscript*, that the movement of faith 'is least of all once and for all [*eengang for alle*]', or the comment in *Philosophical Fragments* that, to say that God gives an individual faith 'once and for all [. . .] is the eternal Socratic presupposition [. . .] which is incommensurable with the categories of temporality': in other words, it is paganism and not Christianity.[84]

And in fact, we find that it is on just this point (that is, on the infinitely reiterable character of the movement of faith) that Deleuze reconsiders his initial assessment of Kierkegaard, fifteen years later, when he writes in *Cinema I* (which we will discuss in Chapter 4) that the movement of faith

> is not defined by what it chooses, but by the power that it possesses to be able to start afresh at every instant, of starting afresh itself, and in this

way confirming itself by itself, by putting the whole stake back into play each time. And even if this choice implies the sacrifice of the person, this is a sacrifice that he only makes on condition for knowing that he will start it afresh each time, and that he does it for all times [*pour toutes les fois*] (here again, this is a very different conception from that of Expressionism for which the sacrifice is once and for all [*une fois pour toutes*]).[85]

Consequently, we ought to understand Kierkegaard's conception of faith not as something that brings about a return to identity through a repetition that takes place only once, but rather as a movement which elevates the individual's identity 'to [a] second power', according to which one's present way of being reflects a mere object of chance, in which an infinite diversity of identities are equally reflected.[86]

To Deleuze's second point, on the notion of the 'exclusive' function of the either-or in Kierkegaard, we might observe, again, how such an account ignores the gratuitous character of the movement of faith. Whereas Deleuze likes to suggest, on his account, that in making the movement of faith a person of faith anticipates a desirable outcome from this movement – one which is perhaps maximally unlikely or impossible but nonetheless hoped for – in fact we will see that Kierkegaard's knight of faith makes such a movement not out of expectation of achieving something once considered impossible, but rather specifically for the sake of proving her own willingness to participate in this trial. In other words, the movement of faith is done not for the sake of its outcome, but rather the outcome is there (as lost, in advance) for the sake of affirming the chance involved in the movement of faith. As we will see concretely in the next chapter, it is in the individual's ability to recognise the impossibility of success, and yet act in full consciousness as though this were not the case, that turns the desire for a particular outcome into a desire to participate in the trial of faith itself. As Johannes de Silentio puts it in *Fear and Trembling*, the reason why Abraham makes the movement of faith is not because he expects to thereby secure some good which he deems otherwise impossible to obtain, but rather 'for God's sake and – the two are wholly identical – for his own sake. He does it for God's sake because God demands this proof of his faith; he does it for his own sake so that he can prove it.'[87] In other words, any conditioned division of possible outcomes in the movement of faith does not serve to establish an exclusive outcome that the individual expects to realise, but rather as a condition for the possibility of affirming the whole of chance as the faithful person does when she bets on an impossible outcome. Unlike, as Deleuze says, the player who 'distribute[s] [probability] over several throws' (which he associates with *ressentiment*) the knight of faith affirms 'all of chance at once' in the absolute gratuitousness of her test.[88]

And finally, to address the element of the 'ascetic' character of Kierkegaardian faith, we might notice an important but perhaps overlooked hermeneutic element of Kierkegaard's authorship: namely, that Kierkegaard's pseudonymous representations of faith, especially the 'anguished' representations put forward by authors like Climacus and Silentio (the latter of whom claims, for example, that he 'cannot make [. . .] the paradoxical movement of faith, although there is nothing [he] wish[es for] more'), are precisely bracketed in these representations.[89] In other words, for Kierkegaard, these accounts of faith do not simply serve as a theoretical presentations, but additionally as representations of their pseudonymous authors' orientations towards faith, such that – when we consider these representations as involving a marked dissatisfaction – it is because these pseudonymous authors are intended to portray an important limitation in their 'aesthetic' relationships to faith. One important passage, in this regard, is Kierkegaard's introduction to the upbuilding discourse, 'Look at the Birds of Air, Look at the Lily of the Field', where he distinguishes between the way in which the 'poet' relates to the task of faith, and the way in which the single individual relates to the task of faith. There, he writes:

> Underlying the poet's life there is really the despair of being able to become what is wished, and this despair feeds *the wish*. [. . .] In the poet the wish comes to existence in pain, and this wish, this burning wish, rejoices the human heart more than wine cheers it, more than the earliest bud of spring [. . .]. When the poet thinks about the bird and the lily, he weeps. Meanwhile, as he weeps, he finds relief; the wish comes into existence, and with it the eloquence of the wish [. . .]. But the Gospel dares to command the poet, dares to order that he *shall* be like the bird. And so earnest is the Gospel that the poet's most irresistible invention does not make it smile.[90]

In this passage, what we see is the essence of the critique that Kierkegaard levels even against his own pseudonyms in their praise of faith. The critique that Kierkegaard levels is to understand these depictions precisely as aesthetic: they reflect a kind of deliberate distancing between the individual and faith, so that rather that partaking of the pleasures of faith, they instead produce encomia that emphasise their own failure or inability to obtain it. In this way,

Kierkegaard's pseudonymous authors make use of their suffering to produce art, rather than becoming knights of faith. Thus Deleuze's critique – to the effect that the repetition of faith is represented in Kierkegaard as something difficult or torturous – may well be the same critique that Kierkegaard intends to make: Kierkegaard's pseudonymous representations of faith are not wrong in their basic coordination of the ways in which faith problematises conventional secular philosophy and ethics, but they are misrepresentations to the extent that they depict faith as a torture to their authors rather than as a source of persistent joy.

Conclusion

For all these reasons, we can see that Kierkegaard's account of faith – as a movement of affirmation of singularity that liberates the individual from her calcified sense of identity – is sufficiently different from the negative picture that Deleuze paints of it to actually coincide quite nicely with many of the elements of the latter's account. The claims that Kierkegaardian faith represents an affirmation of theological presuppositions, that it affirms identity over difference, or that it is grounded in *ressentiment*, overlook the affirmative features of his account. And consequently, there are good reasons to suspect that a more charitable reading of Kierkegaard will evoke ideas and themes valuable to a reader coming from a Deleuzian perspective, just as a reading of Deleuze's conception of repetition can helpfully inform an understanding of Kierkegaardian faith. In what follows, we will take up this notion of repetition as a normative ideal to consider a broader account of Deleuze and Kierkegaard's conceptions of ethics. In so doing we will see how, for both Deleuze and Kierkegaard, a radical rejection of prescriptive ethics lies at the basis of their normative ideals, so that to accomplish a movement of self-overcoming will mean to affirm something like the unique singularity of the individual in question.

Notes

1 Deleuze, *Difference and Repetition*, p. 70.
2 On the concept of repetition in Deleuze, see Williams, *Gilles Deleuze's* Difference and Repetition, pp. 91–117, as well as Williams's more extended account of repetition in *Gilles Deleuze's Philosophy of Time*. Keith Faulkner, from a more psychoanalytically influenced perspective,

gives an account of the three syntheses of time in *Deleuze and the Three Syntheses of Time*, and Henry Somers-Hall gives a concise account of the three syntheses in *Deleuze's* Difference and Repetition.
3. Deleuze, *Difference and Repetition*, p. 70, trans. slightly modified. Deleuze is of the opinion that the contemplating mind is strictly speaking first established in the contraction of the elements that it thus contemplates – so that there is a simultaneous determination of the contracting mind along with the elements thus contracted. See ibid., p. 78.
4. Ibid., p. 70: 'Time is constituted only in the originary synthesis which operates on the repetition of instants.'
5. Ibid., p. 79. Note that in Deleuze, *Nietzsche and Philosophy*, p. 48, it is the Eternal Return that grounds the material passage of time.
6. Deleuze, *Difference and Repetition*, p. 79. See also ibid., pp. 59–63, and *What is Grounding?*, pp. 21–24 for an account of the present in terms of its 'claim' to pass.
7. These three characteristics of the 'pure past' Deleuze derives from Henri Bergson's reflections in *Matter and Memory*, where the paradoxes of time are represented as necessitating a re-envisioning of the concept of time. Deleuze obscurely references these paradoxes in *Nietzsche and Philosophy* as well (p. 48).
8. Deleuze, *Difference and Repetition*, p. 80.
9. 'Transcendental memory [in contrast to the empirical exercise of memory] grasps that which from the outset can only be recalled, even the first time: not a contingent past, but the being of the past as such and the past of every time', ibid., p. 140. See also, on this topic, Bergson, *Matter and Memory*, p. 152: Habit is only 'the pointed end' of the past.
10. Ibid., pp. 82–83.
11. Ibid., pp. 83–84.
12. 'Habit' or – as we have said – 'sensibility' grasps the being of the present *qua* empirically imperceptible, as thought does the being of the future (see below), cf. ibid., pp. 139–140.
13. Ibid., p. 88. See also p. 145: '[The ambiguity of the ground is] to represent itself in the circle that it imposes on what it grounds, to return as an element in the circuit of representation that it determines in principle.'
14. Ibid.
15. On the notion of the 'groundless' or 'unground' (*Ungrund*) towards which sufficient reason always points, see ibid., pp. 67, 88 and 274. See also, Deleuze, *Coldness and Cruelty*, p. 114: 'No sooner have we reached the condition or ground of our principle than we are hurled headlong beyond to the absolutely unconditioned, the "ground-less" from which the ground itself emerged.'

16 Kant, *Critique of Pure Reason*, pp. 271–277 [A137–147/B176–187]. Kant's time-determinations are the 'time series' (*Zeitreihe*), 'time content' (*Zeitinhalt*), 'time order' (*Zeitordnung*) and 'totality of time' (*Zeitinbegriff*).
17 Deleuze, *Difference and Repetition*, p. 89. Deleuze also discusses the 'time-order' as distinct from the 'time-series' mentioned below, in *Cinema II*, p. 155.
18 Ibid.
19 See Kant, *Critique of Pure Reason*, p. 276 [A146/B185]. Guyer and Woods translate '*Zeitinbegriff*' as 'sum total of time'.
20 Deleuze, *Difference and Repetition*, p. 89.
21 Ibid. Deleuze links this concept of becoming-equal to the Aristotelian concept of 'recognition' (*anagnoresis*), at *Difference and Repetition*, p. 15.
22 Ibid., pp. 89–90.
23 Ibid., p. 88.
24 As we will see in what follows, the association of a certain 'idea' with the disordering of identity was already drawn in Klossowski's *Nietzsche and the Vicious Circle*, where Klossowski describes the Eternal Return as '[a] thought that is so perfectly coherent that it excludes me *at the very moment I think* it', Klossowski, *Nietzsche and the Vicious Circle*, p. 64. In this we see already the idea that Deleuze articulates, linking this 'futural' category of repetition to the faculty of thought (as compared to the faculties of sensibility and memory above), as well as the notion of the *Zeitinbegriff* to the Eternal Return, Deleuze, *Difference and Repetition*, p. 90.
25 Quoted in de Launay, 'Introduction' to *Le Gai Savoir*.
26 Nietzsche, *The Gay Science*, p. 273.
27 Nietzsche, *Thus Spoke Zarathustra*, p. 126.
28 Deleuze, *Nietzsche and Philosophy*, p. 68.
29 Ibid., p. 69.
30 On the absence of the 'doer' behind the 'deed' see *On the Genealogy of Morality*, 'First Essay' §13.
31 Nietzsche, *On the Genealogy of Morality*, p. 20.
32 Deleuze, *Nietzsche and Philosophy*, p. 57; see also Nietzsche, *On the Genealogy of Morality*, p. 26.
33 Deleuze, *Nietzsche and Philosophy*, p. 57.
34 Ibid., p. 68.
35 Ibid., pp. 68–69.
36 Ibid., p. 70.
37 Ibid., pp. 70–71 and 174–175.
38 Nietzsche, *Thus Spoke Zarathustra*, pp. 7–9. Deleuze describes the affirmation described here as the *ratio essendi* of the will to power, in the sense that it captures something proper to the unique way of being

of the will to power, whereas negation is merely its *ratio cognoscendi* – that is, the only form under which the will to power is ever known to us as reactive and life-deprecating creatures. See, Deleuze, *Nietzsche and Philosophy*, p. 173.
39 Deleuze, *Nietzsche and Philosophy*, pp. 64–65. We will see how this notion of 'sensibility' or 'way of being affected' plays an important role in Deleuze's 'ethology' of immanent ethics in the next chapter.
40 Deleuze, *Nietzsche and Philosophy*, p. 48; Nietzsche, *Will to Power*, pp. 330 [617].
41 Kierkegaard, 'Supplement'. pp. 283–319. The critic was J. L. Heiberg (1791–1860).
42 Kierkegaard, *Concept of Anxiety*, pp. 17–18 and 90.
43 Hong and Hong, 'Historical Introduction', p. xxxiii; Eriksen, *Kierkegaard's Category of Repetition*, p. 5.
44 Hong and Hong, 'Historical Introduction', p. xxxiii.
45 Eriksen similarly claims that the concepts of 'the paradox' and 'the moment' – just as much as the concept of repetition – can be taken as rearticulations of the central thought and concern of Kierkegaard's body of work, *Kierkegaard's Category of Repetition*, p. 5.
46 Clair, *Pseudonymie et Paradoxe*, pp. 66–68. It is worth noting that the category of spiritual repetition (as opposed to mere 'material' repetition) is used across *Difference and Repetition*; see pp. 24, 25, 83, 84 and 106.
47 Clair, *Pseudonymie et Paradoxe*, p. 67, fn. 52. The three 'spheres' or 'stages' of existence are most famously accounted in Kierkegaard, *Stages on Life's Way*, p. 476.
48 Deleuze, *What is Grounding?*, p. 77.
49 A broad survey of the concept of repetition in Kierkegaard is available in Emmanuel, McDonald and Stewart (eds), *Kierkegaard's Concepts, Tome V: Objectivity to Sacrifice*, where the entry focuses on an explication of the pseudonym Constantius's encomium to repetition, Kierkegaard, *Repetition*, p. 149. Both Niels Eriksen, in *Kierkegaard's Category of Repetition*, and Stephen Crites compare Kierkegaard's repetition to the Eternal Return, although only Eriksen pursues these similarities so far as to say that Nietzsche's Overman and Kierkegaard's 'believer' actually maintain some strong correspondence (see Erikson, *Kierkegaard's Category of Repetition*, p. 154). Both Clair and Eriksen reference Deleuze's comments on Kierkegaard, but neither pursue a comparison. For a schematic of correspondences between Deleuze and Kierkegaard's accounts, see Appendix B.
50 Kierkegaard, 'Supplement', pp. 301–302.
51 Kierkegaard, *Either/Or I*, p. 292. Kierkegaard's 'Constantius' refers to the Aesthete in 'Supplement', pp. 301–302.
52 Deleuze, *Difference and Repetition*, p. 70: 'One can speak of repetition

only by virtue of the change or difference [. . .] that the mind *draws from* repetition', emphasis in original.
53 Kierkegaard, 'Supplement', p. 302.
54 Clair, *Pseudonymie et Paradoxe*, p. 68.
55 Kierkegaard, *Fear and Trembling*, p. 43.
56 Ibid.
57 Deleuze, *Difference and Repetition*, p. 140.
58 Kierkegaard, 'Supplement', pp. 302 and 326.
59 Ibid., p. 320.
60 Kierkegaard, *Concept of Anxiety*, p. 19.
61 Kierkegaard, 'Supplement', p. 320.
62 Kierkegaard, *Concept of Anxiety*, p. 17.
63 Ibid., *Concept of Anxiety*, p. 17, fn *.
64 Kierkegaard, *Philosophical Fragments*, pp. 1 and 13.
65 Ibid., p. 14.
66 Kierkegaard, *Concept of Anxiety*, p. 17.
67 It is worth noting, in this context, that Kierkegaard correlates this concept of faith specifically with an exercise of thought, *Philosophical Fragments*, p. 37. 'Faith' – which makes possible the comprehension or understanding of the paradox of Christ – emerges in the space where the understanding confronts something that it is unable to understand, and consequently steps aside in order to make room for the faithful grasping of the paradox. In this sense, Kierkegaard's conception of faith is an articulation of what Deleuze describes in *Difference and Repetition* when he speaks of the paradox as the 'highest pathos of thought', *Difference and Repetition*, p. 227. In *Nietzsche and the Vicious Circle*, Klossowski similarly defines the Eternal Return as such a paradoxical object, owing to the way in which it perplexes the identity of the one who thinks it, Klossowski, *Nietzsche and the Vicious Circle*, p. 64.
68 Kierkegaard, *Philosophical Fragments*, p. 17.
69 Ibid., p. 19, emphasis in original.
70 Ibid., p. 87: 'The historical is that the god *has come into existence*'; 'the god's eternal essence is inflected into the dialectical qualifications of coming into existence', emphasis in original.
71 In this sense, Eriksen concurs that Nietzschean recurrence and Kierkegaardian repetition both figure distinct ways of 'historicizing the eternal and eternalizing the historical', although he argues that the two philosophers differ on the role of the Other in their conceptions, *Kierkegaard's Category of Repetition*, p. 153, quoting Kierkegaard, *Philosophical Fragments*, p. 100.
72 For the explicit association of faith with the future, see *Concept of Anxiety*, p. 90. For the notion of faith as a kind of potentiation of thought, see *Philosophical Fragments*, p. 37.

73 On this theme, see Deleuze, *Difference and Repetition*, p. 95; and also Deleuze, *Logic of Sense*, pp. 300–301.
74 Ibid. Deleuze's phrases, *'une fois pour toutes'* ('once and for all') and *'pour toutes les fois'* ('for all times'), seem to be references to Klossowski's use of these same phrases, as early as his 1935 article, 'Temps et Agressivité', pp. 101–102, and, later, in *Nietzsche and the Vicious Circle*, p. 58
75 Deleuze, *Logic of Sense*, p. 300–301.
76 Klossowski, *Nietzsche and the Vicious Circle*, p. 224. The phrase appears in relation to the question of identity in *Nietzsche and the Vicious Circle* at least a dozen times.
77 The opposition between repetition performed 'once and for all' and repetition that takes place 'for all times' is perhaps the most readily repeated element of Deleuze's comparison between Kierkegaard and Nietzsche, appearing (for example) in Williams's, *Gilles Deleuze's* Difference and Repetition, p. 49; Bogue, 'To Choose to Choose', pp. 120–121; Carlisle, *Kierkegaard's Philosophy of Becoming*, p. 139; and Somers-Hall, *Deleuze's* Difference and Repetition, p. 14. As we note below, only Justo, 'Gilles Deleuze: Kierkegaard's Presence in his Writings', identifies any evolution in Deleuze's thought on this topic.
78 Deleuze, *Nietzsche and Philosophy*, p. 37.
79 Deleuze, *Logic of Sense*, p. 296.
80 Deleuze, *Nietzsche and Philosophy*, p. 36.
81 We will discuss this concept of singularity at length in the following chapter.
82 Kierkegaard, *Concluding Unscientific Postscript*, p. 267.
83 Clair, *Pseudonymie et Paradoxe*, p. 340.
84 Kierkegaard, *Concluding Unscientific Postscript*, p. 488; *Philosophical Fragments*, p. 62. For other references, see also *Concluding Unscientific Postscript*, pp. 44, 175 and 525, *Fear and Trembling*, p. 37, and *Either/Or II*, p. 139.
85 Deleuze, *Cinema I*, p. 115. So far as I am aware, this shift in attitude towards Kierkegaard's concept of repetition has only been noted by Justo in his meticulous 'Gilles Deleuze: Kierkegaard's Presence in his Writings', p. 98.
86 Kierkegaard, *Repetition*, p. 229.
87 Kierkegaard, *Fear and Trembling*, p. 60.
88 Deleuze, *Nietzsche and Philosophy*, p. 27.
89 Kierkegaard, *Fear and Trembling*, p. 51.
90 Kierkegaard, 'Look at the Birds of the Air; Look at the Lily in the Field', pp. 8–9, emphasis in original.

3

Kierkegaard as a Thinker of Immanent Ethics

Having now established some idea of where Deleuze and Kierkegaard stand on the nature of personal identity, I want to turn more directly towards the two philosophers' ethical thought, insofar as this is related to some of the normative features of repetition from the previous chapter. Having shown that both Deleuze and Kierkegaard are primarily interested in those sorts of practices which serve to free the individual from the stability of their identity, we can here look at the ways in which this normative ideal serves as part of a more general orientation in the two philosophers towards an ethics that we can call – following Deleuze's nomination – 'immanent' ethics. What this means is that in this chapter I am interested in showing how Kierkegaard's ethical thought, which has been read in all sorts of directions by his interpreters, in fact may be best understood in terms of the Deleuzian distinction between so-called 'transcendental morality' and immanent ethics. In making this argument, I will also need to respond to an intuitive criticism of my comparison between Deleuze and Kierkegaard, to the effect that Kierkegaard in fact breaks with Deleuze's basic orientation towards immanence by virtue of his necessarily 'transcendental' orientation. Showing how Kierkegaard can be understood as, in fact, a strong representative of immanent ethics, and moreover how Kierkegaard's very understanding of transcendence can be shown to harmonise with Deleuze's understanding of immanence, will provide us with an important set of tools for the exchange of thought between the two philosophers: Deleuze can be read in terms of a distinctive form of transcendence as it is understood through a Kierkegaardian framework, just as Kierkegaard can be understood in terms of the category of immanence in the way that Deleuze understands it. As I argue at the end of the chapter, this capacity for a more generalised conceptual exchange between the two philosophers on their normative thought offers readers a number of useful consequences; among them, Kierkegaard will be seen to offer to thinkers of Deleuzian ethics a set of ethical concepts and practices that will avoid some of the more nihilistic aspects of Deleuze's thought. Whereas one tradition of Deleuze interpretation might place an emphasis on the concepts of self-destruction and 'nomadism' in his ethics, a Kierkegaardian approach might emphasise the ways in which diverse everyday practices of encounter can solicit forms of becoming that are separable from simple self-destruction. Indeed, virtues such as patience, love and humility can serve to facilitate the kinds of self-overcoming that Deleuze is more wont to describe otherwise.

To these ends, the chapter is comprised of three main elements: first, I look at what Deleuze means by the term immanent ethics, drawing primarily from his accounts in *Spinoza: Practical Philosophy* and *The Logic of Sense* to sketch and illustrate this category. Then, I give an account of Kierkegaard's Christian ethics sufficient to justify my claim that, in fact, Kierkegaard's thought can best be understood in terms of Deleuze's distinction between immanent and transcendental morality. Finally, I address the obvious concern with this account: namely, the idea that by presenting Kierkegaard as a thinker of immanent ethics I violate Kierkegaard's own invocation of the language of transcendence in order to describe his form of Christianity. I conclude by looking particularly at some of the criticisms of Deleuze's 'romantic' ethics from Tamsin Lorraine's *Deleuze and Guattari's Immanent Ethics* and defend a Kierkegaardian account as more adequate to the concern that 'fledgling subjects' might have some guidance to draw from this type of ethics.

The Concept of an Immanent Ethics

So what is an immanent ethics? Perhaps the most concrete explication of this concept comes from Deleuze's short 1970 book, *Spinoza: Practical Philosophy*, where the author distinguishes between the categories of immanent ethics and transcendent morality in Spinoza. Here I will discuss three of the major features of this account.[1]

The first of the major features of Deleuze's conception of immanent ethics has to do with the difference between a prescriptive and a descriptive account of normativity. From the perspective of transcendent morality, a prescription – for example, a command of the sort 'Thou shalt not eat of the fruit from the tree of knowledge of good and evil' – will indicate an normative obligation requiring the obedience of a subject.[2] In this case, to eat of the fruit of the tree of knowledge of good and evil is to violate a duty, one that is intended to constrain the actions of the individual commanded, and the consequences that follow from the violation of this commandment ought to be understood as a kind of punishment. Deleuze writes that, in this commandment, 'Adam thinks that God has shown him a sign' – one which says that the specified action in question violates some transcendental rule, and that its performance is therefore prohibited and punishable by death.³ This sketches a conventional understanding of morality under its 'transcendental' sense, in which moral truths have their basis somewhere outside of our individual desires and wants, and therefore serve to constrain or limit our individual ways of acting.

As Deleuze argues, on an immanent conception of ethics, the commandment that God gives to Adam to the effect that he ought not to eat of the tree of knowledge of good and evil does not in fact present a 'prescriptive' statement of the sort intended to constrain his behaviour, but rather constitutes a descriptive statement related to the implicit interests and desires of the individual in terms of what Deleuze calls that individual's 'singular essence'.⁴ 'God reveals to Adam that the fruit will poison him because it will act on his body by decomposing its relation', writes Deleuze, 'but because Adam has a weak understanding he interprets the effect as a punishment, and the cause as a moral law, that is, as a final cause operating through commandment and prohibition'.⁵ For Deleuze, what God describes to Adam – or what, at least, Adam understands – in the form of a prescriptive commandment is in fact nothing other than a truth about the way in which the world is constructed, insofar as this is related to something about the nature or essence of Adam as a singular individual. 'The divine prohibition against eating of the fruit of the tree is only the revelation to Adam that the fruit is "bad"; i.e., it will decompose Adam's relation: "just as he also reveals to us through the natural intellect that a poison is deadly to us."'⁶ As a consequence of the essentially descriptive nature of God's revelation, Adam will – rather than subjecting his behaviour to a constraint exercised by his free will – instead avoid the fruit of the tree of knowledge of good and evil of necessity under the condition that this truth is adequately understood by him, just as anyone who properly understands the disvalue involved in a particular action that goes directly against their natural instincts and desires will avoid that action as a matter of course.⁷ In other words, in this case the apparent prescription that God presents to Adam is quite simply a misunderstood truth (Deleuze calls it an 'eternal truth') whose content will be immediately integrated into the behaviour of the individual under conditions of adequate comprehension.⁸

Deleuze goes on to explain how it is that this essentially indicative sort of statement ('Do not eat of the tree', and so on) comes to be so often interpreted and experienced as a prescriptive commandment requiring the intervention of a will in order to obey. He writes: 'All that one needs in order to moralize is to fail to understand. It is clear that we have only to misunderstand a law for it to appear to us in the form of a moral "You must."'[9] This is to say that the reason why Adam mistakenly interprets the descriptive content of God's statement regarding the fruit of the tree of knowledge of good and evil as an imperative has to do with Adam's lack of understanding regarding this truth.[10] On an immanent ethical account, when we do not properly understand the relationship between our own interests and the objects or actions that will harm these interests, we experience our otherwise unproblematic avoidance of those particular objects as the consequence of a particular obligation that we ought to obey out of a sense of obedience or fear of punishment. Deleuze elaborates the inverse relationship between understanding and obeying implied in this account in terms of a mathematical example. Speaking of a mathematical rule which describes a proportional relationship between the variables in several fractions (this is the so-called 'Rule of Three' that Deleuze adopts from Spinoza's *Short Treatise*), he writes that, when we do not properly understand how to solve for one of the variables in this equation, we might nonetheless adhere to the method or rule for answering this problem as if it were a duty.[11] In this case, although we might effectively bring about the specific aim that we have in solving for an unknown variable, nonetheless our knowledge of the relationship between the solution arrived at and the behaviour that we adopt is in no way increased, and – furthermore – there is nothing in our practice to indicate a capacity to distinguish between a truthful account of how we ought to arrive at the correct solution and a false account of how we ought to arrive that same solution. Spinoza writes:

> Someone has merely heard someone else say that if, in the rule of three, you multiply the second and third numbers, and divide the product by the first, you then find the fourth number, which has the same proportion to the third as the second to the first. And in spite of the fact that the one who told him could have been lying, he still governed his actions according to this rule, without having had any more knowledge of the rule of three than a blind man has of color. So whatever he may have been able to say about it, he repeated, as a parrot repeats what it has been taught.[12]

Kierkegaard as a Thinker of Immanent Ethics

Here it is because we lack insight into the truth of the relationships between the various elements of our problem that our technique for solving it – the technique we adopt or 'obey' to arrive at the desired result – appears to us as having only as rigorous a relationship to the conclusion aimed at as does a kind of magical ritual or trick. Our behaviour here is effectively identical to the enactment of a kind of superstition, in which, by performing the necessary penance or rites, we arrive at a desirable outcome that we would otherwise arrive at unreflectively if we simply understood, in a comprehensive way, the nature of the relationship between our behaviour and the desired result. In just this way, Deleuze argues, the relationship between a supposedly 'proscribed' behaviour and our own happiness or will seem to have a kind of extrinsic quality when we do not properly understand the truth contained in the relationship between the proscribed behaviour and our own interests. Hence, Deleuze writes, 'one only has to misunderstand an eternal truth [. . .] in order to interpret it as an imperative'.[13] In this way, an immanent ethics cannot take the form of providing a set of prescriptive commandments intended to restrict the behaviour of any individual. Rather, it appears as a mechanism for increasing our knowledge or understanding about the nature of the world – including the nature of our own essences – in a way that is related to the ultimate realisation or expression of individual essences. In this sense, there is a practical value to the descriptive content contained in an immanent ethical science, but it is related to our happiness or well-being through the medium of a richer appreciation of the nature of who and what we are and how we relate to a complex world outside of us.

This distinction between moral obligation and ethical description is linked to another, closely related element of Deleuze's concept of immanent ethics – namely, the idea that such an ethics ought primarily to be understood as an 'ethology' or 'science' of diverse 'ways of existing'.[14] Invoking an element from our account in the previous chapter, Deleuze writes that in Spinoza 'animals are defined less by the abstract notion of genus and species than by a capacity for being affected, by the affections of which they are "capable," by the excitations to which they react within the limits of their capability. [. . .] The *Ethics* is an *ethology* which, with regard to men and animals in each case only considers their capacity for being affected.'[15] Here Deleuze refers, indirectly, to the conception we saw above, in the account from *Nietzsche and Philosophy* whereby a being's 'sensibility' – indeed, what it is to 'be' for a particular individual or kind of individual – refers fundamentally to that individual's particular capacity 'for being affected' or for 'becoming'.[16] Indeed it was this distinctive 'capacity for being affected' that Deleuze emphasised in describing the 'becoming-active' of forces as a transformation of the basic way of being that was 'essentially' constitutive of the human being.[17]

For Deleuze and Spinoza, immanent ethics is an 'ethology' because it belongs to only certain kinds of individuals or ways of being to be affected by, and to 'become' in relation to, specific sorts of events. The sort of individual who is 'capable' of finding joy in making a work of art might be different from, for example, the sort of individual who is 'capable' of finding joy in obtaining political power. Hence, for Deleuze to describe ethics not as an system of judgement but as an ethology means that under an immanent ethics individuals are understood – we might say – 'aesthetically': not simply in terms of their aesthetic 'kind' or as an aesthetic character type, but also in terms of their very 'sensibility' or capacity for being affected and changed under diverse conditions.[18] On Deleuze's account, individuals will be understood – from an ethical perspective – not in terms of their nearness or distance from a necessitated normative ideal, but rather in terms of their diverse ways of existing, including their diverse tendencies to realise or fail to realise what ultimately belongs to their unique 'essence'. It is for this reason that, in another context, Deleuze will talk about the close relationship between an aesthetic, 'critical' account of the character types found in literature and film, and an ethological, 'clinical' understanding of these character types as so many ways of achieving or struggling to achieve one's specific essence. For Deleuze, ethics consists of a careful study of 'how' different individuals can live their lives, rather than constituting a strict canon for one's individual behaviour.[19]

Given that immanent ethics is primarily a matter of a descriptive understanding of diverse ways of existing, one might wonder where this sort of account leaves the conventional categories of moral good and evil. And here we will find that Deleuze adopts an answer to this question that fits perfectly which the above account of ethics as a matter of how individuals seek to express or realise their singular essences in action. This is to say that, rather than posing the difference between good and evil in terms of a universal judgement of kinds of behaviours that ought or ought not to be performed, Deleuze approaches the question of good and evil from the perspective of individuals' interests as finite essences – beings that are capable of being harmed in opposition to their characteristic way of being, or of realising and expressing that characteristic way of being to the fullest possible extent. In *Spinoza: Practical Philosophy*, Deleuze describes this as perhaps the central revision that Spinoza applies to the conventional categories of morality:

> There is no Good and Evil, but there is good and bad [. . .]. The good is when a body directly compounds its relation with ours, and, with all or part of its power, increases ours. A food, for example. For us, the bad is when a body decomposes our body's relation, although it still combines with our parts, but in ways that do not correspond to our essence, as when a poison breaks down the blood. Hence good and bad have a primary, objective meaning, but one that is relative and partial: that which agrees with our nature or does not agree with it.[20]

In this passage, Deleuze reframes the relationship between the evaluative categories good and evil in terms of the specific ways in which individuals achieve or fail to achieve what is in their basic interest. Individuals have distinctive ways of being or capacities for being affected, and it is through their encounters with external objects – through the events that they undergo in time – that they come to either increase their capacities for acting and being affected, or decrease these. To these correspond feelings of joy or sadness:

> When we encounter an external body that does not agree with our own [. . .] it may be said that our power of acting is diminished or blocked, and that the corresponding passions are those of *sadness*. In the contrary case, when we encounter a body that agrees with our nature, one whose relation compounds with ours, we may say that its power is added to ours; the passions that affect us are those of *joy*, and our power of acting is increased or enhanced.[21]

On this framework, 'good' and 'bad' are not evaluations of actions independently of their relationship to ourselves – that is, they are not universal moral evaluations – but rather they are relative evaluations of those encounters or ways of acting that serve or fail to serve our individual way of being. It is only derivatively in relation to this conception of good and bad that individuals themselves can be judged according to such evaluative standards:

> That individual will be called *good* (or free, rational, or strong) who strives, insofar as he is capable, to organize his encounters, to join with whatever agrees with his nature, to combine his relation with relations that are compatible with his, and thereby increase his power. [. . .] That individual will be called *bad*, or servile, or weak, or foolish, who lives

haphazardly, who is content to undergo the effects of his encounters, but wails and accuses every time the effect undergone does not agree with him and reveals his own impotence.[22]

This is to say that, under an immanent conception of ethics, evaluations of goodness and badness are simply descriptive nominations of diverse ways of existing as either tending towards or tending away from the kinds of actions that will increase an individual's power of acting. This is, as we saw above, ultimately what Deleuze means by describing his ethics as an 'ethology': the categories of good and bad can only be applied in terms of the broad classification of those sorts of essences who tend to realise their singular way of being, or who habitually despair of being able to do so.

Having now laid out these features of Deleuze's immanent ethics, let's look at an illustration of this ethics as it appears in Deleuze's 1969 *The Logic of Sense*, where the author brings together a reflection on Stoic metaphysics with his own account of how this metaphysics fits into a broader notion of ethics as a matter of 'willing what happens'. In this, we will see, there is an important precursor to elements in Kierkegaard's account that emphasise a kind of receptivity towards the conditions of one's existence in a way that permits a fuller expression of one's possibilities for living and acting.

Stoic Ethics as 'Willing What Happens'

Deleuze begins his account of Stoic ethics in *The Logic of Sense* by drawing a distinction between the central epistemological orientation of Stoic thought as opposed to various forms of Socratic and idealist epistemology. Here he uses the terms 'humour' and 'irony' to capture an essential difference between these epistemological orientations.[23] 'Irony', writes Deleuze, describes a philosophical orientation away from the concrete world. On an 'ironic' worldview, a philosophical investigation into the nature of the world will point us away from individual concrete instances, and towards the 'Ideas' or categories in terms of which these material cases can be classified. Socrates's enquiry in the *Euthyphro*, for example, is ironic. Euthyphro claims to be acting piously, and can even point to cases of what he considers to illustrate the principle of piety (for example, 'the pious is to do what I am doing now', says Euthyphro) but he cannot, for all that, give an account of what it means to 'be' pious.[24] Deleuze, writes: 'Plato laughed at those who were satisfied with giving examples, pointing and designating, rather than attaining the Essences: I am not asking you (he used to say) who is just, but what is justice.'[25] Here – on the non-Stoic account – the concrete is criticised in the name of an ideal: an example of what is pious (or just) and what it is to be pious (or just) are two distinct things, and the former will always fail to provide an account of the latter. By contrast, the Stoic epistemological orientation, which Deleuze associates with a 'humorous' worldview, employs strategy of 'descent' in relation to the genera. Rather than present a case and ask how it might be possible to classify that case, from a Stoic approach we observe the classification and we ask whether or not it is possible to undermine this abstract classification by an appeal to something concrete. Diogenes the Cynic will serve to illustrate this practice: where the Eleatics rely upon the abstractions of logic to demonstrate the impossibility of motion, Diogenes will simply walk back and forth in front of them. His demonstration here is not one of providing 'evidence' for the existence of movement in a manner than might be integrated into the conceptual debate that the Eleatics are engaging in; rather, his movement back and forth is itself a technique for undermining their reasoning, pointing towards a materiality that always outstrips the orderliness of philosophical thought.[26] As Deleuze writes:

> Every time we will be asked about signifieds such as "what is Beauty, Justice, Man?" we will respond by designating a body, by indicating an object which can be imitated or even consumed, and by delivering, if necessary, a blow of the staff (the staff being the instrument of every possible designation).[27]

This latter technique Deleuze refers to as 'monstration': the designation of a case or object intended to return the abstraction of hypostatised significations back the materiality of bodies from which these abstractions originate.[28]

On Deleuze's account, what the Stoic finds at the level of the raw materiality of things is what Deleuze calls 'the Event' (*l'événement*).[29] Deleuze's 'event' is not some specific occurrence that takes place at a particular historical moment in time, but rather it is what is at once actualised in a state of affairs constituted by a set of bodies or material elements, and also affected by that state of affairs or set of bodies as a distinctive sort of phenomenon. In the second chapter (Deleuze strictly calls his chapters 'Series' in *The Logic of Sense*), Deleuze writes:

> All bodies are causes for one another, in relation to one another, but of what? They are causes of certain things of an entirely different nature. These *effects* are not bodies, but strictly speaking 'incorporeals.' They are not physical qualities and properties, but logical or dialectical attributes. They are not things, or states of things, but events. One cannot say that they exist, but rather that they subsist or insist, having the minimum of being which belongs to what is not a thing, entity or existent.[30]

What Deleuze is describing here is what he will later come to call the 'sense' of a thing: not its denotative content, nor the set of concrete objects designated by a proposition, but rather the incorporeal 'truth' of a state of affairs – its tone or affect as a meaning-bearing phenomenon. Thus when Deleuze speaks of the Stoic 'sage' as pointing us towards 'the ground of bodies and the groundlessness of their mixtures', he means by this to refer us to an equally deliberate movement 'back to the surface [. . .] where pure sense is produced'.[31]

In drawing the distinction between the 'surface' at which pure events take place and the 'ground' where material bodies are mixed among themselves (what Deleuze calls 'the unity of a cosmic present'), Deleuze provides the conceptual tools for an understanding of the manner in which the Stoic sages comes to appropriate the necessity to which her life is subject.[32] In the fourteenth series of *The Logic of Sense*, Deleuze describes the double relation of causality to which all 'events' are subject, owing to their original grounding in the materiality of physical bodies:

> The event has a different nature from the actions and passions of the body. But it *results* from them, since sense is the effect of corporeal causes and their mixtures. It is always therefore in danger of being snapped up by its cause. It escapes and affirms its irreducibility only to the extent that the causal relation comprises the heterogeneity of the cause and the effect – the link of causes among themselves and the connection of effects among themselves. This is to say that incorporeal sense, as the result of the actions and passions of the body, may preserve its difference from the corporeal cause only to the degree that it is linked, at the surface, to a quasi-cause that is itself incorporeal. The Stoics saw clearly that the event is subject to a double causality, referring on the one hand to mixtures of bodies which are its cause, on the other hand to other events which are its quasi-cause.[33]

Here what Deleuze is articulating is a distinction in nature between the manner in which material bodies, on the one hand, serve as causes among themselves, producing the 'events' which are embodied or 'expressed' in those states of affairs; and, on the other hand, the way in which events, among themselves, are linked to one another through a distinctive manner of causation – one in which their autonomy as incorporeal is maintained. In describing the manner in which events, among themselves, connect to one another in relations of 'quasi-causation', Deleuze gives us an account of how the Stoic sage identifies with the events to which her life is subject in a manner that is coherent with the Spinozistic concept of 'understanding' or 'willing' the actions that come to follow from their singular essence. Deleuze writes:

> The Stoic sage 'identifies' with the quasi-cause, sets up shop at the surface, on the straight line which traverses it, or at the aleatory point which traces and travels this line. [. . .] The sage waits for the event, that is to say, *understands the pure event* in its eternal truth, independently of its spatio-temporal actualization, as something eternally yet-to-come and always already passed according to the line of the Aion. But at the same time, the sage also *wills the embodiment* and the actualization of the pure incorporeal event in a state of affairs and in his or her own body and flesh. Identifying with the quasi-cause, the sage wishes to 'give a body to' (*corporealiser*) the incorporeal event, since the effect inherits the cause.[34]

What the Stoic does, on this account, is to put themselves in the position of bringing about the 'event' to which they are subject in the sequence of physical causation. The mixture of material bodies which causes the event at the level of an experienced 'sense' is doubled in the will of the Stoic sage, who treats herself as the 'quasi-cause' of the event that is otherwise unavoidably realised through the actions and passions of the material world. This 'willing' or 'identification' with the event which takes place, Deleuze associates with a kind of performance or – he says – 'representation' of one's fate:

> To know that we are mortal is an apodictic knowledge, but empty and abstract, which real and successive deaths certainly do not suffice to adequately fulfil, to the extent that one does not apprehend dying as an impersonal event endowed with an always open problematic structure (where and when?). In fact, two types of knowledge have often been distinguished, one indifferent and remaining exterior to its object, the other concrete, which will seek out its object there where it is. Representation attains this topical ideal only by means of the hidden expression which it encompasses, that is, by means of the event that it envelops. There is thus a 'use' of representations, without which representation would remain lifeless and senseless.[35]

What Deleuze identifies here is the way in which an individual comes to an adequate understanding of the events to which they are subject

– neither approving nor disapproving of them, but rather 'willing' them through a comprehension of the very necessity they contain. It is this activity of 'willing' the event through a kind of re-performance of it – what he elsewhere calls a 'counter-actualization' of the event – that allows the individual to turn the otherwise alien necessity of one's life into an appropriated and affirmed necessity. Thus Deleuze describes Stoic ethics as a kind of 'willing what happens', in which one moves from a resistant refusal of the events of one's life to a kind of 'longing' in which 'there is [. . .] no change except a change of will, a sort of leaping in place of the whole body which exchanges its organic will for a spiritual will. It wills now not exactly what occurs, but something *in* what occurs [. . .]: the Event.'[36] In this way, the desire to control and modify one's life is replaced with a kind of affirmation of the specificity and facticity of one's life. One does not refuse and resist the life that one leads, but rather confirms this life through a simultaneous comprehension and acceptance, a kind of harmony of willing and understanding.

Kierkegaard's Immanent Ethics

In what sense does Kierkegaardian ethics, then, reflect a conception of ethics as an ethology of different 'types' of existence and a doctrine of 'willing what happens'? A first consideration to bring to bear on this question will have to do with the important relationship between Kierkegaard's concept of faith and the status of moral rules. In perhaps the most well-known of Kierkegaard's pseudonymous oeuvre, *Fear and Trembling*, the pseudonym Johannes de Silentio presents the problem of religious normativity specifically in terms of the conflictual relationship between faith and the necessity of following some set of concrete prescriptive obligations. Speaking of the relationship between conventional, secular morality – what Silentio calls, following Hegel, '*Sittlichkeit*' – and the nature of religious faith, Silentio writes:

> Faith is namely the paradox that the single individual is higher than the universal – yet, please note, in such a way that the movement repeats itself, so that after having been in the universal he as the single individual isolates himself as higher than the universal. If this is not faith, then Abraham is lost, then faith has never existed in the world precisely because it has always existed. For if the ethical – that is, social morality – is the highest and if there is in a person no residual incommensurability in some way such that this incommensurability is not evil (i.e., the single

individual, who is to be expressed in the universal), then no categories are needed other than what Greek philosophy had or what can be deduced from them by consistent thought.[37]

In this passage, Silentio lays out the basic coordinates for his conception of religious normativity. If faith is to be distinguished in any substantive way from other normative principles, it must be of such a kind as to preclude obedience to this principle in the manner of a universal standard. Whereas any number of specific moral obligations can, in principle, find themselves suspended without violating the priority of morality as a normative principle, faith must appear as a suspension of moral obligation in a way that does not install a novel obligation that ought to be followed universally. Here Silentio uses an illustration from the book of Judges, in which Jephthah, who has made a vow to sacrifice 'whatever comes out of the door of [his] house' in exchange for victory over the Ammonites, discovers to his horror that this vow obligates him – against his will – to sacrifice his daughter, 'coming out to meet him'.[38] Silentio emphasises the way in which – under this circumstance – Jephthah is obligated to violate an apparent moral rule which he recognises; namely, not to harm his daughter. And yet in his violation of this moral principle it is evidently not the case that he sets aside something like morality itself, simply because he continues to recognise the primacy of moral obligation as determining how he ought to act in this case. Distinguishing between Abraham, who is 'tested' by God, and Jephthah, who obeys a predominating obligation to sacrifice his daughter, Silentio writes:

> The difference between the tragic hero and Abraham is very obvious. The tragic hero is still within the ethical. He allows an expression of the ethical to have its τέλος in a higher expression of the ethical; he scales down the ethical relation between father and son or daughter and father to a feeling that has its dialectic in its relation to the idea of moral conduct. Here there can be no question of a teleological suspension of the ethical itself.[39]

In other words, what Jephthah does is to recognise a higher or predominating source of moral obligation. Even if this source of moral obligation ends up conflicting with an everyday or conventional form of obligation, he is nonetheless capable of obeying this higher moral obligation in the manner of a moral rule or commandment: indeed it is because this 'higher' moral rule remains a rule that his action never strays from the basic deontological coordinates of his everyday morality. Consequently, when Silentio seeks to distinguish between the kind of action that Abraham, as a representative of religious faith, performs, and the kind of action that someone like Jephthah performs, the mechanism by which he distinguishes these will not appeal to the priority or uniqueness of God's right – as the 'ultimate author of the universe', and so on – to issue commandments to individuals. Instead, it is God's solicitation of Abraham's behaviour outside the bounds of moral obligation – Abraham's recognition of an 'incommensurability' between the universal and his own singularity as an existing individual – that sets him apart as the archetypical representative of religious faith.

So what is it that distinguishes Abraham's way of acting, as a so-called 'knight of faith', from the merely ethical way of acting that Silentio attributes to figures like Jephthah and Agamemnon? Here we see something of the symmetry between the Spinozistic conception of ethics, according to which an action will be judged according to its coincidence with the 'singular essence' belonging to the individual, and the Kierkegaardian concept of faith. Silentio writes: 'Faith is precisely the paradox that the single individual as the single individual is higher than the universal, is justified before it, not as inferior to it but as superior [. . .], that the single individual as the single individual stands in an absolute relation to the absolute.'[40] That is, what the individual does, in their encounter with the divine – and what God solicits from the individual by presenting them with a commandment which, if properly understood, would paradoxically invite the individual to refuse the obedience that the commandment appears to contain – is to isolate, and act in accordance with, their own uniquely singular character, such that this distinguishes them from all those whose ways of acting that can be adequately governed by appeal to universal moral standards. In other words, the individual here identifies with their uniquely 'existential' property; namely, that by virtue of existing, they are not merely a member of a generalisable class of individuals and thereby subject to generalisable moral obligations, but rather they are this particular individual, and therefore responsible ultimately to nothing but themselves as the irreducible standard for their own behaviour.

Here we can see an important resonance with the concept of 'resignation' mentioned in the preceding chapter, when we talked about the nature of ethics as a matter of removing oneself from the finite world in order to inhabit the consistency of eternity. In that place, we understood the category of 'resignation' as a way of separating oneself from the narrow particularistic desires that the individual human being bears, in order to emphasise a sort of universality. Similarly, in this case, faith as a normative principle and faith as a matter of psychological investment will coincide to the extent that the individual's normative principle (to act in such a way that only their 'singular' interests are satisfied through this movement) and their psychological centre (not the 'universality' of their moral obligations, but the particularity of themselves) are united. Silentio writes, in describing the combination of interest and motivation in the movement of faith:

> To the question 'Why?' Abraham has no other answer than that it is an ordeal, a temptation that, as noted above, is a synthesis of its being for the sake of God and for his own sake. [. . .] The paradox of faith has lost the intermediary, that is, the universal. On the one side, it has the expression for the highest egotism (to do the terrible act, do it for one's own sake), on the other side, the expression for the most absolute devotion, to do it for God's sake.[41]

In this, Silentio emphasises the way in which, for Kierkegaard, faith will be a matter of the individual realising the singularity of the singular individual. It is not through obedience to moral rules that one comes to realise the goods of religious faith, but rather faith consists in the challenge to overcome one's natural human tendency to act only under cover of a normative obligation. In this way, the normativity of religious faith, for Kierkegaard, will reflect something of the normativity of an immanent ethics, to the extent that the latter centralises the expression of the distinctive individuality of the individual. Here the apparent 'freedom' of the individual is realised not through a willing of the coincidence between oneself and some moral rules that one takes as a blueprint for how one ought to behave, but rather through the propriety of the event brought about in relation to the individual's essence from which it follows. This, I would claim, is what Silentio means by indicating that Abraham's movement of faith puts him in contact, as a 'single individual' with the 'absolute' insofar as this is represented by God: it is not that God commands Abraham absolutely, nor that Abraham merely voluntarily chooses to do the act that God invites him to do, but rather that Abraham experiences the normative freedom of his own action 'in' the necessitation that follows from his own individuality. For Kierkegaard, therefore, to act under the conditions of religious faith will mean to find the space of liminality between one's freedom and one's necessitation, through a relinquishment of the moral rules that otherwise serve to guide one. Let us now see how this 'relinquishment' appears in several of Kierkegaard's other works, where the kind of immanent ethics principles we have described are at play as well.

The Signed Works: Kierkegaard as Immanent Ethicist

In several of Kierkegaard's signed works we find strong illustrations of what it might mean to act in this liminal space between agency and receptivity as well as strong illustration of the non-prescriptive character of 'immanent' ethics that we spoke of above. In 'Look at the Birds of the Air; Look at the Lily in the Field', a 'devotional discourse' that Kierkegaard published to coincide with the second printing of his pseudonymous *Either/Or*, we find a deliberate proposal that one suspend one's tendency towards reflective obedience to prescriptive obligations in order that the individual should more fully approximate the lessons of 'the birds in the air' and 'the lilies in the field'.[42] In this discourse, Kierkegaard discusses the biblical injunction to 'become' like the birds of the air and the lilies of the field specifically in terms of the skill of 'becoming silent', where it is the distinction of the human being to be able to speak that allows their 'becoming silent' to serve as a kind of normative accomplishment. Kierkegaard connects this art of silence to an injunction which, by persistently forestalling the individual's anxious seeking after a more specific normative obligation, leads the individual towards a posture of openness and receptivity that is coincident with the lessons of 'the birds' and 'the lilies'. Kierkegaard writes:

> 'Seek first God's kingdom and his righteousness.' But what does this mean, what am I to do, or what is the effort that can be said to seek, to aspire to God's kingdom? Shall I see about getting a position commensurate with my talents and my abilities in order to be effective in it? No, you shall *first* seek God's kingdom. Shall I give all my possessions to the poor? No, you shall *first* seek God's kingdom. Shall I then go and proclaim this doctrine to the world? No, you shall *first* seek God's kingdom.[43]

In this passage, we can see Kierkegaard's invocation of a message to resemble the birds of the air and the lilies of the field not in order to provide the reader with a set of responsibilities of requirements that they ought to obey in the manner of a moral obligation. Rather, it is precisely by redirecting one's intentions to find a prescription that Kierkegaard can point the reader towards a receptivity that coincides with resumption of their original nature. 'The advantage of the human being over the animal is the ability to speak, but, in relation to God, wanting to speak can easily become the corruption of the human being, who is able to speak.'[44] It is because the individual is capable of acting in an intentional and morally obedient way that the skill of suspending this intentionality constitutes a normative accomplishment. Indeed, in this context, the skill of learning to 'become silent' in emulation of the unreflective immediacy of birds and lilies is identified as a form of re-insertion into the flow of everyday life:

> But then in a certain sense it is nothing I shall do? Yes, quite true, in a certain sense it is nothing. In the deepest sense you shall make yourself nothing, become nothing before God, learn to be silent. In this silence is the beginning, which is to seek *first* God's kingdom.[45]

Here we can see something of the cultivated non-intentionality discussed in Deleuze's account of Stoic ethics: just as the Stoic sage learns to identify herself immediately with the sequence of events that constitute her necessary fate, so does Kierkegaard's faithful individual learn to suspend her anxious striving in order to 'become nothing' in a way that puts her into immediate contact with surrounding circumstances. In this context, the individual loses her 'self' as an intentionally minded agent in order to 'become nothing' in her relationship to God in the surrounding world.

Kierkegaard's upbuilding discourse 'To Gain One's Soul in Patience' describes a similar theme, that of becoming 'still', in order to consider the relationship between the self and itself in this posture of receptivity. In this discourse, Kierkegaard reflects on the paradoxical injunction to become 'patient' through an exercise of that same faculty which is said to be the achievement of becoming patient:

> 'It grows in patience.' In these words, the condition and the conditioned are again inseparable, and the words themselves suggest duplexity and unity. The person who grows in patience does indeed grow and develop. What is it that grows in him? It is patience. Consequently, patience grows in him, and how does it grow? Through patience. If the person who will gain himself will just be patient, he will surely grow in patience.[46]

Here the paradox that Kierkegaard identifies – that to become patient one must deploy the virtue that one seeks to obtain – serves to problematise the relationship between Christianity normativity and the kind of normativity proper to conventional secular ethics. In the latter case, we can be made responsible for fulfilling those tasks alone of which we are capable, so that it is our exercise of free will in the service of some normative obligation that marks us out as morally good. But under what I am calling the 'immanent' ethics of Christianity, the injunction to become patient comes not through an exercise of some existent capacity, but rather through a kind of temporal loop, in which the individual becomes themselves by drawing on the set of skills that belongs to them in the future. It is because of this apparent circularity that the individual is invited not to exercise their will upon some external object, but rather to move into a posture of receptive appropriation that allows them to realise their own intrinsic capacities. Thus, to achieve the kind of normative aims described under Kierkegaard's framework will mean to practise inhabiting a kind of liminal space between activity and passivity, in which the practice of 'becoming oneself' entails a suspension of one's wilful insistence on choosing what it is that one becomes.

One interpreter who emphasises the non-prescriptive character of Kierkegaardian ethics is David Kangas, who, in this *Errant Affirmations: On the Philosophical Meaning of Kierkegaard's Religious Discourses*, specifies the differences between a moral-theological reading of Kierkegaard's discourses – one in line with conventional understandings of morality – and a reading that more properly approximates Kierkegaard's own intentions.

> In the prefaces to his discourse Kierkegaard makes a clear distinction between 'edifying discourses' and 'discourses *for* edification.' The latter would take edification, the state of being or feeling edified, as the end-goal toward which the discourse is supposed to lead; the discourse would then be a means to that end. [. . .] Kierkegaard, however, could not be clearer: the author of these discourses *is not a moral or theological teacher*. [. . .] The author relinquishes it from any purposive horizon: the discourse becomes, as Kierkegaard stresses, *superfluous*.[47]

And he goes on: 'This indeed is where the discourses really tend: toward an affirmation of reality that is unconditioned, that is, without cause or occasion.'[48] In other words, as with Deleuze's non-prescriptive account of ethics, Kierkegaard's upbuilding discourses essentially refuse to provide any prescriptive canon. Instead, they function, in their superfluity, for the development of the reader's own affirmative posture, through their depiction of the kinds of practices and virtues characteristic of a Christian way of being. M. Jamie Ferreira, in her commentary on Kierkegaard's *Works of Love*, draws a similar attention, adapted from Martin Luther, to the distinction at play between an 'imperative' and 'indicative' ethics: 'Imperative ethics is meant to refer to the rigorous demand of the law ("you are required to do this") as opposed to the indicative ethics, which describes our ability – through grace – to fulfil the law ("You are enabled to do this").'⁴⁹ In employing this distinction, Ferreira points us towards the way in which, in Kierkegaard, the kind of account one typically finds is oriented towards an indication of the capacities one has and one's ability to exercise those capacities in a fuller realisation of their essential nature:

> There is a sort of commandment that is not an assertion of duty but rather a sort of exhortation. The idea of intimacy with the commandment means at the very least that it does not feel like a duty. Indeed, one could even consider the apostles exhortation to be a form of invitation – 'I invite you to love one another.' It contains within it the multivalence of the Danish word *Lov*, which means both law and permission.⁵⁰

Thus, for Ferreira, the basic orientation of Kierkegaardian ethics is not towards a constraint or limitation on how the individual behaves, but rather towards an unfolding of the capacities of the individual beyond the limitations of obligation. In this, we can see something of the Spinozistic principle which takes the realisation of the individual's 'singular essence' a primary ethical value, and – moreover – which sees the project of ethical reflection not as the establishment of a moral canon, but as a practice of reflection on the diversity of human beings' ways of being. Rather than defining ethics in terms of a misrelation between the individual and the world around them, Kierkegaardian ethics, like immanent ethics, serves to bring the individual into a greater appreciation of their own unique way of existing.

The Problem of Transcendence

Having shown how Kierkegaard's Christian ethics reinstates certain central features of a Deleuzian conception of immanent ethics, I now want to consider one fairly obvious objection to this reading. This would have to do with the way in which, for Deleuze, to consider normativity in terms of immanence must mean specifically to oppose 'transcendent' values in terms of which an individual's actions can be judged. On a superficial level, then, it would seem that this reading invites a strong rebuttal on the grounds of Kierkegaard's regular invocation of transcendence as a distinctive principle of his Christian authorship. In *The Concept of Anxiety*, the pseudonymous Vigilius Haufniensis describes Christian ethics as a '*secunda philosophia* [second philosophy] whose essence is transcendence or repetition';

and, in the *Concluding Unscientific Postscript*, Johannes Climacus describes the Christian conception of religion as one that 'breaks with immanence and makes existing the absolute contradiction – not within immanence but in opposition to immanence'.[51] In other words, Christianity on this account will specifically involve a principle of transcendence – and in particular the principle of the 'transcendence' of a divine being in time – in a way that violates secular principles of 'immanent' ethics.

To this objection one might reply by emphasising the specific character of the transcendence that Kierkegaard describes. There are two points to be made here in Kierkegaard's favour, both of which, incidentally, ought to reciprocally challenge conventional interpretations of Deleuze's work as fundamentally a philosophy of immanence. When Kierkegaard invokes the concept of transcendence with respect to the paradoxicality of Christianity, the paradox he describes is intended specifically to refer to the reality of an object which cannot be adequately understood in terms of the categories of rational reflection. Speaking of the divine paradox of 'the god in time' in *Philosophical Fragments*, Climacus writes that a relationship with the Eternal 'coming-into-existence' requires faith (*Tro*) because it is something that cannot be grasped according to the principles of rational, reflective understanding. If to know things a priori means to set the principles for the possibility of human experience over and above the singularity of concrete events, then to have faith in an event like the appearance of God in time – something supposed to 'transcend' the immanence of rational reflection – specifically means to orient oneself with respect to what lies beyond the realm of rational knowledge but not beyond the domain of appropriable experience. In this sense, it directs us towards something historical and factual, and therefore towards the irreducibility of concrete, temporally expressed reality, and not, as others would have it, towards something that is 'beyond' experience in the manner of an ineffable abstraction. Here it is the materiality of existence that Kierkegaard intends by the idea of transcendence.

Related to this, when Kierkegaard specifically invokes the concept of transcendence in reference a the kind of 'rupture' or 'transition' brought about through faith, this concept is used in order to indicate the way in which movement and becoming entail real change and novelty in contrast to the immanence of a merely 'logical' movement.[52] Whereas for Deleuze the category of immanence is intended to show how phenomena of change and becoming in fact ground concepts of identity, and thereby to demonstrate that transcendence is in fact an illusion predicated on immanence, for Kierkegaard immanence is understood as what misrecognises the nature of reality for precisely the same reasons – namely, that in what is merely thought or understood dialectically, there is no true movement but the misapplication of a category of existence to a category of reflection. Consequently, when Kierkegaard discusses transcendence as a principle of Christian ethics, he is indicating thereby the relationship between faith as soliciting a form of becoming in the individual, and the real change or novelty that belongs to this transformation. The category of transcendence here functions very differently for Kierkegaard than it does for Deleuze, since for Kierkegaard it is the immanent understanding of reality that suspends the possibility of real change through the logical identity of a *subjectum* or ground. Consequently, when Kierkegaard invokes the category of transcendence to describe faith as a 'transcending' movement, what he means thereby is that faith accounts for a genuine form of becoming which uproots even the conditioning limitations of logical identity. Faith is a form of becoming because it amounts to a transcendence of natural types, in the same way that – for Deleuze – immanence will accommodate forms of radical becoming for the same reason. In this sense, the valorisation of becoming remains an essential feature of accounts, despite the fact that one adopts the language of transcendence and the other adopts the language of immanence when speaking of their highest ethical ideals. For both, their ethics will remain a matter of affirming the forms of becoming that are endemic to human existence which only an 'immanent' ethics – one which rejects the restrictive character of transcendent rule-giving – can accommodate.

Hence it is clear that Kierkegaard and Deleuze not only agree on their conceptions of normativity, but also that a closer look at this apparent point of conflict only deepens our understanding of the similarities between their approaches to ethics. For both, it is the emphasis on the concreteness of existence – on the becoming essential to it, and the principles that guide an individual more profoundly towards this becoming – that underlies both of their conceptions of normativity. For both, the notion that ethics should be a mere accounting of obligatory objects of willing is something straightforwardly rejected.

Why This Account?

So what can be gained from this interpretation of Kierkegaard as a thinker of immanent ethics in this sense? To my mind there are at least two substantive benefits to be gained from such a reading: one from a broadly Kierkegaardian perspective, and the other from a broadly Deleuzian perspective.

For Kierkegaardians, the way in which Kierkegaard thinks about Christian ethics as somehow 'beyond' traditional morality, and the kinds of practical reflection he pursues (for example, in *Works of Love*, where he discusses duties related to love) are objects of perennial interpretive debate. Readers like Edward Mooney see Kierkegaardian ethics as a kind of virtue ethics, where qualities like faith, patience and humility sketch the properties necessary for happiness in a sacred world.[53] Others, like C. Stephan Evans, read Kierkegaard as a kind of 'divine command' theorist, on whose account certain kinds moral obligations will remain unrecognised if they are not disclosed by some source beyond mere secular, rational reflection.[54] On the reading I have presented here, both these lines of interpretation are sublated in the direction of a non-prescriptive immanent ethics that undergirds both the set of virtues and the account of 'commandment' that we find in Kierkegaard's thought. For Kierkegaard, virtue arises precisely through the paradoxical receptivity that one adopts by 'becoming' who one is. Similarly 'obligation' appears not as the source of a prescription that ought to be followed, but rather in the form of a normative ideal that the individual should act in such a way as to eschew their own tendency towards prescriptive moral obligation. By drawing upon the Deleuzian account of an immanent ethics we can accommodate such features of Kierkegaard's thought, as well as numerous other elements that on any other account of ethics would seem obscure or even inexplicable – for example, Kierkegaard's 'ethological' presentation of so many diverse ways of being through his use of pseudonyms; or his refusal to present virtues like patience, stillness or faith in any way that can be voluntarily adopted through one's intentional behaviour. From the perspective of an immanent ethics, we gain a vocabulary and a framework under which such features need not be explained away, but rather can be recognised as essential to the very way in which immanent ethical thought is understood.

The second, and perhaps more substantial, upshot of this reading falls to the Deleuzian side of the equation. It is related to the risks involved in what some have seen as an all-too-Romantic conception of self-overcoming in Deleuze's own account of immanent ethics. As we have already seen, Deleuze's thought of personal identity is shot through with an orientation towards the value of becoming, especially the sort of becoming that serves to undermine or displace one's settled conception of personal identity. We saw in Deleuze's reading of Nietzsche in the previous chapter that such a becoming is often facilitated by an event of self-overcoming that entails, or seems to entail, a destruction of the self in which the individual is cast out from a stable sense of identity into an open-ended field of becoming. And yet, as some critics have pointed out, this valorisation of self-abnegation can easily fall prey to an overly Romantic evaluation of one's loss of orientation as an intrinsically desirable or laudable quality. As Tamsin Lorraine argues, in *Deleuze and Guattari's Immanent Ethics*,

> There may [. . .] be a strain of Nietzschean elitism in Deleuze and Guattari's work that speaks to those 'strong' enough to pursue schizoanalysis without worrying about those subjects too traumatized and silenced to be welcomed or supported by their prose. The subaltern subject yet to give voice, the problematic subject struggling to make affirming sense of the 'abnormal' experiences of a marginalized subjectivity, the border-crossing or transnational subject attempting to fit together the lived experience of dissonant perspectives, the traumatized subject attempting to heal ruptures in her sense of a shared humanity, the anxious subject struggling to come to grips with her implication in perpetuating oppression, the raced subject confronting systematic patterns of oppression or entitlement: It is with these subjects that progressive politics must be concerned.[55]

On this account, if the best that Deleuze can offer us in his model of ethics is a practice of subjective dissolution or collapse – a kind of chaotic emotional Rumspringa desirable only to those who have enjoyed 'too much' stability in their lives rather than too little – it will be hard to imagine what this account can offer to that large majority of individuals still struggling to establish liveable modes of existence or to find acceptance for ways of being that most properly express their distinctive sense of self.

In this connection I would argue that Kierkegaard's ethics of faith can potentially serve as a tool for understanding something like an immanent ethics in ways that eschew Deleuze's overt emphasis on self-destruction and destabilisation, while nonetheless maintaining a space for the processes of growth and becoming that remain invaluable in Deleuze's account. On Kierkegaard's account, principles like love and patience can serve as opportunities for self-transformation in ways that remain integrated with forms of social connectivity and political empowerment. Rather than seeking out dramatic and esoteric circumstances that will 'destroy' a self, Kierkegaard provides us with a strong appreciation for the kinds of experiences that serve to liberate individuals from overly calcified forms of identification, but without the implication that these experiences must come through dramatic and unpleasant encounters with dangerous 'events'. Consider, in this regard, Lorraine's own comments on the sorts of values that might better serve to accommodate individuals in processes of collective growth and self-discovery: here she cites Kelly Oliver, for her proposal that philosophy ought to replace its traditional emphasis on the Hegelian notion of 'recognition' – with its subtly interpolative and exclusionary implications – with a novel emphasis on 'witnessing', in which 'love' plays a key role. Lorraine explains:

> Loving eyes facilitate the connection necessary for allowing the circulation of energy that makes things happen. [. . .] The power of an individual subject cannot unfold without connecting to other energy flows. It is the ability to affect and be affected that allows energy to circulate. It is the double becoming-other of genuine encounters where each allows self-transformation through being open to affecting and being affected by the other.[56]

This concept of love as both a liberatory and an integrating virtue – one that permits becoming, allows for individuals to grow in relationship and also gives motives for transformation and becoming – is just the sort of thing that Kierkegaard is properly equipped to theorise. This is because love, for Kierkegaard, serves not only as a central value for his Christian ethics (witness his major book, *Works of Love*) but also as a key illustration of what it might mean for an individual to undergo an everyday movement of faith: in love human beings learn to risk and accept themselves all at once, disclosing themselves to others in ways that require a courage that only faith can sustain.

The idea that Kierkegaard can offer a radical critique of substantial identity that is nonetheless compatible with forms of social and historical situatedness is one that Christine Battersby illustrates in her book *The Phenomenal Woman*. Speaking of Kierkegaard's reading of Antigone in *Either/Or* she writes:

> For feminists to opt in to the Deleuzian version of [. . .] ontology would be to opt for a system in which self is just a surface phenomenon, and

hence agency (and also political agency) cannot be thought. [...] For Kierkegaard, by contrast, Antigone is a model for a self that is created in the moment: in the 'nook' of present, future and past. This self is not created solely by itself, nor is it a passive victim of circumstance or of the 'system' as a whole. Political agency is possible; but the agent has to live with radical ambiguities; an infinity of potential 'realities'; with power discrepancies; and with relational dependence on others.[57]

In framing Kierkegaard in this way, Battersby emphasises the ways in which, on Kierkegaard's account, movement and becoming is adopted in harmony with one's historical and social context. Rather than simply uprooting oneself in a way that is intended to undermine settled notions of identity, Kierkegaard emphasises a creative reappropriation of one's extant circumstances, looking for those dimensions of freedom available under conditions of regularity and repetition. In this way we are asked not to dramatically transform or radicalise our ethical ways of behaving, but rather to open ourselves to the forms of becoming already available within our everyday ways of being and being with others. This, I would claim, might not obligate us to dispense with any of the critical features of a Deleuzian conception of ethics, but it might allow us to develop a greater sensitivity to the manifold ways in which Deleuzian ethical values can – and are – realised in everyday life.

Conclusion

From what we have seen, we can say that Deleuze and Kierkegaard's philosophical grounding in the post-Kantian problem of personal identity continues to orient the current picture of their relationship. Having laid out some of the basic metaphysical coordinates of their thought in the previous chapter, in this chapter we saw a correlation in these philosophers' work between the undermining of traditional notions of personal identity and the reorganisation of traditional notions of morality. Rather than remaining entangled within the framework of rational ethics as the only possible solution to the problem of personal identity, both Deleuze and Kierkegaard accepted a radical emphasis on change and becoming and adapted a notion of immanent ethics sufficient for the normative dimensions of this kind of change.

In the next chapter, we will take off from our picture of personal identity, left behind with the account of self-overcoming in Chapter 2, and move towards a tentative account of what it might mean to 'be' a self on Deleuze and Kierkegaard's accounts. In doing so, we will attempt to fulfil the requirements of a tentative notion of stability in their conceptions, at the same time as we show the radicality of their transformed notions of selfhood. As much as there will be conditions for coherence in their understanding of the self, there will be conditions adequate for the inevitable processes of becoming and growth that necessarily belong to one's existence as a finite human being.

Notes

1. Discussions of the basic principles of Deleuze's immanent ethics can be found in Smith 'Three Questions of Immanence' and 'Deleuze and the Question of Desire', both found in Smith's *Essays on Deleuze*. Tamsin Lorraine pursues a theory of immanent ethics in *Deleuze and Guattari's Immanent Ethics*, which I discuss below. Note that the three features I identify here are not isomorphic with the three '-isms' that Deleuze attributes to Spinoza in that chapter: mine are extrications of several properties specifically intended to distinguish immanent ethics from a conventional (transcendental) understanding of morality.
2. Gen. 2:17.
3. Deleuze, *Practical Philosophy*, p. 106.
4. Ibid., 27: 'An individual is first of all a singular essence, which is to say, a degree of power.'
5. Ibid., p. 106.
6. Ibid., pp. 71–7, quoting Spinoza, 'Letter to XIX to Blyenberg' and *Theological-Political Treatise*, chapter 4.
7. Ibid., p. 70: 'What defines freedom is an "interior" and a "self" determined by necessity. One is never free through one's will and through that on which it patterns itself, but through one's essence and what follows from it.'
8. Ibid., p. 106.
9. Ibid., p. 23.
10. See also Deleuze's 1956–1957 lectures in Gilles Deleuze, *What is Grounding?*, p. 61: 'The moral law is ultimately nothing but a badly understood natural law (cf. Adam and the apple: an indigestion).' Note that in the following paragraph Deleuze describes a continuity between Spinoza and Kierkegaard: 'With Kierkegaard this philosophy will be able to call itself a veritable philosophy of the absurd.' We will see why this is below.
11. Deleuze, *Practical Philosophy*, p. 23.
12. Spinoza, *Short Treatise*, p. 97.
13. Deleuze, *Practical Philosophy*, p. 106.

14 Ibid., p. 23.
15 Ibid., p. 27.
16 Deleuze, *Nietzsche and Philosophy*, p. 62: 'For Nietzsche, the capacity for being affected is not necessarily a passivity but an *affectivity*, a sensibility, a sensation', emphasis in original.
17 See pp. 53–54 above. Deleuze, *Nietzsche and Philosophy*, p. 64: 'Is not [. . .] man essentially reactive? [Is not] becoming-reactive [. . .] constitutive of man?'
18 Deleuze, *Practical Philosophy*, p. 27. On this topic see Uhlmann, 'Deleuze, Ethics, Ethology, Art'.
19 On the concept of a 'clinical' evaluation of types, see Deleuze's *Essays Critical and Clinical*, and in particular Daniel Smith's wonderful essay discussing the relationship between the clinical project and Deleuze's literary studies: Smith, 'Deleuze's "Critique et Clinique" Project', pp. xi–liii. See also, by way of illustration, Deleuze's early *Coldness and Cruelty*.
20 Deleuze, *Practical Philosophy*, p. 22.
21 Ibid., pp. 27–28.
22 Ibid., p. 23, emphasis in original.
23 Deleuze, *Logic of Sense*, pp. 134–141. Deleuze also employs the categories of irony and humor in *Coldness and Cruelty*, pp. 81–90 and *Difference and Repetition*, p. 245.
24 Deleuze, *Logic of Sense*, pp. 137–138; Plato, *Euthyphro*, p. 5 [5d].
25 Deleuze, *Logic of Sense*, p. 135.
26 See Diogenes Laertius, *Lives of Eminent Philosophers*, Book 6, chapter 2.
27 Deleuze, *Logic of Sense*, p. 135.
28 Ibid. Deleuze associates this dimension of Stoic ethics with the Zen school of Buddhism, which famously distinguishes itself from other schools of Buddhism by its emphasis on the 'direct' or non-verbal transmission of enlightenment. See Waddell and Abe, 'Translators' Introduction,' to *The Heart of Dōgen's Shōbōgenzō*, p. xi, and Deleuze, *Logic of Sense*, p. 136.
29 Deleuze, *Logic of Sense*, p. 136: 'By the same movement with which language falls from the heights and then plunges below, we must be led back to the surface where there is no longer anything to denote or even to signify, but where pure sense is produced. [. . .] What does the wise man find at the surface? Pure events considered from the perspective of their actual truth, that is, from the point of view of the substance which sub-tends them, independent of their spatio-temporal actualization in a state of affairs.'
30 Ibid., pp. 4–5, translation slightly modified.
31 Ibid., pp. 135–136.
32 Ibid., p. 144. Strictly speaking, bodies do not have effects 'among'

themselves, given that they always coincide in a single, non-sequential present that Deleuze designates by the term 'Chronos', despite the fact that they do 'act' (*agir*) and 'suffer' (*pâtir*), *Logic of Sense*, p. 77.
33. Ibid., p. 94, translation slightly modified.
34. Ibid., pp. 146–147, emphasis in original.
35. Ibid., pp. 145–146, translation modified.
36. Ibid., p. 149, emphasis in original.
37. Kierkegaard, *Fear and Trembling*, p. 55.
38. Judges 11:31 and 11:34. Silentio discusses the Jephthah story at *Fear and Trembling*, p. 58.
39. Ibid., p. 59.
40. Ibid., p. 56.
41. Ibid., p. 71.
42. Kierkegaard, 'Look at the Birds of the Air; Look at the Lily in the Field', p. 10. The biblical passage discussed is Matthew 6:24–34.
43. Ibid.
44. Ibid., p. 11.
45. Ibid., pp. 10–11.
46. Kierkegaard, 'To Gain One's Soul in Patience', p. 169.
47. Kangas, *Errant Affirmations*, pp. 3–5.
48. Ibid.
49. Ferreira, *Love's Grateful Striving*, p. 242. Here we might also invoke a terminological distinction that Victor Goldschmidt draws between 'optative' and 'indicative' ethics in Stoicism, Goldschmidt, *Le Système Stoïcien*, pp. 68–69, translation my own. Deleuze cites Goldschmidt in Deleuze, *Logic of Sense*, p. 348.
50. Ibid., p. 242.
51. Kierkegaard, *Concept of Anxiety*, p. 21; Kierkegaard, *Concluding Unscientific Postscript*, p. 573.
52. See, for example, Kierkegaard, *Concept of Anxiety*, p. 82, where 'transition' is described as a property of 'historical freedom' rather than a category of dialectics.
53. Mooney, *Knights of Faith and Resignation*, p. 100.
54. Evans, *Kierkegaard's Ethic of Love*.
55. Lorraine, *Immanent Ethics*, p. 138.
56. Ibid., p. 144.
57. Battersby, *Phenomenal Woman*, p. 196.

4

Kierkegaard, Deleuze and the Self of Immanent Ethics

> ... but if the world has become a bad cinema, in which we no longer believe, surely a true cinema can contribute to giving us back reasons to believe in the world and in vanished bodies?[1]

A primary theme of the previous chapter had to do with the nature of Kierkegaard's conception of ethics as 'immanent'. Although we found, in Deleuze's work, several places where themes of willing, affirmation and choice guided the concepts of normativity, I also pointed out that Kierkegaard's reflections on practical virtues like patience and faith served as a valuable counterweight to some of the more Romantic tendencies of Deleuze's work which emphasised values of self- and identity-destruction. In making this claim, I looked, in particular, at Tamsin Lorraine's call for some alternative values adequate for selves in process of being formed or re-formed under conditions of exclusion or marginalisation.

In this chapter, I want to pursue this theme and – in doing so – return to a central concern of this book by addressing the question of the nature of selfhood insofar as it corresponds to the modified conception of ethics we discussed in the previous chapter. Recall that we began this book by reflecting on the ways in which a Kantian response to the impossibility of noumenal self-knowledge led to a choice for moral judgement as sufficient for the determination of the nature of the self. The persistence of identity across time (known as 'personality', in Kant's vocabulary), the immortality of the soul as sufficient for an endless process of moral self-improvement, and unconditional freedom sufficient for an attribution of moral responsibility or blame became, at least, postulates of human selfhood, such as were necessary for a framework of moral judgement. If, however, such a set of ethical coordinates – in particular the values of moral judgement and deontological obligation – are absent from Kierkegaard and Deleuze's ethical accounts, what might remain of a concept of selfhood? How might the nature of the self be understood under this new ethical paradigm, in which becoming is more closely integrated with the kinds of ethical ideals that these philosophers propose? Moreover, if (as we argued in the previous chapter) Kierkegaard provides an at least superficially more palatable illustration of immanent ethical practice than Deleuze, how might Kierkegaard's work helpfully expand upon some of Deleuze's ideas of self-overcoming in order to offer a more robust picture of selfhood amenable to the concerns of subjects in process of constructing novel forms of identity? In this chapter, I will sketch the rudiments of a concept of selfhood independent of the assumptions of a 'substantive' concept of the self, but also amenable to the concerns described in the preceding chapter, to seek a notion of ethics that can provide a desirable quantum of stability and coherence. In so doing, we will see that a Deleuzian/Kierkegaardian notion of the self will have much common with an 'aesthetic' picture of identity, where experimentation and novelty are balanced by the relative stability of artistic coherence, while nonetheless avoiding the kinds of closure endemic to substantial notions of the self. In other words, the Deleuzian-Kierkegaardian self will appear as a genuinely 'composite' self, one adequate to the open-endedness of finite, factical existence.

To develop these elements, in this chapter I look at a set of moments from Deleuze's later works, especially in those places where Deleuze specifically invokes Kierkegaardian concepts in order to think about the nature of selfhood. In addition, I will look at a handful of places in Kierkegaard's work where he explores concepts discoverable in Deleuze's thought. In this way we will develop some of the methodology of this argument, by finding those places where Deleuze and Kierkegaard enter into an indirect and yet immensely productive dialogue. From this, we will see what happens when we pursue these two philosophers' ideas in conjunction, somewhere 'between' their thought and in a way that might be compared to the kinds of becoming that Deleuze describes later in *A Thousand Plateaus* – a kind of 'becoming-Deleuze' of Kierkegaard, and a 'becoming-Kierkegaard' of Deleuze.

The Cinema *Books: Belief in the World and the Self of Modern Cinema*

At first glance Deleuze's *Cinema* books may give the impression of being a novelty. In them, Deleuze claims to pursue a 'Peirce-ian' classification of 'images and signs' by rifling through an extensive canon of cinema, from the earliest works of the Lumière brothers to contemporary works by Straub and Huillet, Godard and Kubrick.

Kierkegaard, Deleuze and the Self of Immanent Ethics

And yet – as we will see – within this critical account of the history of cinema there is a parallel reflection on the interrelated categories of time, subjectivity and truth, as Deleuze moves from 'classical' cinema preoccupied with the representation of movement, to a 'modern' cinema in which time is presented for itself – appearing on the screen independently of movement – with a corresponding dismantlement of conventional relationships between truth and falsity, cause and effect and sound and image. In marking this transition within cinema, Deleuze simultaneously articulates a revision in the notion of identity as a corollary of these different aesthetic projects: the 'critical' representation of film will serve as an opportunity to present a 'clinical' account of the selves understood under these forms as so many ways of feeling and existing. Hence, within Deleuze's classification of images as invoking novel conceptions of identity and temporality, there appears an equally important account of the place of the self. Rather than placing an account of identity or subjectivity somewhere outside these films and therefore insulated from the effects of cinematic evolution, here Deleuze depicts the self as appearing 'within' cinema. Rather than seek for the truth of subjectivity somewhere beyond art, we ought to find it there where it is represented, 'in' the work of art. But in order to arrive at the radicality of Deleuze's account of subjectivity in these works, it will be necessary first to present some of the basic coordinates that both link and distinguish the so-called 'classical' image of cinema from its 'modern' correlate.

CINEMA I: 'AFFECTION-IMAGES' AND KIERKEGAARDIAN CHOICE

Amongst the many 'images' of classical cinema presented in *Cinema I*, an important case for understanding the nature of immanent-ethical subjectivity will be the case of the so-called 'affection-image'. Beginning in chapter 6 of *Cinema I* Deleuze discusses the concept of what he calls an 'affection-image' as the second of three 'movement-images' endemic to classical forms of cinema. For Deleuze, the affection-image presents viewers with a set of affects that are incarnated in the materiality of a body or a face, not unlike the relationship described in *The Logic of Sense* chapter between Events as incorporeal insistences and the material states of affairs which subtend and cause these Events, and in which – reciprocally – these Events come to be embodied or actualised.[2] Speaking of the emergence of the close-up in early cinema as the ideal cinematic shot, Deleuze writes: 'The affect is an entity, that is Power or Quality [*la Puissance ou la*

Qualitè]. It is something expressed: the affect does not exist independently of something which expresses it, although it is completely distinct from it. What expresses it is a face, or a facial equivalent (a facefied object [*un objet visagéifié*]).'[3] In Carl Theodor Dreyer's 1928 masterpiece, *The Passion of Joan of Arc*, for example, the affect is precisely what is on display. Dreyer persistently scans the faces of the characters present at Joan of Arc's prosecution: long, tight shots of Joan's face – played incomparably by Renée Falconetti – serve to present a drama of affect, as Joan transitions between terror, ecstasy and resignation while the faces of her prosecutors transition between satisfaction, fury and – at least in in the case of one character, played by Antonin Artaud – sympathy. And yet, Deleuze goes on to point out, despite this early fascination with the close-up, that classical cinema would need not to rely on the face alone to express the affects embodied in the film:

> Take, for example, [Robert] Bresson's *The Trial of Joan of Arc*. Jean Sémloué and Michel Estève have clearly indicated its differences with, and similarities to, Dreyer's *Passion*. The major similarity is that it concerns the affect as complex spiritual entity: the white space of conjunctions, meetings and divisions; the part of the event which is not reducible to the state of things, the mystery of this begun-again present. However, the film is primarily made up of medium shots, shots and reverse-shots; and Joan is perceived at her trial rather than in her Passion, as a prisoner who resists rather than as victim and martyr. [...] In this way Bresson can achieve a result which in Dreyer was only indirect. The spiritual affect is no longer expressed by a face and space no longer needs to be subjected or assimilated to a close-up, treated as a close-up. The affect is now directly presented in medium shot, in a space which is capable of corresponding to it.[4]

In cinema of the 'medium' shot – Deleuze claims – the affect which was previously only incarnated in the representation of a face is now capable of being realised or embodied 'without the face, and independently of the close-up, independently of all reference to the close up'.[5] A pure Event of fear, horror, despair or dismay can appear instead in a concrete space or territory from which even the human body is absent. Amongst the variety of forms under which this 'affective' space would come to be realised, Expressionistic cinema deserves a particular pride of place: in Robert Wiene's *The Cabinet of Dr. Caligari*, for example, the horror and disorientation of the film – in which a sleepwalker is hypnotised to commit murder – is incarnated not merely in the ragged appearances of its

Kierkegaard, Deleuze and the Self of Immanent Ethics

characters, but just as distinctively in the material composition of its setting. Jagged, abstract, chiaroscuro lines evoke a sense of anxiety and dread without, for that reason giving the audience any orientation as to the specific location (is it a hallway? A mountain pass? A rooftop?) in which the events of the film take place. In this way we are taken away from the particularity of the location represented, in order to experience a concrete space as an affectively embodied 'kind' of place: what Deleuze will come to call affective 'any-space-whatevers [*espaces quelconques*]'.

These 'any-space-whatevers' Deleuze uses to sketch out some of the ethical and anthropological stakes involved in his account of cinema. Deleuze links these black and white images of 'any-space-whatevers' to a new style, that of 'lyrical abstraction', in which the pairings of black, white and grey serve to represent a spiritual conflict – not a conflict in which good 'struggles' with evil in the manner of Expressionism, but rather a conflict within the individual over what they will choose and, even more importantly, over the manner in which they will choose it:

> From its essential relation with the white, lyrical abstraction draws two consequences which accentuate its difference from Expressionism [...]. On the one hand, it is the white-black alternation: the white which captures the light, the black at the point where the light stops and sometimes the half-tone, the grey as indiscernibility which forms a third term. The alternations are established between one image and the next, or in the same image. [...] On the other hand, the spiritual alternative seems to correspond to the alternation of terms, good, evil and uncertainty or indifference but in a very mysterious way. It is indeed doubtful whether one 'must' choose the white.[6]

Here Deleuze sketches an important distinction between Expressionistic cinema and the cinema of lyrical abstraction, in terms of the uniqueness of the affect or quality embodied in the alternation of black, white and grey. In 'lyrical abstraction', it is no longer the case that these tones are used in order to sketch the everyday affects involved in a conflict between moral good and evil, but rather they are used to present an affect in which the nature of our choice – our capacity to choose freely, in full knowledge of our choice, or to choose under the impulse of necessity and constraint – is emphasised. Here Deleuze invokes Kierkegaard in order to understand the nature of this novel affect as it is represented in the cinema of lyrical abstraction:

> A fascinating idea was developed from Pascal to Kierkegaard: the alternative is not between terms but between the modes of existence of the one who chooses. There are choices that can only be made on condition that one persuades oneself that one has no choice, sometimes by virtue of a moral necessity (good, right), sometimes by virtue of a psychological necessity (the desire that one has for something). The spiritual choice is made between the mode of existence of him who chooses on the condition of not knowing it, and the mode of existence of him who knows that it is a matter of choosing. It is as if there was a choice of choice *or* non-choice. If I am conscious of choice, there are therefore already choices that I can no longer make, and modes of existence that I can no longer follow – all those I followed on the condition of persuading myself that 'there was no choice.'[7]

In this passage we see Deleuze's masterful appropriation of the themes of Kierkegaardian faith: unlike the model of moral choice in which what matters most is the duty and the sense of responsibility with which one chooses duty, on the Kierkegaardian account, represented in films like Dreyer's *Ordet*, Bresson's *Pickpocket* or (later) Rohmer's *My Night at Maud's*, all of which depict protagonists who struggle with their own freedom to choose, freedom to will, or freedom to believe, it is the nature of the individual as an agent of choice - their freedom to choose in a way that nonetheless returns responsibility for the choice to themselves – that is reflected in the composition of the film. This, Deleuze argues, is what is ultimately represented in the 'lyrical abstraction' of classical cinema: the nature of the spiritual choice involved in faith, such that this unique affect or power is represented through a character's struggle to liberate themselves from the closure of black and white, good and evil, necessity and impotence. The black and white of the cinema, used so effectively to stage this conflict, makes the 'any-space-whatevers' of these films reflective of their ethical and psychological conflict.

CINEMA II AND THE COLLAPSE OF THE SENSORY-MOTOR SCHEMA

In describing classical films as involving 'any-space-whatevers' Deleuze links this account of faith in classical cinema to an important set of reflections from the second volume of the *Cinema* books, where he returns to the category of 'any-space-whatevers' in order to describe the conditions of modern cinema, where a collapse of the traditional 'sensory-motor schema' leads to precisely such a liberation of such spaces after the destructions of World War II. Deleuze writes:

It is therefore shadows, whites and colours which are capable of producing and constituting any-space-whatevers, *deconnected or emptied spaces*. But with all these means and with others as well, after the war, a proliferation of such spaces could be seen both in film sets and in exteriors, under various influences. The first, independent of the cinema, was the post-war situation with its towns demolished or being reconstructed, its waste grounds, its shanty towns, and even in places where the war had not penetrated, its undifferentiated urban tissue, its vast unused places, docks, warehouses, heaps of girders and scrap iron. Another, more specific to the cinema, [. . .] arose from a crisis of the action-image: the characters were found less and less in sensory-motor 'motivating' situations, but rather in a state of strolling, of sauntering or of rambling which defined *pure optical and sound situations*. The action-image then tended to shatter, whilst the determinate locations were blurred, letting any-spaces-whatever rise up where the modern affects of fear, detachment, but also freshness, extreme speed and interminable waiting were developing.[8]

Here Deleuze describes the way in which 'sensory-motor images' – the mechanisms according to which predictable events can be represented as having predictable or necessary consequences in a narrative cinema of conflict and resolution – were replaced under the conditions of post-war society with a kind of disordering of conventional ways of being and acting. Under these circumstances, an environment no longer solicited a programmable response from an actor, whether because the familiar environment had been destroyed (see, for example, *Germany Year Zero*, in which the film takes place within the real-life rubble of Berlin), or because even familiar environments were seen to confront the actor as alien, unbelievable or intolerable (*Europe '51*, where, after the death of her son, Irene can no longer live her familiar bourgeois lifestyle). In these cases, Deleuze writes, film characters suddenly find themselves ineffective, floating: they become 'seers [*voyants*]' in a territory that is now foreign and unsettling.[9]

Under these circumstances of reactionless 'seeing', the traditional function of cinema, as presenting time 'indirectly' though the intermediary of movement, brought about through actions and reactions, is replaced by a new function. Now, in the aberration or disorderliness of movement, Deleuze argues, time ceases to be represented indirectly in cinema, and comes to be instead presented directly, for itself, as an independent phenomenon. We experience time not as an epiphenomenon of movement, where movement remains a function of predictable or programmable responses, but rather as it exists 'for itself', in its disruptive or dissociative character. Here we see the obvious connections between Deleuze's account of time in modern cinema and the account of time appearing 'for itself' in the third repetition of *Difference and Repetition*. At the same time as the world becomes 'intolerable' or 'unthinkable' from a historical point of view, cinema comes to present the subjectivity of a seer in their raw encounter with time, no longer reacting to a system of regular movement, but living in a state of disorderliness or abstraction from their everyday subjectivity.

Deleuze accounts three major phenomena that follow from this 'breakdown' of the cinematic sensory-motor schema, each of these has, we will see, particular significance for how we ought to understand the nature of self under such conditions of transformation and disorder. These will be: (1) the replacement of the faculty of knowledge with a faculty of 'belief' as the basis for a relationship between the individual and the world; (2) an elimination of interiority and autonomous power over one's thought in favour of a 'theorematic' or 'automatic' subjectivity that places the individual outside herself in what Deleuze calls a 'free indirect discourse'; and finally (3) the replacement of an orientation towards the world as an 'open whole' in favour of what Deleuze calls the 'whole' (*tout*) as an 'outside' (*dehors*).[10] In each case we will see that it is a Kierkegaardian relationship to what is radically other that is figured in this account.

With respect to the replacement of knowledge by 'belief', we recall that modern cinema has, as its presupposition, a 'suspension of the world' or 'disturbance' of the domain of images such that what is presented to the individual is no longer something that can 'thought' (as in the classical conception of cinema) but rather reflects something that 'does not let itself be thought in thought' or 'what does not let itself be seen in vision'.[11] In other words, in modern cinema the subject is brought 'face to face with [thought's] own impossibility' in the sense that the individual no longer knows how to react or what to do in the face of a collapse of the traditional sensory-motor schema through which one had inhabited the everyday world. With this replacement of a programmable, thinkable and therefore re-act-able schema, the actor or agent of the film is replaced by a 'seer' (*voyant*) who now inhabits the world as a 'purely visual [or sound] situation', unfamiliar, uninhabitable, or at best recognisable, but entirely intolerable in its inhuman, exhausting banality.[12] In Roberto Rossellini's *Europe '51*, for example, the death of the protagonist's son demystifies the entire architecture of her everyday life, so that where she once saw a normal, inhabitable world, she now sees the impossibly dehumanising patterns of work, poverty and suffering that lead her to struggle to help those whom she meets outside of her home. In this situation, Deleuze writes, 'thought looks for a subtle way out', from which the alternative to an intellectual comprehension of the world and knowledge of what to do is rather to 'believe in the world' in the sense of being capable of invoking or discovering unknowable or not-yet-existent possibilities for life.[13] In this sense, confronted with the impossibility of acting according to a programmable, coherent pattern of behaviour, the individual is put in an entirely different relationship to the world, that requires a kind of openness to possibility: the individual must 'believe, not in a different world, but in a link between man and the world, in love or life, to believe in this as in the impossible, the unthinkable which none the less cannot but be thought: "something possible, otherwise I will suffocate"'.[14] In Rossellini's *Stromboli*, for example, Karin's refusal to flee her adoptive home, coupled with the intolerability of the same, compels her to throw herself to the ground of a volcano as if clinging to the forces of her suffering, while she cries out in faith to a God who will offer no clear answers. In *Germany Year Zero* it is the little boy's despair of leading a liveable life – his inability to muster the kernel of faith necessary to look past the horrors of everyday life – that causes him to throw himself to his death. In these cases, it is the absence of a coherent, programmable response to the world (a world predicated on the regularity of movement or change) that presents the opportunity for a new form of encounter between self and world, one in which belief replaces knowledge, so that the very generative forces behind what exists become the primary object of human contact.[15] It is through the short-circuit of faith or belief (Deleuze uses both the terms '*foi*' and '*croyance*' to refer to this category) that the individual restores an engagement with the world, no longer on the basis of a rigorous distinction between self and world (as we will reiterate below) but now on the basis of a kind of coupling or integration of one's pre-conscious forces with the forces of the earth.

The second feature of modern cinema referenced above has to do with an abandonment of what Deleuze calls the metonymic or metaphoric figuration of the subject, by which he means those traditional methods of establishing psychological continuity within the world of film.[16] Here, in the absence of a programmable, and therefore narratable or predictable reaction to a world become unfamiliar, there emerges instead a 'dislocation of [...] internal monologue' and its replacement by a 'theorematic' or 'problematic' conception of subjectivity instead.[17] Under the breakdown of the sensory-motor image, rather than finding a series of associations between images governed by the principles of contiguity or cause and effect, the individual's reaction to the images presented to her follows instead a certain 'deductive and automatic' necessity, a set of 'formal linkages of thought' that serve to replace the continuity of active reflection with a kind of forced or unconscious behaviour.[18] Where once we found a conventional, psychological sequencing of narrative continuity (doubts, concerns or fears that led to new resolutions and consequently revised situations), in modern cinema we find rather an 'automatism' of the self, in which the protagonist is 'hollow[ed] out' or 'mummif[ied]', so that the reflective relation to the world is replaced by an immediate engagement with what happens.[19] In Pier Paolo Pasolini's *Teorema*, each of the main characters responds in an unconscious, almost mechanical, way to the appearance of a Christ figure whose existence and disappearance they are unable to rationally accept. The patriarch of the group gives away his factories to the workers, strips himself naked in a train station, and wanders into the desert, overtaken by an impulse to make himself adequate to the unthinkable apparition with which he has been confronted. The son, passionately affected by the Christ's beauty, begins producing art in increasingly aleatory and unconscious ways, blindfolding himself, stumbling around his studio, and ultimately urinating on what he has produced. The most pious of the group, a housekeeper, abandons her post and arrives at a neighbouring town, where she eats thistles, levitates and is eventually buried alive in a scene of passionate transfiguration. What Deleuze highlights with respect to these sorts of cases is the 'theorematic' mode of the self's engagement with the 'Outside': something unprogrammable or inconceivable forces the individual into a pattern of behaviour that divests her of her reflective autonomy – the self is as much brought into engagement and involvement in its world, as it is necessitated in its behaviour as a subject of chance or fortuity. In this sense selfhood reflects a kind of exteriority, by virtue of its direct encounter with the incomprehensible. Here we can see the Kierkegaardian invocation of a faith sufficient to bring the individual into an unprogrammable (but not for that reason inauthentic) engagement with the world.[20] Deleuze cites Pasolini's vocabulary to describe selfhood under the influence of this de-personalising but also singularising force: it is a 'free and indirect' subjectivity, no longer belonging directly to the one who inhabits it, but speculative and impersonal, putting the individual into direct contact with an outside that divests her of her reflective autonomy.[21]

The 'liberation' of speech and behaviour from the reflective interiority of the individual leads us at last to the third quality of modern cinema that Deleuze discusses: namely the replacement of the 'Whole' of the film with an 'Outside'.[22] In the first volume of the *Cinema* books, Deleuze describes film as composing an 'Open Whole [*Tout*]' in which the tendency was – in particular in the 'dialectical' cinema of directors like Eisenstein and Griffith – to produce a changing image of the overall film itself through the perennially shifting content of the several shots we see.[23] We observe, for example, in Eisenstein's 1925 film, *Strike*, a group of workers first get into conflict with the bosses, then go out on strike, then have their strike sabotaged by spies, and so on. The 'Whole' in this emerges above these scenes as a perennially shifting, incorporeal fact: what are we seeing? Is it an encomium to the success of the worker's movement? A eulogy for a failed strike? A pragmatic and cautionary tale? Here the film as a whole is invoked as the indirect representation of the visible scenes, always 'open' and shifting as the product and reciprocal cause of the scenes that we see.[24] In modern cinema, by contrast, to say that the whole is now an 'outside [*dehors*]' means that the film itself now intervenes with respect to the individual shots or scenes we observe, but no longer with the intention of unifying these into a coherent or continuous narrative. The film now emerges unsystematically, invisibly, between the scenes or shots we observe, so that rather than generate an associative sequence of events, the 'outside' now generates a differentiation or disordering of scenes sufficient to scramble the predictability of what happens. In Alain Resnais's *Last Year at Marienbad*, for example, the film emerges less in terms of what actually happened last year at Marienbad than in terms of an endlessly reiterated insertion of difference between possible reformulations of what might have happened (the protagonists slept together, the protagonists did not sleep together, the protagonists did sleep together but one of them forgot it, and so on). Here, as in the case of the Kierkegaardian 'encounter' with a divine paradox intended to disrupt or challenge the continuity of 'immanent' historical progress, the Outside appears as the primary Other of selfhood: an unprogrammable or knowable difference that serves to undermine the regularity of subjective continuity. It is for this reason that Deleuze's account of the cinematic principles of exteriority are shot through with Kierkegaardian references: 'Kierkegaard says "the profound movements of the soul disarm psychology" precisely because they do not come from within.'[25]

In this, our first visitation of the principles of selfhood that appear where Deleuze considers Kierkegaard's ideas directly, we see a set of concepts arising already adequate to a conception of selfhood belonging to the two thinkers. Here subjective orientation as a mode of knowledge is replaced by a kind of self in direct contact with the outside world through belief, just as much as the individual, divested of an autonomous, reflective consciousness, is engaged with an always-generative outside. A kind of impersonality, or 'fourth-person' perspective is generated here, at the same time as the individual is brought into direct contact with the world around it for the sake of generating new, unforeseen possibilities of life and experience.

A Thousand Plateaus: *Becomings and Haecceities*

Deleuze's notion of selfhood as somehow displaced from itself, linked in a direct way to an Outside that solicits a disordering of subjectivity, appears with even greater metaphysical systematicity in the co-authored *A Thousand Plateaus*, where Deleuze and Guattari draw on Kierkegaard's work for their reflections on the nature of becoming.[26] In what is perhaps his most sustained direct reflection on the metaphysics of immanent selfhood, Deleuze distinguishes between a kind of 'organic' selfhood composed of various parts oriented towards a single function – the tying-together of a notion of teleology with the notion of identity – and a conception of the self as a 'haecceity', a form of individuation closer to something like a 'patch' of selfhood; an identity that incorporates into its constitution elements drawn from its specific time and place, its unique mood or affect. Deleuze writes:

> We say 'What a story!' 'What heat!' 'What a life!' to designate a very singular individuation. The hours of the day in Lawrence, in Faulkner. A degree of heat, an intensity of white, are perfect individualities; and a degree of heat can combine in latitude with another degree to form a new individual, as in a body that is cold here and hot there depending on its longitude.[27]

In this account, we are presented with a notion of identity or selfhood that is highly specified by its material circumstance, even while this specification is not based on any substantive underpinnings that allow the individual to survive or persist beyond the particular instantiation in which it appears. In articulating this notion of individuation, Deleuze and Guattari employ semiotics as a metaphysical tool: '*Indefinite article + proper name + infinitive verb* constitute the basic chain of expression, correlative to the least formalized contents, from the standpoint of a semiotic that has freed itself from both formal signifiances and personal subjectifications.'[28] The verb in the infinitive corresponds to a type or sort of action, one which is imaginable independently of an agent who enacts it, presented in the form of an event: rather than someone running, we have 'running' as its own independent phenomenon, capable of being realised in a particular place and time, but existing independently of this instantiation. The proper name refers to quite the opposite of a specific substantial individual. It refers instead to a sort of characterisation: scientific phenomena bear proper names, 'Brownian motion', 'the Doppler effect'. Proper names here refer to a classification of an event, rather than to a distinctive set of objects that enact some effect. They therefore serve simultaneously to specify types whose distinctiveness corresponds to a whole class of events, while at the same time lacking the grounding of a subject or set of subjects that bear them. Finally the category of the indefinite article evokes the impersonality of the individual: an individual is not this particular individual, but rather is an 'instance' of individuation. 'One' goes to the store; 'a' person falls in love; 'one' just does not behave in such ways at dinner parties. Hence any particular individual occurs as an instantiation of the impersonality of the indefinite article, but only at the expense of their particular identity. When 'one' dies, they die only in the manner in which no one in particular ever dies. They suffer and live through the death that dis-individuates the individual by allowing their participation in an event to which everyone and no one is destined.

This category of haecceity is closely related to another concept that Deleuze and Guattari will ultimately link to the aesthetic nature of selfhood in this case. This is the category of 'becoming' that describes, in this context, the nature of the relationship between haecceities as instantiations of identity beyond the limits of substantialist notions of identity. 'Becoming', the authors repeatedly emphasise, has nothing to do with a kind of emulation or imitation of the natural type towards which the individual in question is 'becoming'. Rather than indicating the way in which coherent subjects can behave in a manner reflective of the organic composition of another coherent subjects (we can 'act' like Katherine Hepburn, just as we can 'pretend' to be a tree by raising both arms and one leg and freezing in place), becoming here refers to a particular relationship of movement that happens in a sense 'between' individuals – it is the consequence of a solicitation that takes place on the part of both related individuals, making each of them into something they were not before. When, for example, a child undergoes a process of 'becoming-animal' in relation to a dog or a wolf, it is not that the individual comes to emulate or adopt the appearance of dog. Rather the child experiences the dog as invoking moods, affects and ways of being in the child that – at the same time – will change what it is to 'be' a dog as far as that child is concerned and even as far as the dog itself is concerned. In this way, just as in the individual is changed in the encounter of becoming, so does the object one 'becomes' in this way undergo its own transformation: experiencing the proximity between themselves and the other, their own way of being is transformed and solicited in a direction that it had not taken before.

Deleuze and Guattari talk about this space 'between' individuals as a 'zone of proximity' or 'zone of indetermination' in some sense prior to the specification of entities into their several natural types.[29] This is not to imply the existence of some pre-existent archetype in relation to which several later-distinct individuals share a common origin (like Goethe's *Urpflanze* from which all individual species must have derived), but rather to refer to a territory in which such determination has not yet taken place – where components of a coherent identity remain abstracted from a specification according to type or function. In discussing these zones of indetermination and the ways in which they solicit forms of becoming, the authors identify three 'segments' or stages of becoming, implying a kind of progression of types of becoming to which individuals are subject beyond the limits of personal identity: first, 'becoming-woman, becoming-child'; second, 'becoming-animal, -vegetable or -mineral'; and finally, 'becoming-molecular of all kinds, becoming-particles'.[30] Becomings first take place amongst human beings: one 'becomes-woman' or 'becomes-child' in the manner of dis-identifying with the majoritarian organisation of one's subjectivity. To 'become-woman' or 'become-child' means to experience oneself otherwise than in terms of a dominant mode of identification, eschewing conventional notions of selfhood that measure subjectivity in terms of distance from a social norm.[31] Subsequently one moves beyond the purview of the species: 'becoming-animal, -vegetable, or -mineral'. One identifies or feels oneself drawn by a common territory between the self and the organic world around oneself. Deleuze and Guattari cite in this context the long tradition of 'becoming-animal' of music, a pull towards bird song or the sound or twittering – a 'becoming-bird' of music. And finally one arrives at the ultimate aim of all becomings – what in a way can already be said of all becomings, that they 'are already molecular', pointing towards the all-but-invisible being of particles, of molecules in movement.[32]

It is in this place that Deleuze and Guattari (again) discuss Kierkegaard's knight of faith as representing the kind of subjectivity that belongs to this becoming-molecular. The self that 'becomes-molecular' enters into a particular relationship with the imperceptibility of the molecular mode of being. For the knight of faith this becoming is manifest in the unique way in which, through faith, the individual becomes once again capable of being 'like everybody else'.[33]

> To be like everybody else. That is what Kierkegaard relates in his story about the 'knight of faith,' the man of becoming: to look at him, one would notice nothing, a bourgeois, nothing but a bourgeois. That is how Fitzgerald lived: after a real rupture, one succeeds ... in being just like everybody else.[34]

Here Deleuze and Guattari refer the reader to an important element of Johannes de Silentio's account of faith in *Fear and Trembling*: the case of the knight who, despite the normative accomplishment that makes that individual unique and even incomprehensible, 'looks just like a tax collector'. Kierkegaard writes:

> Here he is. The acquaintance is made, I am introduced to him. The instant I first lay eyes on him, I set him apart at once; I jump back, clap my hands, and say half aloud, 'Good Lord, is this the man, is this really the one – he looks just like a tax collector!' But this is indeed really the one. I move a little closer to him, watch his slightest movement to see if it reveals a bit of heterogeneous optical telegraphy from the infinite, a glance, a facial expression, a gesture, a sadness, a smile that would betray the infinite in its heterogeneity with the finite. No![35]

Kierkegaard's tax collector is unique not in his external qualities – that he stands out within a social context by some visible marks or idiosyncratic mode of behaviour. Instead, the tax collector reflects those aspects of faith that allow the individual to live happily, delicately, within her own life through the absence of anxiety that is endemic to the power of faith. The knight of faith lives from moment to moment, enjoying with a degree of frivolity all those goods that the average person is unable to enjoy. Rather than fearing the loss of his status, or desiring some unattainable good, the tax collector is capable of appearing like everyone else simply because he can enjoy all the fruits of human finitude without any of the fear that generally separates an individual from her own everyday environment. Here, what sets the knight of faith apart in terms of her becoming is not something that marks her as unique, but rather her ability to enter into a relationship of becoming with everything, just as it is. As Deleuze and Guattari read this figure, there is no circumstance which distinctively solicits the knight of faith's subterranean movement of change, and in this sense the knight finds this very point of indistinguishability between herself and everything outside of herself (Deleuze and Guattari will say '*tout le monde*': 'the whole world'/'everyone').

Deleuze and Guattari, in speaking of this relationship of indiscernibility that takes place between the knight of faith and 'the whole world', highlight an important element of this that will have a bearing on our discussion in the next chapter of the political stakes of this notion of selfhood, for which reason it is worth highlighting here. This is the idea that – in this process of 'becoming everybody' – the individual inaugurates at the same time a kind of becoming belonging to the world itself. Deleuze and Guattari write: 'Becoming everybody/everything is to world (*faire monde*), to make a world (*faire un monde*). [. . .] It is by conjugating, by continuing with other lines, other pieces, that one makes a world that can overlay the first one, like a transparency.'[36] In this account, what the knight of faith, the 'imperceptible' self does, in its mode of becoming, is to solicit or extract a becoming from the world as such: 'If one reduces oneself to one or several abstract lines that will prolong itself in and conjugate with others, producing immediately, directly *a* world in which it is *the* world which becomes, then one becomes-world.'[37] In other words, in this form of selfhood – as in the account of the self of 'belief' who believes in and thereby engages a new and different world from their conventional experience – it is through one's capacity for identifying and engaging with this other world that we make or 'effect' something new. This, on Deleuze and Guattari's account, is the ultimate aim of the self of becoming: to 'make a world' through the opening of one's identity to the forms of becoming already contained in that world, and in so doing engage a dual process of self- and world-shaping capable of bringing about new ways of being and experiencing. Hence (as we will explore at greater length in the next chapter) the externality to which this notion of immanent selfhood is

Art and the 'Standing Up' of Selfhood

Having already raised some of the concerns regarding an overly Romantic element in Deleuze's thought above, it will be worth mentioning, in presenting this account, one particular element of Deleuze's conception that we have only hinted at so far: namely, the element of aestheticism in Deleuze's account that, in spite of that figuration of selfhood as, in many ways, porous, temporary and transitive, nevertheless prevents this account from entailing a mere chaotic change or dissolution for the self. Instead, on our reading, the criterion under which a self comes into existence under the framework of immanent ethics will bear much in common with the way in which Deleuze and Guattari talk about the creation of a work of art in *What is Philosophy?*, where art is understood not as a mere representation of some organic phenomena that are reproduced through an independent material means.[38] Rather, according to Deleuze and Guattari, a work of art is a 'monument', '*a bloc of sensations, that is to say, a compound of percepts and affects*'.[39] For a work of art to be a compound of percepts and affects means that it instantiates – independently of the subject who observes or produces it – a kind of perspective or experience of the world in itself. It is not that the work of art reflects a possible point of view that the viewer can adopt or reject; rather, the work of art places fragments of perception or feeling directly on view. The work of art is a composite of the world 'as seen'; it is not a tool for seeing the world through itself. And as Deleuze and Guattari specify, the primary issue for the composition of a work of art is not to make something that is recognisable or familiar to the subject who views it (indeed they rail against the work of art which depends upon the author or artist having 'experienced much' in order to compose an effective work of art). Rather, the issue for the composition of a work of art is to make it such that that work can '*stand up on its own [tenir debout tout seul]*' even when what this requires is 'from the viewpoint of an implicit model, from the viewpoint of lived perceptions and affections, great geometrical improbability, physical imperfection, and organic abnormality'.[40] In other words, what Deleuze and Guattari describe here is a work of art which does not survive because it represents something empirically likely or empirically conventional, but rather a work of art which has its own intrinsic stability or integrity, in which its composition attests to a singular coherence or aesthetic sense. 'These sublime errors accede to the necessity of art if they are *internal* means of standing up.'[41] The enigmatic smile, for example, on the face of Rosasharn at the end of the *Grapes of Wrath*, as she gives her breast to a dying man to suck, her own child now dead, represents a monumental effort of narrative and linguistic technique in order to make it 'stand up'. How to convey all that is contained in this single affect which is embodied only as a 'mysterious smile' in the text? But the sense we have of that smile – its unique evocativeness, containing the bitterness and ecstasy of the human experience – entails its very coherence: we know what it is to have that smile, enigmatic and unimaginable though it is. This is what Deleuze and Guattari mean in describing art as a 'monument': it contains an internal coherence that rests upon its present material conditions for its existence, even while it transcends and inevitably outlasts the material conditions in which it is instantiated.

From this we can imagine the nature of what it means to possess a haecceic selfhood which is the accomplishment of an immense effort of subjective becoming. It will mean – rather than establishing something like the substantial identity that guarantees or secures indefinitely a single sense of personality – that the individual finds and constructs a sufficiently coherent sense of self to instantiate itself within the particular material and contextual conditions that surround it. In other words, for a self to be a haecceity will mean for it to have found the unique 'sense' or 'meaning' of its identity – the aesthetic quality that makes possible its appreciation and affirmation, even while it anticipates a transformation into other temporary and semi-stable forms of identity. This is to say that, for Deleuze, the selfhood we embody need not remain permanently throughout our temporal existence, so long as its realisation incorporates, for however long or short a duration, *'the eternity that coexists with this short duration'*.[42] Hence what we find, beyond the categories for substantial identity and responsibility that had condemned individuals to choose between coherence and chaos, is a coherence within chaos – one open to the possibilities of change and becoming while at the same time infused with the sense of accomplishment and approbation belonging to all great works of art.

From what has been said, we can see how the 'Kierkegaardian' subjects we spoke about above – figures of faith or externalisation in confrontation with a world otherwise intolerable – can be capable of a kind of consistency proper to a post-Kantian conception of self. Selfhood, rather than grounded on a kind of pre-existing substantiality – nor itself the object of a moral 'resurrection' – has its place in the multiple rearticulations of aesthetic becoming, each of which circulates around the viability of the self as an aesthetic creation. Selves here are neither cut off from the world, nor utterly dissolved, but rather sewn into the world, in such a way as to permit multiple and diverse reformulations of the self across time: stable, porous and responsive to the world around them. Ethically, we find a practice of appropriation, at the same time as a project of transformation, guiding the principles of the self's involvement in the world that surrounds it. And rather than grounding itself on a pre-supposed knowledge of the way in which such selfhood should affect the world, the self here finds itself engaged in the generation of new forms and possibilities of life through struggle. Selves will be created, and will create a world, by virtue of this unforeseeable grappling with the conditions for the possibility of aesthetic creation.

Kierkegaard: Transparency and Immediacy

Having indicated some of the themes that arise in Deleuze's considerations of Kierkegaardian belief, I want to now highlight, as illustration of the possibility of a 'synthetic' account of selfhood between Deleuze and Kierkegaard, a few concepts from Kierkegaard's work that can helpfully deepen what has been said above by drawing out some themes that remain under-elaborated in Deleuze. The concepts of 'transparency' (*Gjennemsigtighed*) and 'immediacy' (*Umiddelbarhed*) both appear in off-handed ways in Deleuze's oeuvre, and so, to remain close to the encounter between these two philosophers while still elaborating what can be uniquely contributed by Kierkegaard, in what follows I will look at Kierkegaard's presentation of these concepts for a fuller picture of the notion of selfhood that we have been pursuing.[43] What we will see is that, in place of a reflective, internally-oriented subjectivity, Kierkegaard offers a transparency that dissolves subjectivity into a relationship with others, and that in place of abstract, conceptual cognition, he offers us a picture of cognitive immediacy or intuition that bodies forth the singularity of the individual. Both of these concepts, therefore, will highlight a different aspect and a different mode of engagement with the world belonging to the kind of selfhood that I claim Deleuze and

Kierkegaard can both helpfully elaborate: one that is grounded on a metaphysics of temporality, contingency and finitude.

TRANSPARENCY

The Kierkegaardian concept of transparency (*Gjennemsigtighed*) appears primarily in Anti-Climacus's *The Sickness Unto Death*, where the author aims to articulate some properties belonging to the self insofar as it achieves the normative ideal of Christianity – namely, the faith in which despair has been 'completely rooted out' of it.[44] Here, Anti-Climacus presents a formula for faith as a kind of proper relation between the self and itself, including in this formula the fact of the self's dependence upon another for its origin and sustenance. In a famous passage articulating some of the basic elements of Kierkegaardian selfhood, Anti-Climacus writes:

> A human being is spirit [*Aanden*]. But what is spirit? Spirit is the self. But what is the self? The self is a relation that relates itself to itself or is the relations relating itself to itself in the relation; the self is not the relation but is the relation's relating itself to itself. A human being is a synthesis of the infinite and the finite, of the temporal and the eternal, of freedom and necessity, in short a synthesis.[45]

In presenting this picture of the self, Anti-Climacus enumerates several elements of a Kierkegaardian concept of selfhood that will reappear across several of that author's works: first, the notion of the self as a 'synthesis' or composite of both a 'physical' (finite, temporal, necessitated) element and a 'psychical' (infinite, eternal, free) element; second, the notion of 'spirit' (*Aand*) as serving to unite or facilitate this synthetic relationship between two elements (which elsewhere he will identify with our existential 'freedom'); and, finally, the idea that, in some sense, it is a distinctive feature of one's selfhood to be capable of taking a perspective or position on this selfhood. On this picture, the self 'relates itself' to itself, and thereby we do not merely embody the fact of a synthetic, 'composite' identity, but additionally take that fact of synthetic identity as itself of concern or interest for ourselves as individuals (we can notice, for example, that the cold weather has been making it difficult to think, or that we have been pushing our body too hard as of late). In going on to elaborate the nature of the relationship between the self and itself – all the ways in which the self can enter into a variety of proper or improper relationships towards its very nature – Anti-Climacus is clear to first establish an important qualification upon the nature of this synthetic, the reflexively-structured self. He writes:

> The human self is [...] a derived, established relation, a relation that relates itself to itself and in relating itself to itself relates itself to another. This is why there can be two forms of despair in the strict sense. If a human self had itself established itself, then there could be only one form: not to will to be oneself, to will to do away with oneself, but there could not be the form: in despair to will to be oneself.[46]

In this critical passage, Anti-Climacus emphasises an important element of what it means to be a human being on his account, and moreover an important element of what will be necessary for such a human being to achieve a kind of harmony with itself in terms of its basic constitution. In emphasising that the human being, beyond having a relationship of reflection on its own psychical-physical composition, also has an implicit relationship to an outside or 'other' which 'establishes' it, Anti-Climacus incorporates a category of dependence that effectively de-centres the human being from its own relation to self in faith. Here it is the self's basic dependence relationship on something outside of itself that allows for the possibility that an individual can not only fail to affirm or accept itself by refusing the projects that comprise its basic facticity (what Anti-Climacus will call the human tendency to will 'away' from one's fate or to will 'not to be oneself'), but can also – in rejection of its need for the persistent support of one or several others on whom it depends – 'will to be oneself' in such a way that equally obscures or refuses a central element of what it is to be human.

It is because the self can both fail to become itself by virtue of a *ressentiment* directed towards itself, as well as by virtue of a *ressentiment* directed at its dependency, that for the individual to effectively 'become' itself it is necessary that it both comes to identify with the facticity given to it by virtue of being a finite, historically determined and mortal creature, and also comes to recognise its own basic dependence, as a finite and historically determined creature, on something outside of itself for its continued support and empowerment. It is for this reason that Anti-Climacus's account of what it means to 'rout out' the despair that distances the individual from their own essential nature, involves a metaphor of visibility that is noticeably different from the language one might find in a more deontological account. Anti-Climacus writes that 'the formula that describes the state of the self when despair is completely rooted out is this: in relating itself to itself and in willing to be itself, the self rests transparently [*gjennemsigtig*] in the power that established it'.[47]

This vocabulary of transparency, as we mentioned above, is relatively uncommon in Kierkegaard's writings, and yet the visual metaphor that it involves offers much for consideration as far as understanding the nature of the self that corresponds to Kierkegaard's conception of faith. Simon Podmore, in his *Kierkegaard and the Self Before God* draws out Anti-Climacus's optical metaphor in order to highlight the way in which the author's emphasis on 'transparency' serves to undermine the implied relationship of guilt that might obtain between an individual and their own imagining of God as a kind of scrutinising moral judge. Quoting Kierkegaard's comments in a devotional discourse on a passage from the Book of Luke, Podmore writes:

> 'The one who, alone with his guilt and his sin, knows that if he opens his eyes he will see God's holiness and nothing else, that one surely learns to cast his eyes down; or he perhaps looked up and saw God's holiness – and cast his eyes down.' Alone with his guilt and sin, the abyssal distance between the sinner and the Holy seems to bespeak such an incommensurability that the gaze must contend only with this prospect: to see God is to die.[48]

In this context, Podmore highlights the ways in which a gap between one's moral ideals and one's perception of the reality of oneself can lead an individual to conceal themselves – not only from an imagined judge in the image of a disapproving God, but moreover from themself, where one's own faults are made unrecognisable simply by virtue of the fear involved in recognising them. Hence, as Podmore argues, the transparency involved in the individual's exposure to God is not merely a transparency of disclosure, in which the individual supposedly reveals a phenomenon which – by all accounts – must already be known. Rather, the transparency of this exposure coincides with an audacity in the individual to anticipate – in conjunction with the disclosure of one's frailties – a forgiveness of these frailties as both tolerable and forgivable.

> Faith is related to clear-sightedness: the transparency that is aptly described by C. Stephen Evans as being 'willing to stand before God and open myself to his gaze'. But will opening oneself to the gaze of God not induce some form of madness or annihilation, as Anti-Climacus describes in the extreme terms of the 'fantasized religious person' (SUD 32)? [. . .] First, it is a question of how the self perceives its own *sinfulness* – the

consciousness of sin, despair over sin, and sense of the infinite chasmic abyss. But second, the possibility of the self before God is determined by how the self sees itself in relation to the *forgiveness* of sin – the reparation of the infinite chasmic abyss.[49]

What we find in this account of transparency as a function of the courage to expect forgiveness for one's sins, is a notion of visibility that brings together, paradoxically, an exposure of the self to others that coincides at the same time with an extreme imperceptibility or even invisibility to oneself and to others. In the transparent 'resting' in God that anticipates the forgiveness of sins, what the individual does is to pre-emptively disavow the shamefulness or contemptibility of one's failures, so that just as one is made capable and willing to disclose these limitations in an expectation of forgiveness, so are these weaknesses and frailties made invisible through the very disinterest that no longer seeks to hide these from discovery. This transparent willing that allows oneself to become visible to another at the same time as one becomes, themself, invisible, is something that Podmore highlights in reference to another signed discourse, here one in which it is the individual's invisibility – their 'becoming-imperceptible', in a sense – that allows them to enter into a more immediately responsive relationship to God. Podmore quotes:

> Whom should the struggler desire to resemble other than God? But if he is something or wants to be something, this something is sufficient to hinder the resemblance. Only when he himself becomes nothing, only then can God illuminate [*gjennemlyse* – 'light-through'] him so that he resembles God. [...] When the ocean is exerting all its power, that is precisely the time when it cannot reflect the image of heaven, and even the slightest motion blurs the image; but when it becomes still and deep, then the image of heaven sinks into nothingness.[50]

Here we find a concept of transparency that brings together three important elements of the selfhood that Kierkegaard involves with faith: first, a notion of the self as affirming or accepting of the various frailties and weaknesses that constitute an intrinsic element of what it is to be finitely human; second, a notion of self-acceptance as a form of transparency that, perhaps counter-intuitively, eliminates or renders invisible the very self whose anxious self-awareness first rendered the self visible 'for' discovery; and, finally, a concept of selfhood aligned with this notion of invisibility that makes possible a richer and more responsible relationship to others – one absent the anxious striving to conceal oneself that inhibits such a relationship to the other. In this we can see how, in transparency, the subject is made to open itself to a greater form of becoming that coincides with a deeper and more intimate connection with others, precisely for its willingness to leave behind those limitations grounded on a refusal to see and accept one's weaknesses.

Deleuze and Guattari, in describing their own account of becoming-imperceptible in *A Thousand Plateaus*, describe this phenomenon in terms that are remarkably resonant with Anti-Climacus's account. There, they describe a paradoxical form of secrecy in which, by virtue of one's direct self-exposure, one suddenly becomes imperceptible to others. They write:

> It is because we no longer have anything to hide that we can no longer be apprehended. To become imperceptible oneself, to have dismantled love in order to become capable of loving. To have dismantled one's self in order finally to be alone and meet the true double at the other end of the line. A clandestine passenger on a motionless voyage. To become like everybody else; but this, precisely is a becoming only for one who knows how to be nobody, to no longer be anybody.[51]

In this passage we see the three related themes from above: a loss of shame that facilitates one's visibility, a 'dismantling' of the self that coincides with an acceptance of those elements that had previously remained concealed, and finally an intimacy that arises precisely through this virtual absence of the self, by allowing that self to enter into a process of becoming with another. We can see here that to 'be transparent' as a property of selfhood means both to overcome the limitations of shame and disavowal that inhibit processes of becoming, as well as to lose oneself as a perceptible, indexable object of surveillance. Hence transparency, more than merely illustrating something about one's relationship to oneself, implies a kind of distribution of selfhood to others as well, in which we are better able to be carried away in our relationships.

IMMEDIACY

An additional category that can helpfully elaborate what it might mean for a self to exist under faith is the category of 'immediacy', which Kierkegaard and his pseudonyms regularly use in order to distinguish between the several 'stages' or 'spheres' of existence.[52] On Kierkegaard's account, the category of immediacy is primarily to be understood in terms of its relationship to several related or opposed terms – in particular the categories of 'innocence' (which will have a complex, we might say 'ambiguous' relationship to the category of immediacy) and 'mediacy' or 'reflection', which have a much more straightforward dialectical relationship to the category of immediacy.

In both cases what we find in the category of immediacy as it is related to the concept of faith is the notion of a kind of simplicity or intuitiveness that allows the individual to suspend their anxious, language-mediated reflection, although in such a way as to at the same time include or sublate this reflection into a novel form of instinct. In other words, with the category of immediacy Kierkegaard offers us a way to think about the spontaneity of the individual without for this reason appealing to Rousseau-esque beliefs about the greater perfection of the uncorrupted subject. Instead, immediacy will serve to link Kierkegaardian notions about the responsiveness of the individual to her immediate and material environment with an appreciation for the role of consideration, thoughtfulness and even the conventions of ethics in everyday human experience. But let us begin with the category of immediacy as it appears in its initial shape as a term of aesthetic 'dreaminess' or un-conscientious behaviour.

Kierkegaard's most common account of the nature of immediacy is represented in his work on the 'aesthetic' stage of existence, where immediacy is connected to a kind of instinctual or pre-ethical manner of behaving. In *Either/Or II*, the quintessential representative of the 'ethical' frame of mind, the pseudonym Judge William, writes of immediacy as what precludes the aesthetic individual from participation in the category of genuine choice, and – therefore – precludes the aesthetic frame of mind's participation in the framework of moral right and wrong at all. William writes that 'to choose is an intrinsic and stringent term for the ethical. Wherever in the stricter sense there is a question of an Either/Or, one can always be sure that the ethical has something to do with it.'[53] On the other hand,

> aesthetic choice is either altogether immediate, and thus no choice, or it loses itself in a great multiplicity. For example, when a young girl follows her heart's choice, this choice, however beautiful it is otherwise, is no choice in the stricter sense, because it is altogether immediate. If a man aesthetically ponders a host of life tasks, then he [...] does not readily have one Either/Or but a great multiplicity, because the self-determining aspect of the choice has not been ethically stressed and because, if one does not choose absolutely one chooses only for the moment and for that reason can choose something else the next moment.[54]

What Judge William here describes is something that the pseudonym Frater Taciturnus will later emphasise in the *Stages on Life's Way*, namely the close association between the aesthetic stage of immediacy and the uncorrected 'drives and natural impulses' of the individual.[55] Indeed the unreflectiveness built into this category of immediacy comprises much of the reason as to why aesthetic consciousness is unable to achieve a truly ethical qualification: on the one hand, the 'choices' made under the impulse of one's immediate desires and inclinations lack sufficient constancy – the intention to commit to a decision and therefore suffer the ramifications or enjoy the benefits of such a commitment – as is necessary for these to be properly understood as genuine choices; on the other hand, (relatedly) the pursuit of one's immediate desires and inclinations lacks the necessary conscientiousness to these movements to properly count as imputable to the individual. Hence, as William states: this aesthetic stage 'is not evil but [. . .] indifferent'; in other words it lacks the necessary qualifications to properly choose for evil simply because the nature of authentic ethical choice has not been made present to it.[56]

Hence it is because the ethical stage is facilitated by a form of reflection or conscientiousness that immediacy as a source for one's normative motivation is precluded in the stages above the aesthetic. Because a conscientious, ethical person entails a kind of rational reflection – the ability to step outside of one's mere inclinations – in order to both make responsible moral choices and also in order to constitute oneself as responsible 'for' one's moral choices. And yet, as Kierkegaard goes on to say, the category of immediacy is not merely lost in the normativity of ethical reflection and the 'higher' stage of faith that takes the individual beyond this ethical level: there is indeed a return of the category of immediacy in the religious sphere of existence that brings something of the 'primitivity' of the aesthetic stage to bear on what is means to live in faith and be guided by one's 'absolute relation to the absolute'.[57] In *Fear and Trembling*, Johannes de Silentio articulates it this way: 'Faith is not the first immediacy but a later immediacy. The first immediacy is the aesthetic [. . .]. But faith is not the aesthetic, or else faith has never existed because it has always existed.'[58] In his own notes, Kierkegaard uses similar language to talk about the relationship between faith and immediacy: '[. . .] faith is immediacy or spontaneity after reflection'.[59] But what might it mean to achieve an immediacy 'after' reflection in the way that Kierkegaard refers to faith? One way of thinking of this relationship might have to do with something that M. Jamie Ferreira describes in her account of Kierkegaard's Christian love (*Kjerlighed*) where she distinguishes between the merely 'preferential' character of erotic or romantic love (what Kierkegaard calls '*Elskov*'), and a more properly responsible love that attends to the basic humanity and needs of the love object.

> Kierkegaard identifies erotic love [*Elskov*] and friendship [*Venskab*] as love based on preference, inclination, drives, feelings, as love that is therefore '*umiddelbar Kjerlighed*': spontaneous or immediate love. His crucial contrast, therefore, between preferential love [*Forkjerlighed*] and non-preferential love [*Kjerlighed*] can be seen as a contrast between immediate and non-immediate love (WL 52; SV 3 12, 56).[60]

In this account we might get the impression that the kind of love that Kierkegaard classifies under 'non-preferential love' – something closer to the Christian ideal of 'neighbourly love' – would be a particularly attenuated or abstract love. If we are committed to the kind of love that we can offer to those we have no particular attraction to or inclination towards, where does this put our most intimate relationships with those with whom we intend to build a life? Is this an example of something like a Kantian duty which, just insofar as it obligates us to show respect and concern for each individual, equally starves our closest relationships of their unique beauty and importance?

Ferreira addresses such question by specifying the ways in which non-preferential or 'neighbourly' love does and does not reflect something of the immediacy of romantic *Elskov*. On the one hand, non-preferential love does not reflect the aesthetic immediacy of *Elskov* if by this category we mean something like the mere inclination-satisfying that belongs to romantic love. On this account we do not show Christian love to others – including love to our closest relations and our partners – owing to their possession of some property by means of which they earn this love. And yet there is something of the aesthetic attunement to the specificity or 'distinctiveness' of the other, if by this we mean to include in our love a sense for the ways in which individuals will move in and out of their diverse set of priorities and properties over the course of a lifetime, their way of being uniquely themselves through their course of change and growth.[61] What this means is that the nature of non-preferential love is not contingent upon any one or several properties belonging to the other in terms of which this kind of love can be lost once these properties have changed. And yet just for this reason one is even more capable of recognising and remaining attentive to the singularity of the love-object, just because these properties no longer serve as sources of potential anxiety or concern: unlike Kierkegaard's 'poetic' lovers, who run the perpetual risk of falling 'out' of love, Christian lovers are capable of remaining with what is truly unique to the other – namely, the process of becoming for which the care and support of a lover is an invaluable condition. In this sense neighbourly love retains something essential to the category of aesthetic love, namely the 'immediacy' that allows us to enter into a singular and intimate relationship with the one loved.

On the other hand, one might wonder what, if anything, of reflective, universalistic love remains in such an account. Here Ferreira suggests an opportunity for reversing the traditional relationship between the categories of romantic immediacy and Christian neighbourliness: 'The question of whether the aesthetic is preserved [in neighbourly love] already prejudices the discussion, putting a priority on aesthetic immediacy. It assumes that erotic love or friendship is paradigmatic caring, the caring that most exhibits what caring should be.'[62] And she goes on to specify the terms of the Kierkegaardian reversal: 'in erotic love and friendship, preserve love for the neighbour'.[63] In other words, Kierkegaardian *Kjerlighed* invites us to reconsider the relative weaknesses of preferential love for the other: do the weaknesses of such a love consist, primarily, in an inability to properly distinguish the other from our generalised responsibilities? Is our concern to ensure that we do not merely respect the other as a human being, but rather demonstrate our preference as a lover? Or, on the contrary, is our concern to navigate our preferential forms of love – the kind of love that satisfies its own needs through others and therefore risks losing sight of the others' best interests – by means of a conscientiousness of this kind of neighbourly love, the love which places the other on equal footing with ourselves, and even resists a temptation to treat those we love the most intimately as though they were not also human beings on their own journeys of growth and change. In this sense, Ferreira argues, the conventional relationship between neighbourly types of love and preferential types of love is reversed, so that *Kjerlighed* is not an attenuated form of *Elskov*, but rather *Elskov* will restrict or limit the full expression of *Kjerlighed*. Thus, '*Kjerlighed* is immediate caring, but with the qualification that it is not arbitrary or exclusive. One could conclude that in the case of love the so-called "second immediacy" is really the paradigm of immediacy.'[64]

On this account we have a better understanding what it might mean to speak of religious existence as a kind of 'second' immediacy. Here the nature of immediacy is not merely the immediacy of our unconscious predilections which are given to us, but rather a capacity for a greater sensitivity and attunement to the world around us – other human beings included – by means of a learned distance from our anxious self-interest. Indeed it is by allowing ourselves a form of appreciation and enjoyment that does not 'depend' upon states of affairs in a way that leads to an inevitable disappointment, but rather expresses a gratitude for the finite in its endless change and transformation, that we can balance the kind of aesthetic appreciation that can only come from a sensitivity to the concrete with the reflective appreciation that forestalls our selfish inclinations. In this sense the category of immediacy perhaps paradoxically 'mediates' between our own singularity as subjects – the fact of our sensitivity to the world outside of our personalistic desires and inclinations – and the singularity of the world around us in its temporal fecundity. Here immediacy accounts for something like the dual-becoming that Deleuze describes: the ways in which the suspension of our naked rationality permits a simultaneous growth and letting-grow with the world around us.

Conclusion

From these qualities we have the sketches of a clearer image of a Deleuzian conception of selfhood, insofar as the latter is linked, through faith and a desire to increase one's capacity of acting and of being affected, to Kierkegaard's work. Deleuze's work, when approached through the lens of his own reflections on Kierkegaard, provides complementary details of the nature of the self as conceived under this paradigm: the self 'becomes-imperceptible' or appears 'like everybody else', while expressing a kind of 'dislocation' with respect to its own internality and intentionality, so that its individuality somehow makes contact with an extreme impersonality with which it now identifies.[65] These qualities differ substantially from those properties relevant for a thinking about the self in the context of traditional conceptions of morality, just as much as they differ from the properties of a metaphysically substantial self. Deleuze and Kierkegaard both present a selfhood organised around ephemerality, provisionality, change, a kind of un-self-consciousness that allows for a more natural set of reflections on how human beings actually navigate their worlds. Moreover, we see in these qualities a certain conception of selfhood that is both more adequate to the preceding chapter's conception of normativity, as well as adequate to a thinking of selfhood that avoids the dual pitfalls of an overly substantialised and overly 'dissolved' conception of the self. What we find is that selfhood here figures certain normative evaluations that individuals can achieve (a desire to fit well, struggle with or relax into, one's environment) without for this reason being predicated on a moral necessity of achieving these ideals. More importantly, we have begun to sketch a way of thinking about the self that does justice to the dual interests of individuals to shape and reshape their identities, to be affected by and to engage with the conflicts and struggles of the world around them, all the while maintaining a provisionally stable image of self that gives a human being something to aspire towards. Looking more closely at Kierkegaard's thought – and also at how Deleuze takes up and is influenced by Kierkegaard's thought – has shown us what can be found along a more humanistic line than might have been supposed: where once we saw mere self-destruction, dissolution or abdication of identity, here we find the recurring process of self-shaping and evolution that traces the fluctuations of a human life.

Notes

1. Deleuze, *Cinema II*, p. 201.
2. Deleuze draws an explicit connection between 'affection-images' and Stoic 'events' at ibid., p. 97.
3. Ibid.
4. Ibid., pp. 108–109.
5. Ibid., p. 108.
6. Ibid., p. 113.
7. Ibid., p. 114. On the concept of choice in *Cinema I*, see Bogue, 'To Choose to Choose', pp. 115–132. Bogue links Deleuze's reflections on choice here to his discussion of repetition in *Difference and Repetition*.
8. Deleuze, *Cinema I*, p. 121.
9. Deleuze, *Cinema II*, p. 169.
10. Deleuze, *Cinema II*, pp. 187–188. Some explicit references to Kierkegaard in this chapter of *Cinema II* appear in the context of the principles of 'theorematic selfhood' and 'the outside' that we will discuss below. The principles of 'belief' (*croyance*) that Deleuze discusses manifestly owe their basis to Kierkegaard's concept of faith as we will see in what follows. They are also book-ended by oblique references to Kierkegaard's work – for example, the famous 'something

possible, otherwise I will suffocate' mentioned in our Introduction, and a reference to making 'the unthought the specific power of thought, through the absurd', ibid. p. 170. A discussion of incarnation or 'embodiment' (which I will not pursue here for the sake of space) begins with a reference to Kierkegaard ('give me a body, then', pp. 172–173) and reappears as a heading in the following chapter ('"Give me a body then": this is the formula of philosophical reversal', p. 189). For more on the association between Deleuze's conception of modern cinema and Kierkegaard, see Marrati, *Gilles Deleuze: Cinema and Philosophy*, Bogue, 'To Choose to Choose', and Rodowick, 'The World, Time'.

11 Deleuze, *Cinema II*, p. 168. Notice that the description of 'what cannot be thought in thought' matches how Deleuze characterises the transcendental exercise of the faculties in the three repetitions from *Difference and Repetition*: 'Finally, the third characteristic of transcendental memory is that, in turn, it forces thought to grasp that which can only be thought [. . .]: not the intelligible, for this is still just the mode under which we think what can be other than thought, but the being of the intelligible as the last power of thought, as well as the unthinkable', Deleuze, *Difference and Repetition*, p. 141, translation slightly modified.

12 Ibid., p. 169.

13 Ibid. Deleuze gets the concept of the 'subtle way out' from Artaud, *Oeuvres Complètes*, p. 22. On the concept of 'belief in the world', see Hughes, 'Believing in the World', pp. 83–89. Rodowick highlights the link between 'any-space-whatevers' in *Cinema I* and the 'crisis of knowledge' in *Cinema II*, in 'The World, Time', p. 107.

14 Deleuze, *Cinema II*, p. 170. 'Something possible, otherwise I will suffocate', as mentioned earlier, is an adaptation of Kierkegaard, *The Sickness Unto Death*, p. 38: 'When someone faints, we call for water, eau de Cologne, smelling salts; but when someone wants to despair, then the word is: Get possibility, get possibility, [. . .] for without possibility a person seems unable to breathe.' The original source is Fondane, '*Traité du Désespoir*', pp. 42–43.

15 That Deleuze in fact describes 'time' as the particular object of engagement when the sensory-motor schema breaks down is the persistent theme of *Cinema II*. As we will see in the next chapter, Deleuze also characterises Francis Bacon's engagement with the forces 'behind the visible' specifically as an engagement with time at Deleuze, *Francis Bacon*, p. 54. Interestingly (but perhaps to be expected), Kierkegaard describes Abraham as a victor in a struggle 'with time' at Kierkegaard, *Fear and Trembling*, p. 19.

16 Deleuze, *Cinema II*, p. 173.

17 Ibid., p. 173.

18 Ibid., p. 174.

19 Ibid., pp. 169 and 174. Deleuze refers to Jean-Louis Schefer, *The Ordinary Man of the Cinema*, for the concept of the 'mummified' character, although the category of automatism is already there, for example, in *Practical Philosophy*, p. 86.
20 Deleuze, *Cinema II*, pp. 175 and 177.
21 Ibid., p. 183. Deleuze's reference is to Pier Paolo Pasolini, *L'expérience hérétique*. Robert Bresson's films – a frequent reference point for Deleuze – contain many 'automatic' characters, whose speech and behaviour is intentionally stereotyped in order to isolate the exteriority or impersonality of the selves they represent.
22 Ibid., p. 179.
23 Deleuze, *Cinema I*, pp. 18–24.
24 Ibid., p. 19.
25 Deleuze, *Cinema II*, p. 175. The likely reference here is to somewhere in *The Concept of Anxiety*, where Haufniensis circumscribes the limits of psychology as capable of 'explaining' sin: 'The science that deals with the explanation is psychology, but it can only explain only up to the explanation and above all must guard against leaving the impression of explaining that which no science can explain', p. 39.
26 Here I am looking primarily at chapter 10: '1730: Becoming-Intense, Becoming-Animal, Becoming-Imperceptible ...', where there are several pages of reflection on the knight of faith, as well as discussion of a favorite Kierkegaardian dictum, 'I look only at movements', Deleuze and Guattari, *A Thousand Plateaus*, p. 281, quoting Kierkegaard, *Fear and Trembling*, p. 38. There is also mention of Kierkegaard with reference to the concept of imperceptibility in chapter 8, *A Thousand Plateaus*, p. 197.
27 Deleuze and Guattari, *A Thousand Plateaus*, p. 261.
28 Ibid., p. 263.
29 Ibid., p., 273. See also Deleuze and Guattari, *What is Philosophy?*, p. 173.
30 Deleuze and Guattari, *A Thousand Plateaus*, p. 272.
31 On the notion of a minor and major mode of identification, see the next chapter, and especially the section on 'minor' literature, p. 142–148.
32 Ibid., p. 277.
33 Ibid., p. 279.
34 Ibid.
35 Kierkegaard, *Fear and Trembling*, p. 39.
36 Deleuze and Guattari, *A Thousand Plateaus*, p. 280.
37 Ibid., p. 280, emphasis in original.
38 On the self as a work of art, see Surin, 'Existing Not as a Subject But as a Work of Art'.
39 Deleuze and Guattari, *What is Philosophy?*, p. 164, emphasis in original.

40 Ibid., emphasis in original.
41 Ibid.
42 Ibid., p. 166, emphasis in original.
43 Deleuze and Guattari reference subjective 'transparency' at *A Thousand Plateaus*, pp. 280 and 282; and 'immediacy' appears as a function of the contact between inside and outside in faith at *Cinema II*, p. 221.
44 Kierkegaard, *Sickness Unto Death*, p. 14. See also Kierkegaard, *Works of Love*, p. 361.
45 Kierkegaard, *Sickness Unto Death*, p. 13.
46 Ibid., pp. 13–14.
47 Ibid., pp. 14, 49.
48 Podmore, *Self Before God*, p. 153, quoting Kierkegaard, *Without Authority*, p. 130.
49 Ibid., p. 154.
50 Kierkegaard, 'One Who Prays Aright', p. 399; quoted in Podmore, *Self Before God*, p. 178.
51 Deleuze and Guattari, *A Thousand Plateaus*, p. 197.
52 On the concept of immediacy, see, in addition to those sources cited below, Liu, 'Immediacy/Reflection', p. 216, and Schulz, 'Second Immediacy'.
53 Kierkegaard, *Either/Or II*, p. 167.
54 Ibid.
55 Kierkegaard, *Stages on Life's Way*, p. 399.
56 Kierkegaard, *Either/Or II*, p. 169.
57 Kierkegaard, *Fear and Trembling*, p. 56.
58 Ibid., p. 82.
59 Kierkegaard, *Journals and Papers*, Vol. 2, p. 12 [1123].
60 Ferreira, 'Immediacy and Reflection', pp. 107–108.
61 Ibid., p. 115.
62 Ibid., p. 118.
63 Kierkegaard, *Works of Love*, p. 62, quoted in Ferreira, 'Immediacy and Reflection', p. 118.
64 Ferreira, 'Immediacy and Reflection', p. 119.
65 Deleuze and Guattari, *What is Philosophy?*, p. 166.

5

Faith, Creation and the Future of Deleuzian Subjects

Having now established some of the basic elements of a Deleuzian-Kierkegaardian notion of selfhood – one which is adequate to the concept of ethics sketched in the earlier chapters – I want to elaborate some of the ideas discussed there in the direction of a possible political interpretation of these questions, if only for the sake of indicating the kinds of productive directions in which a comparison of the two philosophers might be taken. One recent direction of research that has been interestingly adumbrated in Kierkegaard scholarship has to do with the subtle political value of his thought, showing how the Kierkegaardian emphasis on possibility and embodiment might contribute towards ideas about political materialism and non-teleological thinking. On the other side of things, one element of Deleuze's reading of Kierkegaard that has been taken up in secondary literature (to some extent) is the category of 'belief', which, as we have seen, serves in Deleuze's later writings as a central concept related to the open-endedness of the relationship between the individual and her environment or 'world'. In this chapter, I want to bring some of these themes together in order to show how – for Deleuze – the category of belief can serve to link an implicit political dimension to his ethical thought, and to confirm this account through an indication of some of the recent developments in Kierkegaard scholarship that move Kierkegaard's supposedly individualistic account in the direction of a collective politics. In particular, we will see below how the category of belief, which draws upon notions of identity distinct from private, individualistic concerns as well as from overly generalised 'group' concerns, allows for a mode of political engagement that brings individuals into an immediately political domain, one where political action need no longer be mediated through loci of stereotyped, 'collective' enunciation – that is, it will be possible to draw the radical individuality of actors directly into contact with an immediately political set of effects. Using this account, we can see how contemporary Kierkegaard scholarship has begun to move in similar directions to certain branches of Deleuze scholarship, by emphasising the collective dimensions of individual subjectivity, and therefore opening new possibilities for political engagement through the activity and creativity of individuals.

To present this account, we will begin with a discussion of the complex relationship between the Deleuzian understanding of 'belief' and artistic creation, looking at Deleuze's work on Francis Bacon in order to sketch a normative concept of creation as a function of 'wrestling' with the intolerability of the world around us, and an appeal to 'the future' as a resource for novelty and change. From there we will look at Deleuze's important concept of 'minor' literature and its relationship to modern cinema, especially insofar as this category is linked to a notion of collective subjectivity distinct from conventional ideas about unified group identity – the sort of identity that integrates individuality by supressing it relative to a dominant political perspective. From this, we will see how Deleuzian belief serves as an ethical and existential activity linked to political engagement, where individual subjectivity is brought into immediate contact with the conditions for the possibility of creating new worlds and ways of being. This will serve as the context for reflecting on Kierkegaardian notions of existential freedom as resources for a novel approach to political philosophy, and for offering a novel understanding of political normativity. We will begin with the category of belief as an aspect of artistic creation in *Francis Bacon: The Logic of Sensation*.

Belief, Art and Optimism

In *Francis Bacon: The Logic of Sensation*, Deleuze talks about the creation of works of art in terms of an engagement or encounter with the 'invisible and insensible forces that scramble every spectacle, and that even lie beyond pain and feeling'.[1] The task of painting in this context is not to paint what exists, in the simple manner of an accurate figuration – to render the image of one who screams, for example – but rather 'render visible these invisible forces that are making [the subject] scream, these powers of the future'.[2] But why, according to Bacon, is it important to engage with the forces 'behind' the scream, rather than with the scream itself? As Deleuze understands Bacon, it is important to engage with these forces because to do so is in some sense to 'surprise' the world at its point of emergence, rather than in its calcified form as 'what exists', and in this way one finds once again the possibility of a creation that can divert, reformulate or harness these powers.

> When, like a wrestler, the visible body confronts the powers of the invisible, it gives them no other visibility than its own. It is within this visibility that the body actively struggles, affirming the possibility of triumphing, which was beyond its reach as long as these powers remained invisible, hidden in a spectacle that sapped our strength and diverted us. It is as if combat had now become possible.[3]

Art is the process of breaking beyond an encounter with the deterministic content of the world, in order to encounter the conditions sufficient for a creation of something new. Under this framework, the nature of what exists is to have been reified in the form of a set of necessary relations, in such a way that disempowers human beings to effect any real change. We are no more able to bring about a future which diverges from the present state of affairs than we can reverse time and change the past which has brought us inevitably to the present. And yet, as Deleuze understands Bacon, when artistic creation brings us into contact with the raw forces which subtend the calcified content of the present, we become once again capable of producing a future other than what follows from the way things already are.

In speaking of this aesthetic encounter with the forces behind what exists, Deleuze invokes Bacon's own vocabulary, by talking about the engagement with these forces as the function of a kind of 'faith in life' or a 'vital faith'. Bacon defines himself as a 'pessimist' from the perspective of his intellectual understanding of the world, but as 'nervously optimistic', in the sense of being capable of circumventing his own rational understanding of the way things are in order to persist in the project of aesthetic creation. From the intellectual point of view, everything that happens in the world happens by sheer necessity; yet from the 'nervous' point of view (that is, the point of view of one's embodied or 'nervous' encounter with the materiality of the world around us), the world continues to contain innumerable, as-yet-unarticulated possibilities. In this the artist creates beyond the threshold of reflectively apprehensible experience, in order to create what is new through an encounter with the raw 'vital' forces of reality.[4]

We see here the function of a concept of 'belief' or 'faith' as circumventing one's intellectual encounter with the world, where faith serves to orient the individual towards a generative materiality of the world – the persistent ability of existence to outstrip what can be said and known about it – by replacing our mere reflective apprehension of things with a supra-rational faculty for engaging

Faith, Creation and the Future of Deleuzian Subjects

with the 'paradox' of what exists. To understand the world is to encounter only catastrophe, but to have faith is to remain engaged with this world, beyond its predictable orderliness, beyond even what is knowably 'possible', so as to enable the individual to act and create once more. 'Bacon distinguishes between two violences, that of the spectacle [of what exists] and that of sensation [of what lies behind], and declares that the first must be renounced to reach the second', writes Deleuze. '[This] is a kind of declaration of faith in life'.[5] In this sense we have an anticipation of what Deleuze will specify in the later *Cinema* books, and what he has already indicated in *Difference and Repetition*: that belief or faith functions in order to enable a creative engagement with the world, one that makes possible an invention of the new beyond the predictability of the rational. This kind of unconscious or involuntary engagement carries with it the possibility of a disruption and interruption of the expected course of history.

In this context it is also worth noting the close relationship that we saw earlier between the function of faith in allowing an individual to generate new possibilities of existences, and the function of faith in permitting the individual to appropriate the reality of time as an unpredictable and incomprehensible force. Earlier we saw how something like a Kierkegaardian concept of faith served to enable an individual to reconcile themselves to the inevitability of change and transformation, so that it was only through a kind of suspension of one's reactive insistence upon control that the individual became capable of 'becoming' in a way that allowed them to change their identity. In Deleuze's book on Bacon, this theme of the relationship between faith and time reappears, here in the context of an identification that Deleuze draws between the 'vital faith' that links the artist to life itself, and the ability of the artist to 'render visible' time itself, as the ultimate force at the base of aesthetic creation. In a chapter entitled 'Painting Forces', Deleuze begins to describe a set of such 'forces' that artists like Bacon are capable of 'rendering' in the practice of painting. He identifies, among them, forces of 'isolation', 'deformation' and 'dissipation', but also a force of 'coupling' – 'which seizes hold of two bodies with an extraordinary energy, and which [those bodies reciprocally] render visible by disengaging from it a kind of polygon or diagram' – and 'a force of unification of the whole, proper to light, but also a force of separation of Figures and panels, a luminous separation which ought not to be confused with the isolation mentioned above'.[6] Deleuze goes on to describe the function of these techniques – a technique of coupling bodies as well as a technique of triptych-painting, stretching a figure across three panels in diverse modes of contortion – as two techniques for rendering time itself visible.

> To render time visible, the force of time – Bacon seems to have done it twice: the force of changing time, through the allotropic variation of bodies, 'down to a tenth of a second,' which takes place through deformation; then the force of eternal time, the eternity of time, though this Unification-separation which reigns in the triptychs, pure light. To render time sensible in itself is the task common to painting, to the musician, sometime to the writer. It is a task beyond all measure or rhythm.[7]

In this sense we see the concluding point of Deleuze's account of art as a function of a kind of 'faith' in life. 'Faith' here serves as the basic orientation of art: artistic practice has the intention of moving beyond the domain of what can be seen and known, towards the grounds of force which can make possible a new reality or a reality worth believing in. And ultimately the force beneath the calcified forms of reality is the same as the one which we found in our earlier exploration of the concept of faith in *Difference and Repetition*: faith or belief serves to make possible an encounter with *time* – to make it possible to bring to the surface the luminescence of time itself as a ground for the possibility of the new. Hence the necessity that art should have a bearing on the nature of history and on the ways in which individuals, no less than collectivities, are situated in time. Art will serve to imagine the present otherwise in order to make possible the elicitation of a future other than what follows necessarily from the present of everyday life.

Kafka, Cinema and the People to Come

Having already invoked a notion of time and historicity in his account of art in *Francis Bacon*, Deleuze will go even farther in the direction of a politicisation of art in his reflections on the work of Franz Kafka – an author whose work he invoked in *Francis Bacon* in terms of the 'diabolical powers of the future' that Kafka was capable of recognising.[8] In Deleuze and Guattari's book on Kafka, the authors will link the rendering of time proper to art in the broadest sense to a political de-centring of subjectivity that will link the artist to a political community or 'people to come'. The creation of art will constitute a form of political activity that brings the subjectivity of the individual into a collective domain so as to short-circuit the problematic nature of the relationship between individuals and communities ('to what extent can an individual adequately speak for the community?') by instead formulating a notion of politics through which the individual is herself in some sense 'immediately' collective. In this way the individual will invoke a non-unified 'people to come' whose very function is to displace dominant notions of power and identity. This feature is what Deleuze and Guattari will discuss in terms of the creation of a 'minor' literature in *Kafka*, no less than Deleuze will himself discuss it in connection to so-called 'third-world' cinema in the final chapters of *Cinema II*.

To begin with Kafka's minor literature: in *Kafka: Toward a Minor Literature*, Deleuze and Guattari describe three features of a 'minor literature' sufficient to undermine majoritarian discourse. The first of these is simply the phenomenon of deterritorialisation attributable to minor literature, by which an extant language – even a language representing political power and institutional authority like German – is made to function and behave in ways other than its conventional institutional purposes. 'Deterritorialised' language is language separated from its simple descriptive or representative functions, so that it is brought more into contact with the non-signifying or expressive functions intrinsic to language itself. As Deleuze and Guattari point out, practices of deterritorialisation are frequently undertaken under conditions of constraint. For Kafka, his language of authorship is German: a minority language proper to the Jewish community in Prague, despite the fact that this language refers to a majoritarian nationality from which Kafka is de-centred by virtue of his Judaism. 'Kafka marks the impasse that bars access to writing for the Jews of Prague, and turns their literature into something impossible – the impossibility of not writing, the impossibility of writing in German, the impossibility of writing otherwise.'[9] Here the problem of writing is a problem of escape: how, for Jews living in Prague, can one write in a German that is not 'territorial' to the country (Czech being the 'vernacular' language of the region), and yet not in a German from which Jews are excluded by virtue of their minority status? One can neither write in Czech (to speak in a language which is not one's own), nor can one write in German (to speak in a language from which one is excluded or de-centred), nor yet can one refuse to write entirely.

The answer, as Deleuze and Guattari put it, is to 'deterritorialise' this majoritarian language: to cause it to say and do things for which it is not intended – to turn the language away from its everyday function by speaking with a broken syntax, carrying words and phrases towards their purely expressive and onomatopoeic functions.[10]

> Kafka is a Czech writing in German, and Beckett an Irishman (often) writing in French, and so on. They do not mix two languages together, not even a minor language and a major language though many of them are linked to minorities as a sign of their vocation. What they do, rather is, invent a *minor* use of the major language within which they express themselves entirely; they *minorize* this language, much as in music, where the minor mode refers to dynamic combinations in perpetual disequilibrium.[11]

This technique of using a major language in ways other than its purely referential and representational purposes is what Deleuze and Guattari mean by saying that within minor literature language is 'affected with a high coefficient of deterritorialization'.[12] Here it is by carrying language away from its conventional, practical functions that language begins to do something other than represent a dominant mode of subjectivity – it becomes capable of expressing other moods and ways of being than those whose subject-positions tend to be represented through this language.

To the deterritorialising function of minor literature Deleuze and Guattari add another: the function which minor literature serves of undermining of a supposedly rigorous distinction between the private and the political, so that the content of a domestic or personal drama is immediately imbued with a political sense and significance. Here Deleuze and Guattari invoke a concept that will later appear in Deleuze's *Cinema II*: 'The private affair merges with the immediately social or political.'[13] In this context, what Kafka does is to break down the distinction between the merely Oedipal domestic conflict and the political world beyond the home; conflict with the Father is not merely an internalisation of a political conflict, nor the starting point for a movement to an external political world, but itself blends and problematises the supposed distinction between the personal and the political. In *Cinema II*, we see this confusion of the boundary between the political and private in a rejection of the trope of 'becoming-conscious' traditionally taken as essential to the relationship between the public and private spheres. For 'classical' cinema the problem of the relationship between the private and the political is a problem of the recognition of the illusory nature of one's domestic concerns, linking them at last to a political context which awakens a character and moves them beyond the four walls of their household. In this regard Pudovkin's *Mother* (1926) is exemplary: the eponymous long-suffering mother naively turns her son over to the Tsarist police, only to arrive, after his death, at an awareness of her political predicament such that she can raise the red flag of socialism while charging a wall of Tsarist cavalry. Deleuze highlights, by contrast, the tendency of modern cinema to eschew such 'consciousness' in favour of a notion of automatic or 'trance-like' behaviour. In Yılmaz Güney's *Yol*, for example, a prisoner's leave of absence allows him to engage in a complicated political negotiation with a neighbouring family, so that he can retrieve and ultimately punish his divorced wife. In this context, we no longer need a mechanism of 'becoming-conscious' in order to draw a connection between the political and personal spheres: the political is immediately blended throughout one's personal life, so that it is more often in a hallucinatory or trance-like state (Seyit drags his wife, zombie-like, through the blinding cold) that one can navigate the blending of diverse domains.

A third – and perhaps most important – property of minor literature consists of what Deleuze and Guattari identify as its immediately 'collective' significance. Here Deleuze and Guattari reiterate reflections on subjectivity that we saw in *A Thousand Plateaus*: the articulations of an individual within the context of a minor literature are more than the articulations of a pre-existing subject possessing a coherent identity and therefore capable of representing a coherent set of experiences or beliefs. Instead, the subject of a minor literature involves a mode of collective enunciation that is closer to the 'invention' or the 'fabulation' of a collective identity: collective identity does not 'pre-exist' the speech of the individual but is instead created through it. It is for this reason that Deleuze and Guattari will write about minor literature as a function of the non-existence of a 'people' who are nonetheless incorporated, through storytelling, in an act of aesthetic creation.[14] This non-existence of 'the people' is manifest in the transition from so-called classical cinema to modern 'third-world' political cinema, where one no longer claims to speak in the name of a coherent minoritarian or majoritarian position, but rather aims to undermine or fragment the notion of subjective coherence that belongs to every majoritarian political structure. In John Ford's *The Grapes of Wrath* (which, it is worth noting, wildly abandons the political ambivalence of Steinbeck's novel by its political optimism) Ford can have Ma Joad unironically intone, after her family survives a narrow brush with destruction, 'They can't wipe us out. They can't lick us. We'll go on forever, Pa, because we're the people.'[15] In this context, 'the people' refers to some generalised set of interests or beliefs, for which an individual can serve as a mouthpiece, conveying or representing these interests in an enforceable way. In modern cinema, by contrast, the problem is precisely the perennial absence of this supposed-coherent 'people' in whose name as much revolutionary good as reactionary evil can be done. In Glauber Rocha's *Entranced Earth* (1967), we are presented with all the problems and stupidities of a populist political movement, including the opportunism of its leaders and the gullibility of the masses who follow them. At one point someone urges a representative of the 'people' to speak, giving him a chance to finally address himself directly to the camera: 'Don't be afraid! Speak! You are the people! Speak!' the character urges. But when the worker steps before the camera, he is only capable of expressing political banalities: 'I'm a humble man, a worker. I'm the leader of my Union. I've been in the class struggle. Things are very wrong. I really don't know what to do. The country is in crisis and the best thing is to obey the President's orders', whereby he is immediately interrupted by another of the film's protagonists, who puts a hand over his mouth. He looks directly into the camera: 'Do you see what the people are like? Idiots!'[16]

In this context, the significance of the immediately 'collective' nature of a 'minor' utterance becomes clear. This is to say that, in the absence of a 'people' who can serve as the condition for the possibility of political speech – the ability to 'represent' or advocate for a coherent set of beliefs or interest – the collective utterance of the individual becomes less a mechanism for mediating between a mythical 'people' and the world, and instead reflects a form of immediately political speech, one in which 'the people' are invoked as an always-displaced position from which one can advocate for a change to the current state of affairs. In this sense, the function of a minor literature – no less than that of a modern political cinema – is not to replace one political power with another political power. The function of a revolutionary practice is not to assume the majoritarian position, now with the corrected voice of a coherent 'popular' subjectivity from which an analogous power can be exercised. Rather, it will be to undermine the majoritarian structure of politics through an act of creation which opens new possibilities of social organisation.[17] Pierre Perrault's 1963 *Pour la Suite du Monde* ('For Those to Come') features a community of Québécois fishermen who stage a re-enactment

Faith, Creation and the Future of Deleuzian Subjects

of their traditional porpoise-trapping technique, but this time with all the ambiguities proper to the non-existence of a coherent 'tradition' from which they can univocally draw. They are compelled to 'fabulate' or perform the collective identity which they no longer or do not yet possess, invoking a displaced source of identity in order to stage their own political sovereignty and facilitate their economic independence.[18] This practice of 'fabulative' storytelling is ultimately what Deleuze means when he speaks about aesthetic creation as involving the 'powers of the future' and making possible novel ways of becoming. The utterance of the minor subject, no less than the work of a painter like Bacon, invokes the open-ended character of history, through which novel political organisations and novel subject-positions can emerge. In this way, the function of aesthetic creation which Deleuze initially associates with a faculty of 'belief' or 'vital faith' in the forces of life serves equally to enable a political subject-formation which undermines established notions of identity as much as to invoke a novel conception of time intended to interrupt the predictable flow of political history.

These properties – the deterritorialisation of language, the deconstruction of the boundary between the personal and the political, and the collective form of minoritarian speech-acts – provide the coordinates for a radical reversal of conventional understandings of political agency and power. Here, rather than seeking for a future somehow 'different' from the present state of affairs but ultimately contiguous with it, and contiguous with the historical progress that is supposed to lead to it, artistic creation sets the conditions for the emergence of novelty within history in a way that refuses notions of political utopia. Political utopia, in this context, will link together a concept of coherent political subjectivity (the subjectivity which will come to power in the future) with a reified notion of history (the history which will effectively end with the subject's assumption of power). Here, instead, we have the resources to think an imperfect, broadly distributed but immediately political form of engagement, in which the undermining of conventional notions of power and authority itself serves as a revolutionary political goal. Thus, as we will elaborate in the next section, we have the connection of several critical elements in a Deleuzian notion of political possibility as they arise in his reflections on 'minor' art: the close association of political possibility with an artistic practice of engagement with the materiality of existence, the 'forces' which always undergird the current state of affairs; the relationship between individuals, in their de-centred subjectivities, as 'immediately' in contact with a political outside, an outside that scrambles the notion of collective subjectivity in a 'double becoming' of self and community; and, finally, a notion of faith or belief which makes possible an encounter with these forces, liberating a quantum of novelty sufficient for the creation of something new.[19] Truly, 'belief' is not a merely private and individual matter, but the condition for the possibility of a revolutionary politics in a world in which revolutionary politics has become virtually unimaginable.

Kierkegaard as Political Philosopher

Having now laid out some of the importance of 'belief' for Deleuze's notion of politics, I want to approach the same issue from a different direction, by looking at two recent efforts at drawing Kierkegaard's thought in the direction of a radical materialist politics – attempts that I believe to be in sympathy with the Deleuzian account presented above. In this way I will single out two philosophers whose work goes far in the direction of liberating Kierkegaardian thought from a superficial religious/secular divide, as well as bringing Kierkegaardian notions of open-endess and indeterminacy into dialogue with issues of political ontology and praxis. As we will see, the basic impulse of drawing the notions of subjective embeddedness and contingency in the direction of collective politics reflects an important insight into the nature of subjectivity under the conditions of Kierkegaard's non-substantialist metaphysics: on these accounts, to speak of a normative ethical project that links notions of personal identity to problems of situatedness and relatedness will necessarily entail a relevance for political and collective questions, and yet – as we know from the preceding discussions of selfhood in Kierkegaardian and Deleuzian ethics – these will not be political and collective questions that can ground themselves on an essentialising notion of 'authentic' identity. Rather, a Kierkegaardian notion of selfhood, coupled to a notion of faith as belief in the unthought possibilities of the future, will entail a reconsideration of what it means to engage in collective praxis and what it means to inhabit a political subject-position in an interdependent context. It will mean drawing oneself into contact with those mechanisms of change that remain unpredictable and uncertain, so that politics will be a matter of individual growth as much as a matter of collective empowerment.

Faith, Creation and the Future of Deleuzian Subjects

BURNS: THE POLITICS OF FRACTURE

Michael O'Neill Burns, in his *Kierkegaard and the Matter of Philosophy*, proposes a radical materialist interpretation of Kierkegaard's thought in terms of a link between the 'ontological' presuppositions of Kierkegaard's account of the self and the possibilities of politics contingent upon those same ontological presuppositions. Here, Burns is interested to demonstrate how, despite the superficially individualistic concerns of Kierkegaardian anthropology, the ontological premises at the heart of Kierkegaard's 'fractured dialectic' – in particular the ontological 'abyss' or *Afgrund* that serves as the basis for the radical contingency of Kierkegaard's philosophy – will be the same premises that make possible a radical political reading of Kierkegaard as potentiating a revolutionary politics of the future. Burns accounts his own approach to the political stakes of Kierkegaard's thought this way:

> Through a recasting of the religious sphere and form of existence in ontological terms, I am able to arrive at an underlying account of concepts such as possibility, contingency and relationality which anchor the dynamic nature of Kierkegaard's existential categories. After this reverse engineering of the ontological out of the existential, I [can] consider the way in which this ontological interpretation allows us to reconceive the political potential at play in Kierkegaard's authorship.[20]

In this context, we can see that it is by recasting Kierkegaardian thought, away from groundings in notions of unity or authenticity, and towards notions of open-endedness and becoming, that Burns can link the kinds of existential projects that Kierkegaard promotes – the forms of becoming and self-transformation irrevocably tied up with notions of faith and self-overcoming – to a notion of politics as a involving the 'possibility-of-possibility' that allows for reconfigurations of social organisation.[21]

In the next section we will speak more directly to the ways in which a Kierkegaardian notion of identity blurs the distinction between self and community in a manner reminiscent of the 'minoritarian' model in Deleuze. For the time being, however, we can see how Burns uses the notion of ontological contingency in Kierkegaard to enable a politically progressive navigation of the relationship between individuals and collectivities within forms of political action. On Burns's account, the basis for the political potentiality in Kierkegaard's philosophy rests not just on the historical presupposition that elevates contingency and possibility above necessity in political accountings, but moreover rests upon the condition that a 'fractured' ontology can provide for a mode of relationship between individuals as participants of collective political projects such that these collectivities will avoid calcifying into reified 'group' identities, in which individuals submerge their political consciousness for the sake of a herd-like dis-individuation.[22] As Burns argues, a 'tension' at the heart of the Kierkegaardian notion of choice makes it necessary that individuals will always have to reconsider and revise their investments in meaningful projects and plans, and this tension reiterates itself at the level of collective political projects: individuals committed to common political ideals must not only consistently reconsider and correct their own ways of relating to those ideals, but must moreover consistently re-navigate and reconsider their relationships to others sharing their common political projects. Thus, avoiding Kierkegaard's fear that interpersonal projects will slip into a form of 'herd'-like behaviour, collective projects grounded on the open-endedness of a contingent ontology allow for the realisation of both individual and collective aims in pursuit of new forms of social organisation and modes of equity. As Burns writes: 'The work of the political, just like the work of becoming a self, or participating in a relationship, can never be completed and instead requires that I am constantly reaffirming a commitment to a particular project as I/we aim at actualizing an ideal into reality.'[23]

On this account, a materialist and ontological line of interpretation of Kierkegaardian ideas can point towards a democratic politics that undermines the dichotomy between self and collective, so that the praxis of political activity can more naturally partake of the open-endedness and contingency to which imperfect human projects are always anyway subject. Political activity will find new resources for the creative construction of social forms by acknowledging the unsettled way in which individuals are forced to navigate their own political projects as much as the projects they pursue in conjunction with similarly minded collectives.

JAARSMA: THE SELF AS COLLECTIVE ASSEMBLAGE

In Ada Jaarsma's *Kierkegaard After the Genome*, we find an even more explicitly 'Deleuzian' appropriation of Kierkegaardian values for the sake of reflection on radical political projects. There, Jaarsma links the categories of contingency, finitude and openness in Kierkegaard to an undermining of the conventional distinction between secular and religious philosophical projects, highlighting the ways in which a genuinely 'Kierkegaardian' politics would refuse the theological elements frequently at play in secularised notions of progress.

> Kierkegaard and his pseudonymous authors explore case after case of examples in which adherence to social norms enables individuals to dissemble about the dynamics of faith, not only to other but to themselves. These examples are deftly rendered as preposterous in Kierkegaard's texts, both because of how they deceive individuals about their own behaviour and because of how they miss the entire dynamics of faith, freedom and subjectivity. In this way, Kierkegaard is an early proponent of what we might today identify as a queer and post-secular critique [...]. Refusing the terms by which the religious/secular boundary is drawn, Kierkegaard's existentialist critique from within Protestant Christianity [...] is one that resonates with contemporary projects that protest against the secularizing logics of modernity as not only misguided but existentially and politically destructive.[24]

On this account, Kierkegaard's Christian critique of Christianity functions not only to undermine the 'idolatry' of religious political projects, but moreover to critique the kinds of teleological thinking already at play in rationalistic progress-narratives of liberal capitalism and scientific optimism. From this perspective, to deploy a Kierkegaardian conception of becoming means precisely to refuse the triumphalist politics that aims to foreclose questions about the conditions of genuine human and collective liberation, in the service of an open-ended notion of history and time that renews the possibility of political action.

As one dimension of this politicised reading of Kierkegaardian becoming, Jaarsma emphasises the political potential involved in an undermining of conventional notions of identity that Kierkegaard can point towards:

> According to Kierkegaard and to eco-evo-devo theories [ecological-environmental-developmental thinking] we cannot point to one efficient cause when we are thinking about development and the movement of becoming. [...] There is no untangling ourselves from our environs, [...] but we can both *indict* inflexible designs for how they inhibit becoming and *cultivate* more flexible relationship between organisms and environments.[25]

In this picture, human beings are no longer regarded as simple, enclosed subjectivities, nor as mere 'effects' of (say) their genomic predispositions – something Jaarsma refers to as a 'god trick', intended to foreclose rather than open sources of possibility in human experience – but rather as complexes of activity and passivity, distributed across causative factors (one's genes as much as one's environment, and so on), as well as across scales of influence, navigating biological, social and political elements in creative and open-ended ways.[26] Here we have an even stronger sense of the connection between a Kierkegaardian notion of selfhood and the 'immediacy' that Deleuze attributes to relationships between individuals and their political environments: subjects of the sort that Jaarsma describes do not suddenly begin to engage in political activity when they work together to achieve common ends (although this may indeed remain as a preferred mode of political engagement); rather they are already in contact with, incorporating and revising, political dimensions of human experience in their own personhood. Selfhood, distributed across sources of influence and activity, will have an immediately political valence owing the ways in which these political dimensions are immediately present within one's self's very composition. Hence the resources are there for the possibility of revising and affecting extant political structures, and doing so in a way that does not assume any linear causal efficacy from agent to patient but rather acknowledges the complex interplay between activity and passivity involved in all kinds of human behaviour.

Between Burns's and Jaarsma's materialist readings of Kierkegaard, what we find are possible lines of interpretation corresponding to a Deleuzian impulse towards selfhood and politics. Rather than pursuing conventional ideas about Kierkegaardian existentialism that understand the self as closed off to the outside world, these materialist readings of Kierkegaard notice the ways in which ideas about the relationship between the physical and psychical, and between the finite and infinite, can serve to undermine subjects' theoretical isolation from the world around them, elaborating resources for greater freedom and creativity in the ways that individuals navigate their political milieux. Given the emphasis, moreover, on the possibility of possibility in Kierkegaard – the idea that even the inconceivable can serve as an important resource for human creativity – the domain of free human action in creating novel forms of social organisation is broadened that much more by incorporating Kierkegaardian ideas into our political thinking.

Faith, Creation and the Future of Deleuzian Subjects

Conclusion

It should be clear that the accounts presented above regarding the ethical and political stakes of both Deleuze's and Kierkegaard's thought have only begun to touch on the possibilities contained within these philosophers' work. Here it is by reconsidering the nature of subjectivity, away from the closed-off pictures of substantialist metaphysics, and towards a notion of the self as already incorporated into a political and collective environment, that we can arrive at a notion of identity open to possibilities of political action. In this way we are moving away from a narrower conception of the self in terms of its engagement in a complex ethics of 'becoming' and towards a notion of selfhood that links ethical and political normativity together. Selves, no longer circumscribed in their private normative projects of growth and becoming, are also intimately involved in the collective and political dimensions of their own selfhood. They seek new modes and manners of 'being', new ways of becoming recognisable as selves, and they seek ways to shape their social environments so as to better facilitate such ways of being and becoming. In this way, we cannot help but elaborate the notion of selfhood beyond the boundaries of the individual, and link our very sense of identity to a set of political stakes.

Notes

1. Deleuze, *Francis Bacon*, p. 60.
2. Ibid., p. 61.
3. Ibid., p. 62.
4. Ibid., p. 42.
5. Ibid., p. 61.
6. Ibid., p. 63, translation modified.
7. Ibid., translation modified. Notice that Deleuze links the concepts of time and faith to the notion of light ('pure, immanent or spiritual light') in *Cinema I*, p. 117.
8. Deleuze, *Francis Bacon*, p. 61.
9. Deleuze and Guattari, *Kafka*, p. 16. See Updike, 'Forward', p. xiii.
10. See also Deleuze, 'He Stuttered', p. 109.
11. Ibid., p. 109, emphasis in original.
12. Deleuze and Guattari, *Kafka*, p. 16.
13. Deleuze, *Cinema II*, p. 218.
14. Deleuze and Guattari, *Kafka*, p. 18: 'There isn't a subject; *there are only collective assemblages of enunciation,* and literature expresses

these acts [. . .] insofar as they exist only as diabolical powers to come or revolutionary forces to be constructed.' See also Deleuze, *Cinema II*, pp. 215–216.
15 Ford, *The Grapes of Wrath*, 2:08:30–2:08:39.
16 Rocha, *Terra em Transe*, 1:20:37–1:21:31.
17 Deleuze, *Cinema II*, pp. 217–218.
18 On the concept of 'fabulation' as a political practice, see Bogue, 'Fabulation, Narration, and the People to Come'.
19 On the rooting of belief in 'the body', see ibid., p. 202. On the 'double becoming' of the 'I' and the 'people', see ibid., p. 221. On the role of belief in the release of the forces of novelty, see ibid., Deleuze, *Francis Bacon*, p. 61 and Deleuze, *Cinema II*, chapter 8, passim.
20 Burns, *Matter of Philosophy*, p. xv.
21 Ibid., p. 124.
22 Ibid., p. 130.
23 Ibid., p. 136.
24 Jaarsma, *Kierkegaard After the Genome*, p. 26.
25 Ibid., p. 38.
26 Ibid., p. 55.

Conclusion: Kierkegaard and Deleuze – Philosophers of Existence

What have we accomplished in this book? A few things. We looked at a particular trajectory within the history of philosophy that led from the Kantian problem of noumenal self-knowledge to Kierkegaard's and Deleuze's efforts to grasp and reconstruct a sense of identity beyond the bounds of unity-based notions of selfhood. We saw how both Kierkegaard and Deleuze struggled to reformulate a conception of philosophy and philosophical thought in the wake of this development, as well as to understand what it means to exist, normatively speaking, within a world that has become ineffable to mere rational thought. Moreover, we reformulated both Kierkegaard's and Deleuze's thought in terms of their conceptions of normativity, so that Kierkegaard's understanding of Christianity fell more in line with the non-transcendent account of ethics that Deleuze called 'immanent' ethics. We followed Deleuze's appropriations of Kierkegaardian thought – especially the value of faith or belief 'in the world' – for a deeper understanding of the nature of the self of immanent ethics and supplemented this account with some distinctly Kierkegaardian ideas about selfhood. And, finally, we took this reformulation of normativity in the direction of a political application of the notion of selfhood developed, so that selves had a deeper and more generative contact with the social and political world.

This, at least, concludes a certain arc implied in the opening of this book: that Deleuze's and Kierkegaard's critique of the Kantian account of selfhood – their rejection of a rational morality sufficient to ground stable notions of selfhood in the capacity to impute moral responsibility to the subject – would lead them to reconsider both their broad accounts of ethics, but also to reconsider what kind of subject or self could adequately participate in such a conception of ethics. But I would suggest that this is only one line of thought which links Deleuze and Kierkegaard's thought. Along the way we had the opportunity to discuss ideas about Kierkegaard's pseudonymity, about the role of writing and language in Deleuze, and about the complex relationship between the categories of immanence and transcendence in both philosophers' work. In my view, these aspects, amongst others, can only suggest a richness that exists in the relationship between Deleuze's and Kierkegaard's thought. A full appreciation of Kierkegaard's existentialism – an investigation into his basic orientation towards the concrete as an orienting framework for thought – might, for example, find itself in sympathy with what is sometimes termed Deleuze's 'empiricism' (or his 'immanentism') and can sketch out a whole terrain of reflection, not just on questions of epistemology and metaphysics, but also on materialist ethics, politics and anthropology. We have only begun to consider the relationship between Kierkegaardian philosophy as a mechanism for direct normative influence and the Deleuzian struggle for a form of writing adequate to a metaphysics of difference and value. And this sort of an account can lead us to a reconsideration of what it might mean to think theologically in the wake of poststructuralism – which aspects of theological thought have been left behind in a critique of transcendental metaphysics, and which aspects of theological thought have not been thought adequately enough on account of a tradition of transcendental metaphysics.

From all these perspectives, the question remains of how to do justice to a cross-pollination of thought that incorporates the humanistic and pastoral aspects of Kierkegaard's work with a radical rejection of conventional systems of thought and *doxa* in Deleuze. I have argued that this precise blend of humanism and iconoclasm can serve to produce a uniquely valuable normative philosophy at both the ethical and the political levels, making space for novel forms of creation and praxis that nonetheless remain grounded in the basic needs of everyday lives. It is additionally my belief that this sort of integration of superficially conflicting viewpoints can inform philosophical investigation more generally: through the project of adapting, balancing and confronting disparate philosophical views we are forced to pursue novel lines of philosophical thought. In this sense, this book has been an appeal as much as an argument: it has been an argument for the coherence of an unlikely pairing between Deleuze and Kierkegaard, and it has been an appeal for more such unlikely pairings in the future. It is on such bases, I would argue, that we can read the history of philosophy 'otherwise' – as Deleuze was so famously known to do. And it forces us, as philosophers, into an encounter with an outside where we are required to use creativity to do something novel – a central aspect of Kierkegaard's existentialism. And perhaps this is what it might mean to 'become' in relation to these philosophers, as they do in relation to us.

Appendices

Appendix A: Partial Correspondence Table of Deleuze's References to Kierkegaard [1]

Location of Deleuze's reference	Work referenced
A Thousand Plateaus, p. 537; *Difference and Repetition*, p. 305; *What is Grounding?*, pp. 75–76	*The Concept of Anxiety*
Logic of Sense, p. 347; *What is Grounding?*, p. 57	*The Concept of Irony*
Difference and Repetition, p. 95; *Logic of Sense*, p. 143	*Concluding Unscientific Postscript to Philosophical Fragments*
Difference and Repetition, p. 8; *What is Grounding?*, p. 59	*Either/Or I*
What is Grounding?, p. 59	*Either/Or II*
A Thousand Plateaus, p. 535; *Difference and Repetition*, p. 305; *Dialogues II*, p. 127; *Cinema I*, p. 233	*Fear and Trembling*
What is Grounding?, pp. 58 and 62; *Cinema II*, p. 189	*Journals and Papers*
What is Grounding?, p. 63	*Philosophical Fragments*
Difference and Repetition, p. 305; *What is Grounding?*, p. 58; *Logic of Sense*, p. 301	*Repetition*
The Logic of Sense, p. 341; *Difference and Repetition*, p. 305; *Cinema I*, p. 233; *Cinema II*, p. 170; *What is Philosophy?*, p. 177	*The Sickness Unto Death*
Cinema I, p. 233; *Cinema II*, p. 177; *Difference and Repetition*, p. 305	*Stages on Life's Way*

Appendix B: Correspondence Table of Deleuze's and Kierkegaard's Conceptions of Repetition

	Deleuze	Kierkegaard
First Mode of Repetition	*Conception of Repetition:* Material repetition of identical instants across time; generation of expectation	*Conception of Repetition:* Repetition of identical instants across time; sameness as boredom
	Associated Faculty: Habit/Sensibility	*Associated Subjectivity:* Aesthetic subjectivity; immediacy
	Associated Mode of Temporality: Passing/'Living' present	*Associated Mode of Temporality:* The Present (immediacy)
Second Mode of Repetition	*Conception:* Repetition as repetition of pure past grounding diverse presents	*Conception:* Maintenance of the same in the face of change; Stoicism; 'eternity' vs. temporality
	Faculty: Memory/Reminiscence (Platonic recollection)	*Faculty:* Recollection (Platonic recollection)
	Temporality: Pure past/Platonic past	*Temporality:* Platonic past/Eternity
Third Mode of Repetition	*Conception:* Repetition as affirmation of becoming/attribution of Being to Becoming	*Conception:* Synthesis of temporality and eternity; recollection directed forwards in time
	Faculty: Thought	*Faculty:* Faith (the 'downfall' or 'paradox' of thought)
	Temporality: Future as Eternal Return	*Temporality:* Future as Eternity

Note

1 The purpose of this table is obviously not to exhaustively document the many references to Kierkegaard throughout Deleuze's work, but rather to give sufficient evidence for my claim, in the Introduction to this volume, that Deleuze must have been at least somewhat familiar with nearly all of Kierkegaard's published work.

Bibliography

Artaud, Antonin, *Oeuvres Complètes, Vol. III* (Paris: Gallimard, 1997).
Barber, Daniel C., *Deleuze and the Naming of God: Post-secularism and the Future of Immanence* (Edinburgh: Edinburgh University Press, 2014).
Battersby, Christine, *The Phenomenal Woman* (New York: Routledge, 1998).
Baugh, Bruce, 'Introduction', in *Existential Monday: Philosophical Essays* (New York: New York Review of Books, 2016), pp. vii–xxxv.
Beaufret, Jean, 'Hölderlin et Sophocle', in François Fédier (ed.), *Hölderlin: Remarques sur Oedipe/Remarques sur Antigone* (Paris: Union Générale d'Éditions, 1965), pp. 7–42.
Benjamin, Walter, 'Theses on History', in Hannah Arendt (ed.) and Harry Zohn (trans.), *Illuminations* (New York: Schocken Books, 1968), pp. 253–264.
Bergson, Henri, *Matter and Memory*, N. M. Paul and W. S. Palmer (trans.) (New York: Zone Books, 1991).
Bernstein, Jay, 'Introduction', in Jay Bernstein (ed.), *Classic and Romantic German Aesthetics* (New York: Cambridge University Press, 2003), pp. vii–xxxiii.
Bogue, Ronald, 'The Art of the Possible', *Revue Internationale de Philosophie* 241, No. 3 2007, pp. 273–286.
Bogue, Ronald, 'The Betrayal of God', in Mary Bryden (ed.), *Deleuze and Religion* (New York: Routledge, 2001), pp. 9–29.
Bogue, Ronald, 'To Choose to Choose – to Believe in This World', in D. N. Rodowick (ed.), *Afterimages of Gilles Deleuze's Film Philosophy* (Minneapolis: University of Minnesota Press, 2010), pp. 115–132.
Bogue, 'Fabulation, Narration and the People to Come', in Constantin Boundas (ed.), *Deleuze and Philosophy* (Edinburgh: Edinburgh University Press, 2006), pp. 202–223.
Bouaniche, Arnaud, '"Faire le movement": Deleuze lecteur de Kierkegaard', in Joaquim Henandez-Dispaux, Grégori Jean and Jean Leclercq (eds), *Kierkegaard et la philosophie française* (Louvain: Presses universitaires de Louvain, 2014), pp. 127–151.
Burns, Michael O'Neill, *Kierkegaard and the Matter of Philosophy: A Fractured Dialectic*, (Lanham, MD: Rowman & Littlefield, 2015).
Camus, Albert, 'The Myth of Sisyphus', in Justin O'Brien (trans.), *The*

Myth of Sisyphus and Other Essays (New York: Alfred. A Knopf, 1955), pp. 3–138.

Carlisle, Clare, *Kierkegaard's Philosophy of Becoming: Movements and Positions* (Albany: SUNY Press, 2005).

Carlisle, Clare, *Philosopher of the Heart: The Restless Life of Søren Kierkegaard* (New York: Farrar Straus and Giroux, 2019).

Clair, André, *Pseudonymie et Paradoxe* (Paris: J. Vrin Librairie Philosophique, 1976).

Crites, Stephen, '"The Blissful Security of the Moment": Recollection, Repetition and Eternal Recurrence', in Robert L. Perkins (ed.), *International Kierkegaard Commentary to* Fear and Trembling *and* Repetition (Macon, GA: Mercer University Press, 1993), pp. 225–246.

Deleuze, Gilles, *Bergsonism*, Hugh Tomlinson and Barbara Habberjam (trans.) (New York: Zone Books, 1991).

Deleuze, Gilles, *Cinema I: The Movement-image*, Hugh Tomlinson and Barbara Habberjam (trans.) (Minneapolis: University of Minnesota Press, 1986).

Deleuze, Gilles, *Cinema II*, Hugh Tomlinson and Robert Galeta (trans.) (Minneapolis: University of Minnesota Press, 1989).

Deleuze, Gilles, *Coldness and Cruelty*, Jean McNeil (trans.) (New York: Zone Books, 1989).

Deleuze, Gilles, *Difference and Repetition*, Paul Patton (trans.) (New York: Columbia University Press, 1994).

Deleuze, Gilles, *Essays Critical and Clinical*, Daniel W. Smith and Michael A. Greco (trans.) (Minneapolis: University of Minnesota Press, 1997).

Deleuze, Gilles, *Francis Bacon: The Logic of Sensation*, Daniel W. Smith (trans.) (Minneapolis: University of Minnesota Press, 2003).

Deleuze, Gilles, 'He Stuttered', in *Essays Critical and Clinical*, Daniel W. Smith and Michael A. Greco (trans.) (Minneapolis: University of Minnesota Press, 1997), pp. 107–114.

Deleuze, Gilles, 'Immanence: A Life', in *Two Regimes of Madness: Texts and Interviews, 1975–1995*, David Lapoujade (ed.) and Ames Hodges and Mike Taormina (trans.) (New York: Columbia University Press, 2006), pp. 384–389.

Deleuze, Gilles, 'Klossowski, or Bodies-Language', in Mark Lester (trans.), *The Logic of Sense* (New York: Columbia University Press, 1990), pp. 280–301.

Deleuze, Gilles, *The Logic of Sense*, Mark Lester (trans.) (New York: Columbia University Press, 1990).

Deleuze, Gilles, *Nietzsche and Philosophy*, Hugh Tomlinson (trans.) (New York: Columbia University Press, 2006).

Deleuze, Gilles, *Spinoza: Practical Philosophy*, Robert Hurley (trans.) (San Francisco, CA: City Lights Books, 1988).

Bibliography

Deleuze, Gilles, *What is Grounding?*, Arjen Kleinherenbrink (trans.) (Grand Rapids, MI: &&& Publishing, 2015).

Deleuze, Gilles and Felix Guattari, *Kafka: Toward a Minor Literature*, Dana Polan and Réda Bensmaïa (trans.) (Minneapolis: University of Minnesota Press, 1986).

Deleuze, Gilles and Felix Guattari, *A Thousand Plateaus*, Brian Massumi (trans.) (Minneapolis: University of Minnesota Press, 1987).

Deleuze, Gilles and Felix Guattari, *What is Philosophy?* Hugh Tomlinson and Graham Burchell (trans.) (New York: Columbia University Press, 1994).

Diogenes Laertius, *Lives of Eminent Philosophers*, Volume II: Books 6–10, R. D. Hicks (trans.) (Cambridge, MA: Harvard University Press, 1925).

Emmanuel, Steven M., William McDonald and Jon Stewart (eds), *Kierkegaard's Concepts, Tome V: Objectivity to Sacrifice* (Burlington, VT: Ashgate Publishing, 2015).

Eriksen, Niels Nymann, *Kierkegaard's Category of Repetition: A Reconstruction* (New York: de Gruyter, 2000).

Evans, C. Stephan, *Kierkegaard's Ethic of Love: Divine Commands and Moral Obligations* (New York: Oxford University Press, 2004).

Evans, C. Stephan, *Søren Kierkegaard's Christian Psychology: Insight for Counseling and Pastoral Care* (Grand Rapids, MI: Ministry Resources Library, 1990).

Faulkner, Keith, *Deleuze and the Three Syntheses of Time* (New York: Peter Lang Publishing, 2006).

Ferreira, M. Jamie, 'Immediacy and Reflection in *Works of Love*', in Paul Cruysberghs, Johan Taels and Karl Verstrynge (eds), *Immediacy and Reflection in Kierkegaard's Thought* (Leuven: Leuven University Press, 2003), pp. 107–119.

Ferreira, M. Jamie, *Love's Grateful Striving: A Reading of Kierkegaard's Works of Love* (Oxford and New York: Oxford University Press, 2001).

Fichte, J. G., *Science of Knowledge with the First and Second Introductions*, Peter Heath and John Lachs (eds and trans.) (New York: Cambridge University Press, 1982).

Fichte, J. G., *Versuch einerneuen Darstellun der Wissenschaftslehre*, in *Johann Gottlieb Fichte's sämmtliche Werke*, J. H. Fichte (ed.) (Berlin: Veit und Comp., 1845).

Fondane, Benjamin, 'Søren Kierkegaard: Traité du Désespoir', *Cahiers du Sud* 20, No. 134 January 1933, pp. 42–51.

Goldschmidt, Victor, *Le Système Stoïcien et l'idée de temps* (Paris: Librairie Philosophique J. Vrin, 1953).

Green, Ronald M., *Kant and Kierkegaard on Time and Eternity* (Macon, GA: Mercer University Press, 2011).

Green, Ronald M., *Kierkegaard and Kant: the Hidden Debt* (Albany: SUNY Press, 1992).

Heath, Peter and John Lachs, 'Preface', in Peter Heath and John Lachs (eds), *The Science of Knowledge* (New York: Cambridge University Press, 1982), pp. vii–xviii.

Henrich, Dieter, 'Hölderlin at Jena', in Eckart Förster (ed.), *The Course of Remembrance*, (Stanford, CA: Stanford University Press, 1997), pp. 90–118.

Hölderlin, Friedrich, 'Being Judgment Possibility', in Jay Bernstein (ed.) and Stefan Bird-Pollan (trans.), *Classic and Romantic German Aesthetics* (New York: Cambridge University Press, 2003), pp. 191–192.

Hölderlin, Friedrich, 'Letter to Hegel, 26 January 1795', in Jay Bernstein (ed.) and Stefan Bird-Pollan (trans.), *Classic and Romantic German Aesthetics* (New York: Cambridge University Press, 2003), pp. 188–190.

Hölderlin, Friedrich, 'Remarks on Oedipus', in Jay Bernstein (ed.) and Stefan Bird-Pollan (trans.), *Classic and Romantic German Aesthetics* (New York: Cambridge University Press, 2003), pp. 194–201.

Hong, Howard V. and Edna H. Hong, 'Historical Introduction', in Howard V. Hong and Edna H. Hong (eds), *Fear and Trembling/Repetition* (Princeton, NJ: Princeton University Press, 1983), pp. ix–xxxix.

Hong, Howard V. and Edna H. Hong, 'Historical Introduction', in Howard V. Hong and Edna H. Hong (eds), *The Sickness Unto Death* (Princeton, NJ: Princeton University Press, 1980), pp. ix–xxiii.

Hughes, Joe, 'Believing in the World: Towards an Ethics of Form', in Laura Guillaume and Joe Hughes (eds), *Deleuze and the Body* (Edinburgh: Edinburgh University Press, 2011), pp. 73–95.

Jaarsma, Ada, *Kierkegaard After the Genome: Science, Existence and Belief in This World* (New York: Palgrave Macmillan, 2017).

James, Ian, *Pierre Klossowski: The Persistence of a Name* (Oxford: Oxford University Press, 2000).

Jones, Graham and Jon Roffe (eds), *Deleuze's Philosophical Lineage* (Edinburgh: Edinburgh University Press, 2009).

Jones, Graham and Jon Roffe (eds), *Deleuze's Philosophical Lineage II* (Edinburgh: Edinburgh University Press, 2019).

Justo, José Mirando, 'Gilles Deleuze: Kierkegaard's Presence in his Writings', in Jon Stewart (ed.), *Kierkegaard's Influence on Philosophy, Tome II: Francophone Philosophy*, (Burlington, VT: Ashgate Publishing Company, 2012), pp. 83–110.

Kangas, David J., *Errant Affirmations: On the Philosophical Meaning of Kierkegaard's Religious Discourses* (New York: Bloomsbury, 2018).

Kangas, David J., 'J. G. Fichte: From Transcendental Ego to Existence', in Jon Stewart (ed.), *Kierkegaard and his German Contemporaries, Tome I: Philosophy* (Burlington, VT: Ashgate Publishing Company, 2007), pp. 67–95.

Kant, Immanuel, *Critique of Practical Reason*, in Mary Gregor (ed. and

Bibliography

trans.), *Practical Philosophy* (New York: Cambridge University Press, 1996), pp. 135–271.

Kant, Immanuel, *Critique of Pure Reason*, Paul Guyer and Allen W. Wood (trans.) (New York: Cambridge University Press, 1998).

Kant, Immanuel, *Groundwork of the Metaphysics of Morals*, Mary Gregor and Jens Timmermann (eds and trans.) (New York: Cambridge University Press, 2012).

Kant, Immanuel, *Kant's handschriftlicher Nachlaß, Band V: Metaphysik, Zweiter Teil* (Berlin: Walter de Gruyter & Co., 1928).

Kant, Immanuel, *Religion within the Boundaries of Mere Reason*, in Allen W. Wood (ed.) and George di Giovanni (trans.), *Religion and Rational Theology* (New York: Cambridge University Press, 1996).

Kierkegaard, Søren, *The Concept of Anxiety*, Reidar Thomte (trans.) (Princeton, NJ: Princeton University Press, 1980).

Kierkegaard, Søren, *Concluding Unscientific Postscript to* Philosophical Fragments, Howard V. Hong and Edna H. Hong (trans.) (Princeton, NJ: Princeton University Press, 1992).

Kierkegaard, Søren, *Either/Or I*, Howard V. Hong and Edna H. Hong (trans.) (Princeton, NJ: Princeton University Press, 1987).

Kierkegaard, Søren, *Either/Or II*, Howard V. Hong and Edna H. Hong (trans.) (Princeton, NJ: Princeton University Press, 1987).

Kierkegaard, Søren, *Fear and Trembling*, in Howard V. Hong and Edna H. Hong (trans.), *Fear and Trembling/Repetition* (Princeton, NJ: Princeton University Press, 1983), pp. 2–123.

Kierkegaard, Søren, 'To Gain One's Soul in Patience', in Howard V. Hong and Edna H. Hong (trans.), *Eighteen Upbuilding Discourses* (Princeton, NJ: Princeton University Press, 1990), pp. 159–175.

Kierkegaard, Søren, 'Look at the Birds of the Air; Look at the Lily in the Field', in *The Lily in the Field and the Bird of the Air*, in Howard V. Hong and Edna H. Hong (trans.), *Without Authority* (Princeton, NJ: Princeton University Press), pp. 7–20.

Kierkegaard, Søren, 'One Who Prays Aright Struggles in Prayer and is Victorious – in That God is Victorious', in Howard V. Hong and Edna H. Hong (trans.), *Eighteen Upbuilding Discourses* (Princeton, NJ: Princeton University Press, 1990), pp. 377–401.

Kierkegaard, Søren, *Philosophical Fragments*, in Howard V. Hong and Edna H. Hong (trans.), *Philosophical Fragments/Johannes Climacus* (Princeton, NJ: Princeton University Press, 1985), pp. 1–111.

Kierkegaard, Søren, *Repetition*, in Howard V. Hong and Edna H. Hong (trans.), *Fear and Trembling/Repetition* (Princeton, NJ: Princeton University Press, 1983), pp. 125–231.

Kierkegaard, Søren, *The Sickness Unto Death*, in Howard V. Hong and Edna H. Hong (trans.) (Princeton, NJ: Princeton University Press, 1980).

Kierkegaard, Søren, *Søren Kierkegaard's Journals and Papers, Vol. 2: F–K*,

Howard V. Hong and Edna H. Hong (eds and trans.) (Bloomington: Indiana University Press, 1978).

Kierkegaard, Søren, *Søren Kierkegaard's Journals and Papers, Vol. 6: Autobiographical, Part II, 1848–1855*, Howard V. Hong and Edna H. Hong (eds and trans.) (Bloomington: Indiana University Press, 1978).

Kierkegaard, Søren, *Stages on Life's Way*, Howard V. Hong and Edna H. Hong (trans.) (Princeton, NJ: Princeton University Press, 1988).

Kierkegaard, Søren, 'Supplement', in Howard V. Hong and Edna H. Hong (trans.), *Fear and Trembling/Repetition* (Princeton, NJ: Princeton University Press, 1983), pp. 283–319.

Kierkegaard, Søren, *Two Ages: The Age of Revolution and the Present Age, a Literary Review*, Howard V. Hong and Edna H. Hong (trans.) (Princeton, NJ: Princeton University Press, 1978).

Kierkegaard, Søren, *Works of Love*, Howard V. Hong and Edna H. Hong (trans.) (Princeton, NJ: Princeton University Press, 1995).

Kleinherenbrink, Arjen, 'Art as Authentic Life: Deleuze after Kierkegaard', *Kritike* 8, No. 2 December 2014, pp. 98–118.

Klossowski, Pierre, 'Don Juan selon Kierkegaard', in *Sade, mon prochain* (Paris: Éditions du Seuil, 1947), pp. 135–152.

Klossowski, Pierre, 'Nietzsche, Polytheism, and Parody', in *Such a Deathly Desire*, Russell Ford, (trans.) (Albany: SUNY Press, 2007), pp. 99–122.

Klossowski, Pierre, *Nietzsche and the Vicious Circle*, Daniel W. Smith (trans.) (Chicago: University of Chicago Press, 1997).

Klossowski, Pierre, 'On Some Fundamental Themes of Nietzsche's *Gaya Scienza*', in *Such a Deathly Desire*, Russell Ford (trans.) (Albany: SUNY Press, 2007), pp. 1–16.

Klossowski, Pierre, 'Oubli et Anamnèse dan l'expérience vécue de l'éternel retour du même', in *Cahiers de Royaumont: Nietzsche* (Paris: Les Éditions de Minuit, 1967), pp. 227–244.

Klossowski, Pierre, *Sade My Neighbor*, Alphonso Lingis (trans.) (Evanston, IL: Northwestern University Press, 1991).

Klossowski, Pierre, 'Temps et Agressivité', *Recherches Philosophiques* 5, 1935–1936, pp. 100–111.

Larmore, Charles, 'Hölderlin and Novalis', in Karl Ameriks (ed.), *The Cambridge Companion to German Idealism* (New York: Cambridge University Press, 2006), pp. 141–160.

de Launay, Marc B., 'Introduction', in *Le Gai Savoir*, Pierre Klossowski (trans.) (Paris: Gallimard, 1967).

Liu, Zizhen, 'Immediacy/Reflection', in Jon Stewart (ed.), *Kierkegaard's Concepts, Tome III: Envy to Incognito* (Burlington, VT: Ashgate Publishing Company, 2014), pp. 215–222.

Lorraine, Tamsin, *Deleuze and Guattari's Immanent Ethics* (Albany: SUNY Press, 2011).

Bibliography

Mackey, Louis, *Kierkegaard: A Kind of Poet* (Philadelphia: University of Pennsylvania Press, 1971).
Marrati, Paola, *Gilles Deleuze: Cinema and Philosophy*, Alisa Hartz (trans.) (Baltimore, MD: Johns Hopkins University Press, 2008).
Mooney, Edward, *Knights of Faith and Resignation: Reading Kierkegaard's Fear and Trembling*, (Albany: SUNY Press, 1991).
Murphy, Timothy S., 'Revised Bibliography of the Works of Gilles Deleuze', accessed 12 August 2018, http://www.bibliothequedusaulchoir.org/French/activities/Deleuze/Del-euze%20Bibliogr.pdf
Nietzsche, Friedrich, *The Gay Science*, Walter Kaufmann (trans.) (New York: Vintage Books, 1974).
Nietzsche, Friedrich, *On the Genealogy of Morality*, Carol Diethe (trans.) (New York: Cambridge, 2007).
Nietzsche, Friedrich, *Thus Spoke Zarathustra*, Adrian Del Caro (trans.) (New York: Cambridge University Press, 2006).
Nietzsche, Friedrich, 'To Jacob Burckhardt', in *The Portable Nietzsche*, Walter Kaufmann (ed. and trans.) (New York: Penguin Books, 1954), pp. 685–686.
Nietzsche, Friedrich, *Twilight of the Idols*, in Aaron Ridley and Judith Norman (eds) and Judith Norman (trans.), *The Anti-Christ, Ecce Homo, Twilight of the Idols, and Other Writings* (New York: Cambridge University Press, 2005).
Nietzsche, Friedrich, *The Will to Power*, Walter Kaufmann (ed. and trans.) (New York: Vintage Press, 1967).
Pasolini, Pier Paolo, *L'expérience hérétique*, Anna Rocchi Pullberg (trans.) (Paris: Payot, 1976).
Plato, 'Euthyphro', in John Cooper (ed.), *Complete Works* (New York: Hackett Publishing, 1997), pp. 1–16.
Podmore, Simon, *Kierkegaard and the Self Before God: Anatomy of the Abyss* (Indianapolis: Indiana University Press, 2011).
Rodowick, D. N., 'The World, Time', in D. N. Rodowick (ed.), *Afterimages of Gilles Deleuze's Film Philosophy* (Minneapolis: University of Minnesota Press, 2010), pp. 97–114.
Sartre, Jean-Paul, *The Transcendence of the Ego: An Existentialist Theory of Consciousness*, Forrest Williams and Robert Kirkpatrick (trans.) (New York: Noonday Press, 1957).
Schefer, Jean-Louis, *The Ordinary Man of the Cinema*, Max Cavitch, Noura Wedell and Paul Grant (trans.) (South Pasadena, CA: Semiotext(e), 2016).
Schultz, Heiko, 'Second Immediacy: A Kierkegaardian Account of Faith', in Paul Cruysberghs, Johan Taels and Karl Verstrynge (eds), *Immediacy and Reflection in Kierkegaard's Thought* (Leuven: Leuven University Press, 2003), pp. 71–86.
Shakespeare, Steven, *Kierkegaard and the Refusal of Transcendence* (New York: Palgrave Macmillan, 2015).

Smith, Daniel W., 'Deleuze, Kant, and the Theory of Immanent Ideas', in *Essays on Deleuze* (Edinburgh: Edinburgh University Press, 2012), pp. 106–121.

Smith, Daniel W., 'Deleuze and the Question of Desire: Toward and Immanent Theory of Ethics', in *Essays on Deleuze* (Edinburgh: Edinburgh University Pres, 2012), pp. 175–188.

Smith, Daniel W., 'Deleuze's "Critique et Clinique" Project', in Gilles Deleuze, *Essays Critical and Clinical*, Daniel W. Smith and Michael A. Greco (trans.) (Minneapolis: University of Minnesota Press, 1997), pp. xi–liii.

Smith, Daniel W., 'The Doctrine of Univocity: Deleuze's Ontology of Immanence', in *Essays on Deleuze* (Edinburgh: Edinburgh University Press, 2012), pp. 27–42.

Smith, Daniel W., 'The Place of Ethics in Deleuze's Philosophy: Three Questions of Immanence', in *Essays on Deleuze* (Edinburgh: Edinburgh University Press, 2012), pp. 146–159.

Smith, Douglas, 'Wilful Acts, Diminishing Returns: Deleuze and Klossowski', in *Transvaluations: Nietzsche in France 1872–1972* (New York: Oxford University Press, 1996), pp. 140–184.

Söderquist, K. Briab, 'Friedrich Schlegel: On Ironic Communication, Subjectivity and Selfhood', in Jon Stewart (ed.), *Kierkegaard and his German Contemporaries, Tome III: Literature and Aesthetics* (Burlington, VT: Ashgate Publishing Company, 2008), pp. 185–233.

Somers-Hall, Henry, *Deleuze's* Difference and Repetition (Edinburgh: Edinburgh University Press, 2013).

Spinoza, Benedictus de, *Short Treatise on God, Man, and His Well-Being*, in Edwin Curley (ed. and trans.), *The Collected Works of Spinoza, Vol. I* (Princeton, NJ: Princeton University Press, 1985), pp. 59–156.

Stewart, Jon, 'France: Kierkegaard as a Forerunner of Existentialism and Poststructuralism', in Jon Stewart (ed.), *Kierkegaard's International Reception, Tome I: Northern and Western Europe* (Burlington, VT: Ashgate Publishing Company, 2009), pp. 421–474.

Stewart, Jon (ed.), *Kierkegaard Research: Sources, Reception and Resources, Vol. 6: Kierkegaard and his German Contemporaries*, 3 volumes (Burlington, VT: Ashgate Publishing Company, 2007–2008).

Stewart, Jon, *Kierkegaard's Relations to Hegel Reconsidered* (Cambridge: Cambridge University Press, 2003).

Surin, Kenneth, '"Existing Not as a Subject But as a Work of Art": Task of Ethics or Aesthetics?', in Nathan Jun and Daniel W. Smith (eds), *Deleuze and Ethics* (Edinburgh: Edinburgh University Press, 2011), pp. 142–153.

Sylvester, David, *The Brutality of Fact: Interviews with Francis Bacon, 1962–1979* (New York: Thames and Hudson, 1987).

Uhlmann, Anthony, 'Deleuze, Ethics, Ethology, Art', in Nathan Jun and

Bibliography

Daniel W. Smith (eds), *Deleuze and Ethics* (Edinburgh: Edinburgh University Press, 2011), pp. 154–170.

Updike, John, 'Foreword', in *The Complete Stories*, by Franz Kafka (New York: Schocken Books, 1971), pp. ix–xx.

Waddell, Norman and Masao Abe, 'Translators' Introduction', in *The Heart of Dōgen's* Shōbōgenzō (New York: SUNY Press, 2002), pp. ix–xiii.

Williams, James, *Gilles Deleuze's* Difference and Repetition: *A Critical Introduction and Guide* (Edinburgh: Edinburgh University Press, 2013).

Williams, James, *Gilles Deleuze's Philosophy of Time: A Critical Introduction and Guide*, (Edinburgh: Edinburgh University Press, 2011).

Wuerth, Julian, 'The Paralogisms of Pure Reason', in Paul Guyer (ed.), *The Cambridge Companion to Kant's* Critique of Pure Reason (New York: Cambridge University Press, 2010), pp. 210–244.

Index

a priori past, 43, 49; see also pure past
a priori time, 45–7
Abraham, 66, 67, 69, 88, 89–90, 91
active forces, 52–3
actual self, 18
aesthetic representations of faith, 70–1
aesthetic choice, 129
aesthetic existence, 129–30
aesthetic love, 131, 132
aesthetic picture of identity, 106
aesthetic repetition, 57–8
aestheticism, 121–3
affection-images, 107–8
Afterimages of Gilles Deleuze's Film Philosophy (Rodowick), 5
aiesthesis, 58
alienation, 27, 28, 29, 31, 33
anamnesis, 59, 62
anti-Hegelianism, 1
any-space-whatevers, 109–10, 110–11
art, 121–2
artistic creation
 and faith, 139–42
 as political activity, 142–3, 147–8
 automatic subjectivity, 112, 114
 autonomy, 19

Bacon, Francis, 139–42
badness *see* good and bad
Battersby, C., 6, 100–1
Beaufret, J., 27–8
becoming, 2, 4, 8, 22, 156
 Deleuze, 96–7, 99, 116, 117–20
 Kierkegaard, 68, 96–7, 98, 101, 125, 141, 151
becoming-active, 40, 53–4, 82
becoming-animal, 118, 119
becoming capable, 47
becoming-child, 118

becoming-conscious, 144
becoming everybody/everything, 120–1
becoming-imperceptible, 127, 128
becoming-molecular, 119
becoming oneself, 94
becoming patient, 93, 94
becoming-reactive, 53–4
becoming silent, 92–3
becoming-woman, 118
belief, 9, 112–13
 and political engagement, 138, 146, 147, 148
 see also faith
Bergson, H., 43
Bergsonism (Deleuze), 4
Bogue, R., 6
Bouaniche, A., 3
Burckhardt, J., 33
Burns, M.O., 9, 23, 149–50

Cabinet of Dr. Caligari, The (Wiene), 108
Carlisle, C., 6
causality, 86–7
choice, 109–10, 129–30, 150
Christian ethics, 95–7, 97, 98; *see also* immanent ethics: Kierkegaard
Christian love, 131, 132
Christianity, 61, 124, 151, 155
cinema *see* classical cinema; modern cinema
Cinema books (Deleuze), 3–4, 6, 106–16
 Cinema I, 68–9, 107–10
 Cinema II, 105, 110–16, 134–5n, 144
Clair, A., 56, 59, 68
classical cinema, 107–10, 144–5
close-ups, 107–8

Index

Coldness and Cruelty (Deleuze), 2
collective enunciation, 145–7
collective identity, 9, 145, 147
collective political projects, 150
collective subjectivity, 142–3, 148
composite identity, 124
Concept of Anxiety (Kierkegaard), 60, 95–6
Concept of Irony (Kierkegaard), 2, 23, 61–2
Concluding Unscientific Postscript to Philosophical Fragments (Kierkegaard), 2, 68, 96
consciousness, 25–6
Constantius, 58–9, 60
counter-actualization, 88
coupling, 141–2
Critique of Practical Reason (Kant), 20–2
Critique of Pure Reason (Kant), 13–17, 21, 45–6

death of God, 16–17, 30, 31–2
Deleuze, G.
  becoming, 96–7, 99, 116, 117–20
  becoming-active / becoming-reactive, 53–4
  belief and artistic creation, 139–42
  Eternal Return, 50–1, 52, 64, 66
  forces, 52–3
  human beings, 53–4, 55
  immanent ethics, 8–9, 77, 78–84, 96–7: *Logic of Sense*, 84–8
  importance of Fichte and Hölderlin for, 23
  importance of Klossowski for, 30
  importance of Nietzsche for, 29
  on Kant, 16
  and Kierkegaard: commonalities with, 1–2; on K.'s repetition, 56, 65–71; reading of, 138; reference to, 2, 3–5, 109–10, 115–16, 119–20, 134–5n, 157–8; relationship with, 5–7, 35, 155–6
  popular misreading of, 8
  repetition, 41–9, 54–5, 58, 59
  selfhood, 34–5, 133–4: *Cinema* books, 106–16; and morality, 21–

  2; and politics, 152; *A Thousand Plateaus*, 116–21, 128; *What is Philosophy?* 121–3
  see also individual works
Deleuze and Guattari's Immanent Ethics (Lorraine), 9, 99, 100
description, 79–80, 81
deterritorialisation, 143–4
Difference and Repetition (Deleuze), 3, 15
  reference to Kierkegaard, 2, 4, 8, 65
  reference to Klossowski, 30
  repetition, 41–9
  time, 112
Diogenes the Cynic, 85
dissolved self, 42
dissolved subject, 34–5
distinction, 16
dogmatics, 60
Dreyer, C.T., 108, 110

either-or, 66, 69–70
Either/Or I (Kierkegaard), 57, 100–1, 129
empirical cognition, 13–14
Entranced Earth (Rocha), 146
Eriksen, N., 6, 56
erotic love, 131, 132
Errant Affirmations (Kangas), 94
Eternal Return, 30, 32, 49–51, 52, 64, 66
eternal truth, 79, 81
ethical doctrine, 50–1
ethical frame of mind, 129–30
ethical philosophy, 8–9
ethical reflection, 95
ethical repetition, 58–60
ethical subjectivity, 58–9, 60
ethics, 90; *see also* Christian ethics; immanent ethics; morality
ethology, 81–2, 84, 98
Europe '51 (Rossellini), 111, 112–13
Euthyphro (Plato), 84
Evans, C.S., 98
events, 85–8, 107
evil *see* good and evil
existential property, 90
Expressionistic cinema, 108–9

169

INDEX

faith, 40, 56, 57, 60
  aesthetic representations of, 70–1
  and artistic creation, 139–42
  and freedom, 110
  and immediacy, 129, 130–1
  knight of, 119–20
  and love, 100
  and moral obligations, 88–92: problem of transcendence, 96, 97
  and repetition, 63–5: Deleuze's critique of, 65, 67, 68–9
  and sin, 62, 63
  and thought, 75n
  and time, 141–2
  and transparency, 124, 125, 126
  vital, 140, 141, 147
  see also belief
Fear and Trembling (Kierkegaard), 8, 59, 69, 88–9, 119, 130
Ferreira, M.J., 94–5, 130–1, 132
Fichte, J.G., 22–3
  Hölderlin's reply to, 25–6
  self-positing subject, 24–5
forces, 52–3
'Forgetting and Anamnesis in the Lived Experience of the Eternal Return' (Klossowski), 30
form of time, 15, 46
Foundations of the Entire Science of Knowledge (Fichte), 24–5
Francis Bacon: The Logic of Sensation (Deleuze), 139–42
free indirect discourse, 112
freedom, 19, 57, 60–1, 64, 91, 101, 110
friendship, 132
future, 42, 44, 46, 49, 57

Gay Science (Nietzsche), 49–50
Germany Year Zero (Rossellini), 111, 113
God, 66–7, 68, 90, 91, 126, 127
  death of, 16–17, 30, 31–2
good and bad, 83–4
good and evil, 82–3
Grapes of Wrath (Ford), 145–6
grounding, 3, 45; *see also What is Grounding?* (Deleuze)

Groundwork of the Metaphysics of Morals (Kant), 18–20
group identities, 150

haecceity, self as, 116–17
Hamlet, 48
happiness, 20–1
Hegel, G.W.F., 1
Henrich, D., 26
Hölderlin, F., 22–3
  Klossowski's indebtedness to, 30–1
  self-knowledge, 27–8
  sensibility, 23, 24
  subjectivity, 33
  subject-object distinction, 25–7
Hong, H. and E., 56
Hughes, J., 5–6
human beings, 53–4, 55, 90–1, 125, 151–2
humour, 2

identity *see* collective identity; composite identity; personal identity; synthetic identity
immanent ethics, 8–9, 34, 77
  Deleuze, 78–84, 96–7: *Logic of Sense*, 84–8
  Kierkegaard, 88–92: benefits of interpretation, 98–101; problem of transcendence, 95–7; signed works, 92–5
immediacy, 123, 128–33, 152
immortality, 21
imperative ethics, 94
impersonality, 33, 34
indefinite articles, 117
indicative ethics, 94–5
irony, 2, 84–5

Jaarsma, A., 9, 150–2
Jephthah, 89–90
joy, 83
'Judgement and Being' (Hölderlin), 25, 26, 27
Justo, J.M., 6

Kafka (Deleuze and Guattari), 142–4
Kangas, D., 94

Index

Kant, I., 7
  practical resurrection of the self, 17–22
  self-knowledge, 13–17, 21–2, 33, 105
  time-determinations, 45–6
  see also post-Kantian philosophy
Kierkegaard, S.
  anti-Hegelianism, 1
  contemporary scholarship on, 5–7, 98, 99, 100–1, 138–9, 148–52
  and Deleuze: commonalities with, 1–2; D.'s reading of, 138; as reference point in, 2, 3–5, 109–10, 115–16, 119–20, 134–5n, 157–8; relationship with, 5–7, 35, 155–6
  ethical philosophy, 8–9
  immanent ethics, 77, 88–92: benefits of interpretation, 98–101; problem of transcendence, 95–7; signed works, 92–5
  as political philosopher, 9, 148–52
  popular misrepresentation of, 8, 40
  repetition, 55–65: aesthetic conception, 57–8; Deleuze's criticism, 65–71; ethical conception, 58–60; spiritual conception, 56, 60–5
  reply to Fichte, 23
  selfhood, 28–9, 123–33, 133–4: and collective praxis, 148; criticism, 40; and immediacy, 123, 128–33, 152; and morality, 21–2; and transparency, 123, 124–8
Kierkegaard After the Genome (Jaarsma), 150–2
Kierkegaard and the Matter of Philosophy (Burns), 23, 149–50
Kierkegaard and the Self Before God (Podmore), 126–7
Kierkegaard's Philosophy of Becoming (Carlisle), 6
Kleinherenbrink, A., 6
Klossowki, P., 30–3, 50, 66
knight of faith, 119–20

language, 143–4
larval subject, 42
Last Year at Marienbad (Resnais), 115

'lived present, living present', 41
Logic of Sense (Deleuze), 2, 66, 67, 84–8, 107
'Look at the Birds of Air, Look at the Lily of the Field' (Kierkegaard), 70, 92
Lorraine, T., 9, 99, 100
love, 98, 100, 131–2
lyrical abstraction, 109–10

Marrati, P., 6
memory, 43–4, 49, 59; *see also anamnesis*
metaphysics, 2
metempsychosis, 44
mind, 41–2
  ethical frame of, 129–30
minor literature, 143–7
modern cinema, 107, 110–16, 145–7
monstration, 85
monument, art as, 121, 122
Mooney, E., 98
moral freedom, 60–1
moral judgement, 2, 105
moral obligations, 34, 88–92
moral responsibility, 17, 18, 21–2, 34, 52–3
moral scepticism, 17
morality
  rational, 2, 22, 34
  transcendent, 78–9
  see also ethics
Mother (Pudovkin), 145
movement, 46, 96, 101, 111

negativity, 53
neighbourly love, 131, 132
Nietzsche, F., 1, 29–30, 49–50, 54
  Klossowski's reading of, 30–3, 50, 66
Nietzsche and Philosophy (Deleuze), 4, 30, 50–1, 52–3, 66–7, 81–2
Nietzsche and the Vicious Circle (Klossowski), 30, 66
non-materiality, 16
non-preferential love, 131–2

Oedipus, 47, 48
Oliver, K., 100

INDEX

ontology, 2
Open Whole, 112, 115
order of time, 46
organic selfhood, 116
Outside, 112, 114, 115

painting, 139, 141–2
Passion of Joan of Arc, The (Dreyer), 108
past, 42, 43, 44, 45, 46, 49, 60
patch of selfhood, 116
patience, 93, 98, 100
personal identity
  Deleuze, 12, 21–2, 55, 66, 99
  Kant, 7, 18, 21–2
  Kierkegaard, 12, 62, 151
  see also selfhood
personality, 16, 17, 18, 21, 105
Phenomenal Woman (Battersby), 6, 100–1
Philosophical Fragments (Kierkegaard), 62–4, 68, 96
philosophical writing, 2
Plato, 62
Podmore, S., 126–7
political activity, 142–3
political collectivity, 9
political engagement, 138–9, 147
political philosophy, 9, 148–52
political projects, 150
political speech, 146
political sphere, 144–5
political subjectivity, 147
political utopia, 147
possibility, 152
post-Kantian philosophy, 12, 22–8; *see also* Fichte, J.G.; Hölderlin, F.
post-war society, 110–11
Pour la Suite du Monde (Perrault), 146–7
practical reason, 17, 19–22
prescription, 78–80
present, 41, 42, 43, 44, 45, 46, 49, 60
private sphere, 144–5
proper names, 117
Pseudonymie et Paradoxe (Clair), 56
pseudonyms, 2, 70–1
psychology *see* rational psychology

pure past, 43, 44, 45; *see also* a priori past
pure rational beliefs, 18
pure time *see* a priori time

quasi-causation, 87

rational morality, 2, 22, 34
rational psychology, 15–17, 19, 29, 33
rational theology, 33
reactive forces, 52–3
recognition, 100
recollection, 44, 59; *see also* anamnesis; memory
religious repetition *see* spiritual repetition
religious/secular distinction, 151
repetition, 7–8
  Deleuze, 41–9, 54–5, 58, 59
  Kierkegaard, 55–65: aesthetic conception, 57–8; Deleuze's criticism, 65–71; ethical conception, 58–60; spiritual conception, 56, 60–5
  Nietzsche, 54
resignation, 59, 90
Rodowick, D.N., 5
romantic love, 131

Sade My Neighbor (Klossowski), 31
sadness, 83
sagacity, 57, 58
second immediacy, 132–3
secular/religious distinction, 151
self
  actual, 18
  dissolved, 42
  as haecceity, 116–17
self-consciousness, 25–6
selfhood, 8, 9, 105–6
  Deleuze, 34–5, 133–4: *Cinema* books, 106–16; *A Thousand Plateaus*, 116–21, 128; *What is Philosophy?* 121–3
  Fichte, 24–5
  and God, 30, 31–2
  Hölderlin, 25–8, 29
  Kierkegaard, 28–9, 123–33, 133–4:

Index

and collective praxis, 148;
criticism, 40; and immediacy, 123, 128–33, 152; and transparency, 123, 124–8
and morality, 22
see also subjectivity
self-knowledge, 105
Kant, 13–17, 21–2, 33
post-Kantian philosophy, 23, 24, 25, 27–8
self-overcoming, 40, 47, 48, 49, 53–5, 99
self-positing subject, 24–5
self-reflection, 14, 15–16, 27
semiotics, 117
sensibility
Deleuze, 49, 53–4, 58, 81–2
Hölderlin, 23, 24
Kant, 19
sensory-motor schema, 110–16
series of time, 47–8
Short Treatise (Spinoza), 80
Sickness onto Death (Kierkegaard), 124–6
silence, 92
simplicity, 16
sin, 62, 63
singularity, 55, 60–1, 68, 91
Socrates, 84
speculative reason, 20, 21
Spinoza (Deleuze), 8
Spinoza, B. de, 80, 81, 90
Spinoza: Practical Philosophy (Deleuze), 83
spiritual repetition, 56, 60–5
Stages on Life's Way (Kierkegaard), 130
Stewart, J., 6
Stoic ethics, 84–8, 93
Stoicism, 58–9
Strike (Eisenstein), 115
Stromboli (Rossellini), 113
subjectivity, 41–5, 47–9
automatic, 112, 114
collective, 142–3, 148
ethical, 58–9, 60
political, 147
see also selfhood
subject-object distinction, 25–7

substantiality, 15–16
synthetic identity, 124

temporal events, 62–3; *see also* time
Teorema (Pasolini), 114
theorematic subjectivity, 112, 114
A Thousand Plateaus (Deleuze and Guattari), 3, 4, 116–21, 128, 145
Thus Spoke Zarathustra (Nietzsche), 50
time, 15, 28
and faith, 141–2
in modern cinema, 107, 111–12, 135n
and repetition, 41–9, 54–5
see also temporal events
time determinations, 45–8
'To Gain One's Soul in Patience' (Kierkegaard), 93
'To Jacob Burckhardt' (Nietzsche), 33
totality of time, 46–7, 48, 49
transcendence, 77, 95–7
transcendent morality, 78–9
transcendental God, 67
transcendental memory, 44
transcendental unity of apperception, 13–14
transparency, 123, 124–8
truth, 79, 81, 86

values, 31, 100
verbs, 117
virtue, 98, 100
vital faith, 140, 141, 147
Vocation of Man (Fichte), 23

What is Grounding? (Deleuze), 3, 4, 56
What is Philosophy? (Deleuze and Guattari), 3, 4, 121–3
Wiene, R., 108
willing what happens, 87–8
witnessing, 100
writing styles, 2
Wuerth, J., 16

Yol (Güney), 145

zone of proximity/indetermination, 118

EU representative:
Easy Access System Europe
Mustamäe tee 50, 10621 Tallinn, Estonia
Gpsr.requests@easproject.com

www.ingramcontent.com/pod-product-compliance
Lightning Source LLC
Chambersburg PA
CBHW070358240426
43671CB00013BA/2557